THE KIDNAP PLOT

March 16, 1865. On a deserted stretch of road, six men waited for the arrival of President Lincoln's carriage. Their objective . . . to kidnap the President. Their leader . . . John Wilkes Booth.

And so began weeks of terror as Booth and his companions desperately tried to abduct the President. They would fail on six separate occasions. Then mysteriously on the night of April 14, Booth would succeed—but with a new plan! He would murder Abraham Lincoln.

Did Booth, the President's assassin, act alone or was he a pawn of higher-ups?

Was the man shot at Garrett's farm and identified as John Wilkes Booth actually Booth or a substitute?

Why was the existence of Booth's diary hidden until long after the famous 1865 Conspiracy Trial, and when revealed, why had 18 pages been cut? Who removed those 18 pages, and when?

A surprising collection of newly discovered, unpublished, historical documents answers these and many more questions, solving the most famous political assassination mystery in American history.

ACKNOWLEDGEMENT

The authors and publisher
wish to express
their grateful appreciation
to Lee Roddy
for his editorial assistance
on this book.

THE LINCOLN CONSPIRACY

by

David Balsiger

and

Charles E. Sellier, Jr.

Schick Sunn Classic Books
Los Angeles, California

© 1977 Schick Sunn Classic Productions, Inc.
All Rights Reserved
Printed in the United States of America
Library of Congress Catalog Card Number: 77-73521
International Standard Book Number: 0-917214-03-X

CONTENTS

CAST OF MAJOR CHARACTERS

ABRAHAM LINCOLN — 16th President of The United States

JOHN WILKES BOOTH — Assassin of President Lincoln

Lincoln's Cabinet

EDWIN M. STANTON — Secretary of War

WILLIAM H. SEWARD — Secretary of State

GIDEON WELLES — Secretary of the Navy

SALMON P. CHASE — Secretary of the Treasury, Chief Justice, U.S. Supreme Court

JAMES SPEED — Attorney General

MONTGOMERY BLAIR — Postmaster General

Maryland Planter's Plot Participants

PATRICK C. MARTIN — Blockade runner

SAMUEL COX — Farmer

THOMAS JONES — Farmer and smuggler

DR. WILLIAM QUEEN — Medical doctor

DR. SAMUEL MUDD — Medical doctor-farmer

Confederate Plot Participants

JEFFERSON DAVIS — President of the Confederate States of America (CSA)

ALEXANDER STEPHENS — Confederate Vice-President

JUDAH BENJAMIN — Confederate Secretary of War, Secretary of State

JACOB THOMPSON — Chief of the Confederate Secret Service

CLEMENT CLAY — Confederate diplomat in Canada

BEVERLY TUCKER — Confederate agent and diplomat in Canada

GEORGE SANDERS — Confederate Secret Service agent in Canada

Northern Speculator's Plot Participants

JAY COOKE — Philadelphia financier, Lincoln's Civil War fund raiser

HENRY COOKE — Washington, D.C. banker

THURLOW WEED — New York newspaper publisher, political boss

THOMAS CALDWELL — Chaffey Shipping Company manager-agent

J. V. BARNES — New York cotton broker

ROBERT D. WATSON — Cotton speculator

Radical Republicans Plot Participants

BENJAMIN F. WADE — Senator from Ohio, Chairman of the Committee on the Conduct of the War

ZACHARIAH CHANDLER — Senator from Michigan, Chairman of the Committee on Commerce

JOHN CONNESS	Senator from California, Member of the Post Roads Committee

LAFAYETTE C. BAKER	Chief of the National Detective Police (NDP)
EARL POTTER	Administrative Director of NDP
ANDREW POTTER	Secret Service Division Director
LUTHER POTTER	NDP detective
LT. LUTHER BAKER	NDP detective

Convicted Booth Co-conspirators

MICHAEL O'LAUGHLIN	Feedstore clerk given life
EDWARD SPANGLER	Ford's Theatre stagehand given life
SAMUEL ARNOLD	Commissary clerk given life
DR. SAMUEL MUDD	Medical doctor given life
LEWIS PAYNE	Ex-Confederate soldier hanged July 7, 1865
GEORGE ATZERODT	Carriage maker hanged July 7, 1865
DAVID E. HEROLD	Drugstore clerk hanged July 7, 1865
MARY E. SURRATT	Boarding house operator hanged July 7, 1865

Military Personalities

GEN. ULYSSES S. GRANT	Commander, Union Army
GEN. ROBERT E. LEE	Commander, Confederate Armies
MAJ. THOMAS ECKERT	Chief of the War Department Telegraph Office
CHARLES A. DANA	Assistant Secretary of War
ANDREW JOHNSON	Military Governor of Tenn., Vice President, President
COL. WILLIAM A. BROWNING	Secretary to Vice President Andrew Johnson
CAPT. JAMES WILLIAM BOYD	Confederate spy, Union agent
COL. ULRIC DAHLGREN	Union leader of Dahlgren Raid
LT. COL. EVERTON J. CONGER	Aide to Lafayette Baker
GEN. GEORGE McCELLAN	Union general, Democratic presidential candidate

Miscellaneous Personalities

JOHN PARKER	Lincoln's White House guard
HENRY JOHNSON	Booth's valet and barber
EDWIN HENSON	Drug smuggler - Booth friend
WARD H. LAMON	U.S. Marshal for Washington
SGT. BOSTON CORBETT	Self-styled killer of "Booth"
REP. GEORGE JULIAN	Representative from Indiana

BEHIND THE LINCOLN CONSPIRACY

All the players are gone. The audience is gone. The American scene has changed. Of the 32,000,000 Americans who lived in that day and time, all are long since gone. Not only that generation, but the succeeding generations are dust.

Yet the spirit of Abraham Lincoln, the man conspirators tried to kill, does not die. Embodying the mind, heart and conscience of democracy, America's greatest American, Lincoln lives on.

Some people say the true facts of the kidnap and murder conspiracy will never be unearthed. All participants are, of course, dead. The last surviving witness to Lincoln's assassination—Samuel J. Seymour of Arlington, Virginia—died in 1956. He was five years old when his godmother took him to see the President at Ford's Theatre.

Not only do Lincoln's contributions live on, so do the misdeeds of those conspirators in high government positions who played a role in the assassination of the 16th President of the United States.

The massive cover-up effort by government officials to prevent the American public from ever learning the real truth about the assassination, suppressed evidence which presumably had gone to the graves of those connected with the murder conspiracy, is now surfacing and answers many of the questions still surrounding the tragic drama of the 1860s.

— Was there an organized government conspiracy to

get rid of Lincoln?

— Did the President's assassin, John Wilkes Booth, act alone or was he a pawn of higher-ups?

— Why, despite countless threats and known plots, did the War Department not provide Lincoln with adequate protection?

— Did Edwin M. Stanton, Lincoln's power-obsessed Secretary of War, play a role in the assassination?

— Why did so many invited guests refuse to accept Lincoln's invitation to Ford's Theatre on the night of April 14?

— Why was the President's single bodyguard absent from his post during the murder, and never punished or even questioned?

— Why were all the escape routes out of Washington closed except the route Booth used?

— Who, for hours after the murder, blacked out commercial telegraph lines from Washington?

— Was the man shot at Garrett's farm and identified as John Wilkes Booth actually Booth or a substitute?

— Did Booth escape to freedom and die an old man 40 years later?

— Why was the existence of Booth's diary hidden until long after the famous 1865 Conspiracy Trial, and when revealed, why had 18 pages been cut out?

— Who removed those 18 pages, why and when?

— Were the convicted and hanged Booth co-conspirators scapegoats for higher figures in a massive cover-up?

A surprising collection of newly discovered unpublished historical papers answers these questions.

The new documents used to reconstruct events that took place before and after the assassination include secret service documents, congressmen's diaries, old letters, book manuscripts, deathbed confessions, secret cipher-coded messages, rare photographs, and purported missing pages of the John Wilkes Booth diary and correspondence secretly intercepted by Secretary of War Edwin Stanton.

Without a doubt, Lincoln's assassination is the most infamous political murder in United States history. Even today, more than 112 years later, a majority of Americans (according to a Gallup Poll, 56%) do not think the government told all the facts. More than a century has passed, but the murder mystery is still unresolved for many. It is relatively easy for contemporary government and private investigators to probe such killings as John F. Kennedy's and Martin Luther King's. Many of the people involved are still alive and can be subpoenaed.

But how does today's investigator locate new facts about a century old assassination when historians have spent years researching the subject, generation after generation, and have come up with nothing significantly new?

Traditional historical writers have perpetuated an inadvertent cover-up by using 1865 government data and documents as gospel, in addition to quoting previously published books on the subject.

In writing this book, the premise taken is that 1865 official statements might not be true, in light of what is now known about the Warren Commission investigation of the Kennedy assassination and the Watergate cover-up. If the government statements are true, they can be authenticated through papers in private collections.

The authors' approach to re-examining the Lincoln assassination mystery was to set out on a nationwide investigation to locate the heirs of significant Lincoln era decision makers, to locate private unpublished document collections in the possession of heirs or Americana collectors, and to locate others who might have done investigative research on this murder.

Before writing this book, more than 10,000 hours were spent in research, in addition to using the research of historians who have spent their lives looking into the possibilities of a conspiracy.

Although there were bizarre aspects, the investigation had a highly sophisticated and scientific side. Even though the deed took place over a century ago, every modern investigative police science technique has been utilized, including missing person bureaus, private detective agencies, genealogy libraries, psychological stress evaluators, handwriting analyses, toxicology tests, chemical analyses of possibly altered documents, and special infrared and ultra-violet photography. All these methods were employed to locate and authenticate documents discovered during research for this book.

As the research investigation moved forward, a number of special consultants were sought, including Dr. Ray A. Neff, a professor at Indiana State University, known for his application of scientific methods of analysis to historical research and for his scholarly book on Lincoln, *Wounded in the House of Friends*.

Also consulted was Dr. Richard D. Mudd, of Saginaw, Michigan, who has more than 1.5 million papers in his private Lincoln collection. Dr. Mudd is the grandson of Dr. Samuel Mudd, sentenced to life in prison as a Booth co-conspirator.

Another eminent consultant was Theodore Roscoe, of Arlington, Virginia, who wrote *Web of Conspiracy*, a book suggesting that Col. Lafayette C. Baker, the nation's first secret service chief, was probably involved in such a web. The book, released in the 1950s, came under open attack by the Secret Service during the "your-government-always-tells-the-truth era".

Not only have more than a dozen consultants been questioned, newly discovered documents themselves rewrite the assassination account. For years, the government and traditional historians have said all documents in existence would be found on file in the National Archives, the Library of Congress, Ford's Theatre, or in other public Lincoln shrines.

As new documents in private collections were located, often both the traditional historians and the government challenged their authenticity. In research, a primary document provides greater authenticity and accuracy than the secondary source materials most often used by the traditionalists.

A small sampling of the never before published documents utilized in this book includes:

1. Col. Lafayette C. Baker Papers — Journals and cipher-coded manuscripts written by the Chief of

the National Detective Police (secret service) detailing the Lincoln kidnap-assassination conspiracy plot and its cover-up.

2. Detective Andrew Potter Papers — File documents and secret records smuggled out of the National Detective Police (NDP) files which tell of the mysterious murder at Garrett's farm.

3. Rep. George Julian Papers — A diary account establishing that the John Wilkes Booth diary was intact with no pages missing when delivered to War Secretary Stanton.

4. War Secretary Edwin M. Stanton Papers — Letters from a collection of nearly 6,000 items that include the missing Booth diary pages, along with 161 letters addressed to Stanton or secretly intercepted by him, which describe details of the assassination conspiracy cover-up and the framing of Booth's co-conspirators at their 1865 trial.

5. Booth's purported letter to the *National Intelligencer* — This letter explains why Booth planned to kill the President.

6. The 18 Missing Booth Diary Pages — A 3,000 word transcript mentioning the names of 70 prominent people directly and indirectly involved in Booth's plan to kidnap Lincoln. The purported Booth diary details the various kidnap attempts and also contains some cipher-coded material. The diary is in the possession of Stanton descendants.

Probably the most sensational and valuable document (the actual pages are established as being worth up to $1 million) consists of the missing diary pages, discovered in 1974 by Americana collector and appraiser Joseph Lynch, of Worthington, Massachusetts, who at the time was appraising the Stanton collection.

The authors acquired a full transcript of the contents of the missing pages and had the contents evaluated by historical experts, but have not been able to acquire copies of the actual pages to authenticate the handwriting.

Negotiations broke down for several reasons, including the heirs' desire for total anonymity, a disagreement on a dollar amount for using the papers, excessive contractual restrictions on their use, and numerous legal questions such as who actually owned the pages: Booth heirs with common law copyright to the pages, or the Federal government because the pages amounted to suppressed evidence and stolen property?

Everything possible was done to authenticate the Booth diary transcripts, including performing voice analyses on numerous interviews, using the psychological stress evaluator (PSE), used by many law enforcement agencies and the CIA. (The PSE is said to be more reliable than a lie detector.) Based on PSE results and historical evaluations of the page contents, the authors believe the material to be authentic.

As a matter of fact, more historical discrepancies were found in the existing diary pages on display at Ford's Theatre in Washington, D.C., than in the missing pages' transcripts. The only major "physical" flaw in the missing pages was Lynch's insistence that the diary pages had printed lines on them.

All photographs of the pages, and the diary acquisition card at Ford's Theatre show no such lines, and historians have long contended that no lines exist on the pages, and that therefore, the "found" pages could be a hoax.

A researcher was sent to Ford's Theatre to examine the Booth diary and to photograph its pages, for the first time using a variety of special photographic films and techniques.

In the presence of Michael Harman, Curator at the Ford's Theatre National Historic Site, ruled lines were discovered on every page of the diary. "Some of these lines are obscured by the writing, but nonetheless visible under good lighting," says Harman. The reason they did not appear in normal photographs is because the lines were printed in blue ink and blue is not picked up by most normal photographic methods.

The pages delineate Booth's involvement in the conspiracy plot with trusted Lincoln friends, Confederate leaders, and northern businessmen and his distrust of

Col. Baker, Stanton, and Maj. Thomas Eckert, Stanton's top aide. The names of 70 prominent people are mentioned, and the pages contain some cipher-coded names, including the names of prominent Stanton aides.

Since most of the people mentioned in Booth's diary were people involved in Booth's kidnap plot of Lincoln, it must be supposed that the Stanton aides mentioned in cipher-code were involved in the plot. The three prominent government figures were listed as "Frank Peck—1013" which translated to Charles A. Dana, Edwin Stanton's Assistant Secretary of War; "Benjamin F. Kloue—Special 1011" which decoded to Maj. Thomas Eckert, Chief of the War Department Telegraph Office; and "James P. Carr—1031" the code name for Col. Henry H. Wells of the United States Army. Col. Wells was on the staff of Gen. Christopher Augur, Commander of Washington forces.

In this book, the authors have not altered primary source documents nor suppressed historically sensitive information. No claim is made that the work is without flaw or that facts have been interpreted without possible fault. When claim is made of an infallible historical account. it is not long before someone discovers error.

The authors have attempted to reconstruct accurately the conspiracy events prior to the assassination and during the following cover-up. In the reconstruction, sources are frequently footnoted. It must be explained that these footnotes sometimes indicate a direct quote, but in most cases, are the source of the materials researched in the reconstruction of scenes and incidents.

What you are about to read is an unraveling of the most shocking political assassination in American history. It is so shocking. that the authors have asked Congress to form a joint Senate-House Assassination Committee to re-examine the facts, to subpoena still existing incriminating secret documents, and to draw final conclusions.

Until that congressional committee is formed, you are the judge of the evidence.

Chapter 1

THE DAHLGREN RAID

President Abraham Lincoln looked thoughtfully at his visitors. He stroked his beard and, on that fateful morning of February 13, 1864, looked searchingly at the men who were to lead one of the most daring raids of the Civil War—and one of the most disastrous.

Gen. Judson Kilpatrick tapped the maps that he had spread before the President, Secretary of War Edwin M. Stanton, and young Col. Ulric Dahlgren.[1]

The general cleared his throat. "We should be able to move past the enemy's right flank, enter Richmond, and release Federal prisoners held there. The rebel communication and supply lines will be disrupted. It's a bold plan, Mr. President, and we should succeed because the Confederates won't be expecting it."

The President nodded slowly. He didn't feel well. Up since 4:30 a.m., he had breakfasted, as usual, on a cup of coffee and one egg before beginning the day's work. His feet were in carpet slippers to ease painful bunions that had plagued him most of his adult life. "Do you, Col. Dahlgren, understand your assignment?"

"Yes, Sir." The son of Adm. John Dahlgren straightened before his Commander in Chief. As a captain, Dahlgren had lost a leg in action. He had returned to duty as colonel. "I'll separate from Gen. Kilpatrick's main column near Spotsylvania. With 500 specially picked men, I'll cross the James River and strike Richmond from the south. I'll liberate Union prisoners from Belle Isle and

14

rejoin the General on about March 2 as he strikes from the north."[2]

The President nodded and ran long fingers across his famous beard. No American President had ever worn a beard before. "You'll see that the amnesty posters are posted, General?"

Kilpatrick glanced at Stanton, who sat silently. The Secretary of War was a round, compactly built man. His scowl seemed emphasized by hard eyes, enigmatic behind small, wire frame glasses. Lincoln had appointed Stanton to the cabinet in 1862. He had turned 49 the day before Christmas, and now, less than 60 days into the new year of 1864, he was one of the most powerful, ambitious men in Washington.

In private life, Stanton had been highly uncomplimentary about the new President. He had referred to him as "the original gorilla."[3]

As attorneys, Lincoln and Stanton had locked horns years earlier before the U.S. Circuit Court in Cincinnati. Both had represented a client in a suit brought by Cyrus McCormick for infringement of reaper patents. Stanton had derided the homely Lincoln as a "long-armed baboon" and had threatened, "If that giraffe appears in this case I will throw up my brief and leave."[4] Stanton's brilliance was felt to be so necessary to the case that Lincoln was shelved.

Yet when Simon Cameron stepped down as Secretary of War, President Lincoln had appointed his detractor to the vacancy.

Many tales were spread about Stanton. He seemed to have a phobia about death.[5]

When Stanton's little daughter died, and had been buried for a year, he had the body exhumed. It was kept in a special metal container in his room for another year or more, until his first wife died. Only after some persuasion, did he allow little Lucy to be reburied with her mother.[6]

Stanton's behavior at his wife's death was so strange, friends were at a loss to know how to handle the grieving husband. He first threw his wife's letters and wedding ring

15

into her coffin. Friends retrieved them. He then hid them in her shroud. He was no less peculiar about his wife's burial clothes. The dressmaker was required to re-do one garment several times. Stanton wanted his wife to look exactly as she had on their wedding day. Following her burial, night after night he arranged her nightcap and gown beside him in bed.[7]

Gen. Kilpatrick brought his attention from Stanton to the President's question. "I'll see that the posters are placed, Mr. President."

Lincoln rose slowly to his full six feet, four inches. "The posters are important, General. Anyone from the Confederacy may bring one in and take the oath of allegiance to the Union."

Both Gen. Kilpatrick and Col. Dahlgren assured him that they realized the importance of the amnesty posters which Lincoln had insisted upon.

As the cavalrymen left and Stanton crossed the street to the War Department, where Maj. Thomas Eckert presided over the military telegraph, the President pondered the planned raid into the Confederate capital.

After nearly three years of war, the tide of battle still ran against the Union. Lincoln had tried general after general; he had yet to find one who could win decisive battles. Elections were coming up, and Lincoln's chances of being returned to office were slim. The people were weary of war, especially of losing battles against smaller, less adequately equipped forces.

Price Lewis, a British subject imprisoned by the South on charges of spying for the North, had been responsible for the idea of a raid to win the war in one bold stroke.

With time on his hands in prison, Lewis had dreamed up scenarios. One was to have Union forces raid Richmond, seize Confederate President Jefferson Davis and his two top cabinet members, and hold them for ransom—that would be the end of hostilities.[8]

In Washington, operatives of the newly formed secret service learned of the plan. Col. Lafayette Baker, a man of highly questionable integrity, headed the North's Na-

16

tional Detective Police (NDP), an undercover, anti-subversive, spy organization under the direction of Secretary of War Stanton.

Andrew Potter, one of numerous Potter brothers, half brothers and cousins who were members of Baker's secret police, termed Lewis' daring project "somewhat ludicrous and probably impractical."

Nevertheless, the plan eventually went to Stanton, and the Lewis proposal ended up on Lincoln's desk. The President approved the raid. The morning's final meeting at the White House set the maneuver into motion.

On Sunday, March 6, the *New York Times* carried a long article that hinted at a mysterious action. "That Brig-Gen. Kilpatrick has started on an expedition to the vicinity of Richmond with a considerable cavalry force and some artillery is generally known to the reading public. The special and most important objective of that expedition is not so generally known, and I am not at liberty here to state it,"[9] E. A. Paul wrote under dateline of Williamsburg two days before.

A report from Union Maj. Gen. Benjamin F. Butler stated that he had received from Kilpatrick a dispatch indicating Dahlgren was in trouble. A rebel deserter had informed Butler that a one-legged colonel and about 100 Union cavalrymen had been taken prisoner. Butler closed his report with the words, "I shall hear by *flag of truce* on Sunday night and will telegraph again."

The telegraph room in Stanton's office was quiet. The War Secretary controlled the nation's military news through the nationalization of the wires. He also controlled the transportation system. Under his direction, through Col. Baker, his control over private citizens was almost complete.

Lincoln himself was denied the right to see telegrams that came into the War Department in cipher to be decoded.[10]

As Lincoln studied reports, John Hay, one of Lincoln's two young secretaries, came in. "The Senate has just confirmed Andrew Johnson as Federal Military Governor of Tennessee."

The President nodded and eased his feet from their slippers. "Good. Johnson is a Southerner. He's well liked in the Confederacy. He should be able to work with the Tennesseeans. I believe he can keep Tennessee out of the Confederacy and help us in the November elections."

"Yes, sir." The secretary paused, notebook in hand. "Any special message for Mr. Johnson?"

The President shook his head. "He knows what must be done. His work in Tennessee is crucial to a possible peace. Anything new on Col. Dahlgren?"

"No, sir. Not a word."

The President put on his carpet slippers again and shambled to a window where he stood gazing out. "Something has gone very wrong with young Dahlgren," he mused.

In a small workshop on Tenth Street near the White House and the War Department, NDP operatives watched their secret military telegraph.[11] Not even Stanton knew about this clandestine machine that Col. Baker had put in.

The full-bearded Baker was founder as well as chief of the new secret service. Thirty-seven years old, he claimed he'd belonged to the 1856 Vigilante Committee that had "cleaned up" San Francisco following the Gold Rush.

In his position as NDP head, he had almost unlimited resources at his command. Since the constitutional writ of *habeas corpus* had been suspended, Baker and Stanton had thrown 13,000 people into Washington's Old Capitol Prison and other jails on charges never brought or made known.[12]

Baker had endeared himself to Washington's upright citizenry by instigating vice raids.[13]

Grog shops were everywhere, 3,700 listed in Washington alone. Most of these were no more than board shanties whose stock consisted of a barrel of rotgut whiskey and a rusty tin cup. Drunkenness was rife. On the evening of a major battle, when a 100 wagon supply train was needed, only five teamsters sober enough to stay on a wagon seat could be located.

Baker had given the grog shops notice to close or take the consequences. When the notices were ignored, axe-squads appeared. The skies over Washington echoed to splintering barrels, breaking glass, and the anguished howls of owners.

Baker also had a list of 163 "gambling hells," most of them on Pennsylvania Avenue, where high-ranking officers rubbed elbows with members of Congress and Rebel spies. At 2:30 one morning his raiders descended on 15 of the largest establishments, rushed the employees off to prison, and demolished luxurious equipment and furnishings.

For the brothels flourishing openly on every street, endangering the "virtue, health, domestic peace and highest interests of the men," Baker planned total destruction.

In the dead of night squads of Baker detectives surrounded the houses. At a given signal doors were burst in, windows smashed. "The scenes which transpired in these dens of corruption," Baker said, "defy language."

"What do you make of the Dahlgren situation?" asked Earl Potter, who ran the office for Baker.

Baker pursed his lips. "More to it than meets the eye. Better check it out with our Richmond agents."

The name of John C. Babcock, a Pinkerton detective and Union scout, had appeared in the Richmond papers in connection with the Dahlgren effort. Both Earl and brother Andrew followed up Baker's orders and interviewed Babcock.[14]

"I supplied Martin Robinson as guide for the expedition," Babcock told them.

"The black stonemason?"

Babcock nodded.

Robinson, a freedman, had joined the strike force on Sunday, February 28, when 3,500 carefully picked troops under Gen. Kilpatrick had moved out from the Rapidan River and struck for the capital of the Confederacy.

"Now on the evening of Friday, February 26, Col. William Moore arrived at Kilpatrick's headquarters. He'd

19

had additional instructions for the raid," Babcock went on.[15] Moore was Stanton's personal secretary. Like Maj. Thomas Eckert who supervised the military telegraph, he could be depended upon for his loyalty.

Babcock could not have known what was in those new sealed orders.

When Gen. Kilpatrick had read them, his eyes had widened in surprise. "These orders could wreck Lincoln's peace negotiations." He'd handed the papers to Dahlgren, who read them and passed them back. Kilpatrick then had put the papers into a flame and watched them burn. Slowly, he had ground the ashes into the soil with his boot heel.

"Mount up," he'd ordered.

A *New York Times* correspondent's account revealed part of what happened next.[16]

The early penetration of Richmond's defenses had been accomplished quietly. Prisoners taken indicated Richmond defenders had no knowledge of the expedition sweeping towards them from the north and south. On Thursday, March 3, Gen. Kilpatrick's cavalry pressed on, fighting Confederate guerrillas known as "bushwhackers." "Ten of these rascals were captured. Of our men, one was killed, several were wounded and one or two horses were killed," the *Times*' reporter claimed.

The action was not going as well for Dahlgren. Disguised as a Confederate cavalryman, he had left the main column. His accompanying troopers also wore the Confederate gray.

"Six grist mills in full operation, a sawmill, the canal boats loaded with grain, several locks in the canal, works at the coal pits at Manikin's Bend, and the barns of Secretary James A. Seddon were all destroyed," the *Times* stated. Seddon was a top ranking Confederate cabinet member.

The young colonel's rampage had aroused the Southern countryside. Confederate home guards and "invalids" (soldiers furloughed for medical reasons) were preparing to pick off the small Dahlgren cavalry force when it turned back.

Rains had swollen the Rapidan River to a depth no horse could ford. Pursuing Southerners were closing in. Dahlgren, who knew he was cut off from behind, now realized he could not go ahead.

He had turned to the black guide in a rage. "You've betrayed us!"

"Oh, no, suh!" The free stonemason's protests were cut off as Dahlgren turned to his sergeant. "Hang him!"

In moments, the black man was swinging from a tree, and Dahlgren was spurring his horse east in the hope of finding a crossing farther downriver. His men rode hard behind him—and straight into ambush by home guards and "invalids."

"Dahlgren was killed trying to fight his way out," the Pinkerton detective stated to the Potters. "About 100 of his men were captured. Dahlgren and a lot of his troops were in Confederate gray."

What made the Dahlgren Raid of significant historical importance, and eventually fatefully influenced the assassination plot against Abraham Lincoln, was far more than the fact that Union soldiers were dressed as Confederates. On Col. Dahlgren's body were found two documents— which he was "fool enough to keep on his person," Andrew Potter growled.

Richmond newspapers carried copies. The first was a letter signed by Dahlgren and apparently intended to be read to his troops. The letter stated, "We hope to release the prisoners from Belle Isle first, and having seen them fairly started, we will cross the James River into Richmond, destroying the bridges after us, and exhorting the released prisoners to destroy and burn the hateful city; and do not allow the rebel leader, Davis, and his treacherous crew to escape."

The second document, unsigned, seemed to be an order: "Once in the city, it must be destroyed, and Jeff Davis and cabinet killed."[17]

The South was in a white hot fury. Gen. Robert E. Lee,

heading the Army of Northern Virginia, officially asked his Union counterpart, Gen. George Meade, if the Union's true motives were contained in the papers.[18]

President Lincoln was caught in a tragic predicament. He had ordered that no booty was to be taken in the raid and that the Confederate capital was not to be seized nor burned.

Lincoln, searching out the meaning of Dahlgren's very strange documents, feared that his peace initiatives with the South had been fatally jeopardized.

Secretary Stanton arrived to bring more disturbing news. "Mr. President, I've investigated the Confederate charge about the papers found on Dahlgren's body. These papers were forgeries. The War Department has issued an official denial. The U.S. government had nothing to do with those orders. We have to assume the Rebels placed them on Dahlgren."

"Forgeries!"

"Col. Dahlgren and Gen. Kilpatrick received your orders in your presence," Stanton reminded.

"Yes, I know." But the President went on wondering how it had been possible for Dahlgren not to have followed his President's original orders. Could some high ranking person close to the young man have countermanded Presidential orders to cause Dahlgren to go on such a rampage? Who would give orders in opposition to the Commander in Chief?

A successful raid, it had been hoped, would end the war. Its failure caused even Northern partisans and dissident Southerners to doubt the Lincoln Administration.

The Confederates were so aroused over Dahlgren's expedition that, just as Lincoln feared, secret peace negotiations going on in Nashville, Tennessee, were ruined.[19]

President Lincoln's hope for a pre-election peace was gone, his chance of winning in November slimmer than ever. Even members of his own party were now ready to dump him in favor of Salmon P. Chase. Should Lincoln be lucky enough to win the nomination, rumor had it that Gen. George McClellan would be the Democratic candidate. The red-haired field commander, fired by Lincoln in

1862, would almost surely win the nation's highest office over Lincoln.

The Dahlgren Raid faded from public discussion, but it was far from forgotten. Any plan for peace that was presented was refused by Rebels who now completely distrusted the Lincoln Administration. The people of the North, of course, distrusted the Rebel government. They believed that the Rebels had forged the Dahlgren papers and framed an innocent man.

Repercussions were to contribute to national tragedy. That summer, Col. William A. Browning, secretary to Andrew Johnson, visited his family in Washington. There he met John Wilkes Booth.[20] The two men had known each other for years and went at once to a restaurant to discuss the war and events of the day.

Booth was one of the most popular men in the North and the South. He was an excellent marksman and a superb horseman. He had secretly married stage actress Martha Mills in 1859, but remained the darling of the theatre-going women of the Confederacy and the Union.[21] Five feet, eight inches tall, the actor had such penetrating black eyes, some people glanced away uncomfortably from his gaze. His wavy black hair and a full mustache turned down at the ends added to his dashing appearance. Booth sat at the table, idly striking a riding whip against expensive boots. "Tell me," he asked his old friend. "What's the truth about the Dahlgren expedition?"

"It's just as we said, John. The Confederates forged the papers and put them on the Colonel's body to embarrass the Union."[22]

The actor sighed. "I'm glad to know that. I've heard terrible stories about what was really behind that raid. Too bad about the documents breaking up the Tennessee peace negotiations. This miserable war might now have come to an end!"

"How'd you know about the peace negotiations, John? They were secret."

Booth shrugged. "I have a good many friends."

Browning held up a finger. "John! Perhaps you'd be

23

interested in helping re-establish those negotiations!"

The penetrating gaze turned upon Browning. "How could I do that?"

"I'll give you the details, if you're interested."

"I don't know. I've got many preoccupations right now."

"Think what it would be like if people someday could point to you and say, 'There goes John Wilkes Booth—the man who stopped the war.'"

It was a heady thought for the actor. His famous father, Junius, had long been a household word, even though he was scandalously married to two women at the same time. John's oldest brother, Edwin, had succeeded on the theatrical circuits and was admired even in far away California. John had been so determined to make it on his own talent that he had performed for a long time under the name, John B. Wilkes. Only recently had he requested billing as John Wilkes Booth.

"I don't know," he said soberly. "But I'll think it over. I'll let you know."

Booth was not too interested in Browning's proposal. But he became highly in favor when his pretty wife, Martha, was arrested in Tennessee. She was a known Confederate letter carrier, and drug smuggler.[23]

The actor went to Browning, who arranged for him to see Andrew Johnson. Booth explained that Martha Mills was his wife, Izola Booth. He had come to ask for her release.

The Military Governor of Tennessee was a politician who knew how to handle Booth and accomplish another goal at the same time. "I'll see that your wife is released," Johnson promised.

Booth seized his hand. "Thank you, Governor. I appreciate that."

Johnson waved in modest dismissal. "Perhaps you'd like to do something for me in return, Mr. Booth?"[24]

The actor understood that Johnson wanted his help in re-establishing peace negotiations. "I'll try," Booth said. "I'll need passes to travel to Richmond, which means

I'll also need passes signed by the Confederates to go back to Union lines."

Johnson nodded. "I can arrange it. I'll give you all the help I can. I'm in a position to represent the Lincoln Administration in re-establishing both trade and peace."

"This terrible war," Booth sighed. "It could soon be over."

"And with your help, acting as a private citizen."[25]

"It would give me the greatest satisfaction to serve my country by bringing about that goal," the actor declared fervently.

Johnson stood and offered his hand. Booth shook it and went out, glancing at Col. Browning as he passed his desk. Reading the excitement in the actor's eyes, his old friend smiled. "The man who ended the war."

Booth quietly made the trip to Richmond with proper military passes issued by both Union and Confederate governments. What he learned in the capital of the seceded states sent him back to Browning in a violent temper.[26]

"We've been friends a long time," the actor cried. "But I've just seen the truth for myself! The Confederacy's claims that the Dahlgren Raid was intended to kill Davis and his cabinet were true!"

"Now, John," Browning said soothingly, "you're not going to let smooth-talking rebels convince you, are you?"

"Don't try to fool me again," the actor stormed. "You first told me that the claims of our brothers to the South were false. I believed you. But I can't believe you any longer. I've been to Richmond. I've seen the documents for myself. They were going to *kill* Jeff Davis!"

"John, listen! Dahlgren's actions were those of a madman. Dahlgren was too soon sent to command. He wasn't worthy of the assignment. I swear to you that the intention was his and his alone. His actions were without the sanction of the President."

"Oh, my friend, why are you trying to deceive me? Is it expediency? Or have you also been deceived?"

"I beg you not to leave here angry, John, and wrongheaded!"

25

"My dear Colonel, we have nothing more to say to each other." Booth's voice was cold. "I will not be a party to your sham. No, I'm not leaving angry, but I am hurt, Colonel, deeply hurt by your perfidy. Good day to you, Sir."

When John Wilkes Booth walked out on Col. William A. Browning, a slow-burning fuse had been lit.[27] It would be less than a year before it reached its explosive charge on Good Friday, April 14, 1865.

Chapter 2

PLANTERS PLOT A KIDNAP

In 1864, the Union was close to dictatorship—a danger unrealized because the Civil War drama had taken center stage.

All the elements were in motion: transportation and communications were nationalized, the writ of *habeas corpus* suspended. Military tribunals had replaced civilian trials. Thousands of people were jailed without charge and held without trial. Dictatorship was an evil lurking behind the scenes. The name of the would be dictator was not discernible to the public.

Effective dictatorship controls the military. Such control was evident. Dictatorship also requires a secret police system. Such a system had developed in an unlikely place: the Treasury Department.

The first Internal Revenue Act of 1862 was "framed upon the theory that the taxpayers were the natural enemies of the government."[1] Even though L. E. Chittenden, Registrar of the Treasury during Lincoln's administration, strongly opposed the use of detectives in its enforcement, detectives were hired and shared in the heavy penalties collected from the delinquent taxpayers they arrested. The government would share, too, with informers.

The detectives "were not under the control of the Commissioner of Internal Revenue, or the Commissioner of Customs, as they should have been," Chittenden had stated. "They became known as the National Detective Police, with Lafayette C. Baker as their chief."[2]

In Lafe Baker's NDP, "detectives" were hired without recommendation, investigation, or inquiry beyond the chief's own inspection. How large his regiment ultimately grew is uncertain, but at one time he bragged that he controlled more than 2,000 men.

With this force at his command, protected against interference from the judicial authorities, Baker became a law unto himself. Exercising his authority in all federal departments and throughout the United States, he instituted a virtual Reign of Terror.[3]

He dealt with every accused person, reputable citizen, deserter, or petty thief, in the same manner. No formal written charge was necessary to suggest to Baker that a citizen might be doing something against the law. Immediately arrested on suspicion, handcuffed, and brought to his office in the basement of the Treasury building, citizens were subjected to browbeating examinations by Baker.

Men were kept in his basement for weeks, without warrant or affidavit. If the accused tried to take any measure for his own protection, he was thrown into the Old Capitol Prison, where he was beyond the reach of the civil authorities.

Baker held authority not only by way of the Internal Revenue Act, but because a highly placed Lincoln cabinet official had set in motion all machinery necessary to become dictator of the nation.

But first, Abraham Lincoln had to be removed from office.

On May 31 the "Radical" Republicans met in Cleveland. This small but powerful group within the Republican Party openly proposed Gen. John C. Fremont as its presidential candidate. Brig. Gen. John Cochrane of New York was chosen as his running mate. The generals could not really hope to unseat an incumbent, but the action was clear evidence of the in-fighting going on in the party.[4]

Lincoln had contributed to his party's discontent by backing Ulysses S. Grant as the nation's second lieutenant general since George Washington. The Congress had confirmed Grant in March. By early May, Grant had launched the first major conflict of the year, the Battle of the Wilderness.

Public outcry soon followed. "Why, did you know that on the second day of the Wilderness campaign the Federals lost more than 17 percent of their men? Seventeen percent, dead or wounded!"[5]

"The way to peace is a new President! Lincoln can't even win his own party's nomination this June."

The Battle of Cold Harbor on June 3 made Grant even more of a political liability. In one hour, he lost nearly 7,000 men, over and above the casualties suffered in the first two days of fighting. The General was now only eight miles from Richmond, but his favor with the home folks was at a new low. It was said Grant "has literally marched in blood and agony from the Rapidan to the James River."[6]

Lincoln lost more favor when he allowed the seizure of two newspapers before the Republican Convention.[7] On the morning of May 18, the New York *World* and the *Journal of Commerce* contained what purported to be a proclamation by President Lincoln calling for 400,000 more troops to be furnished before June 15 through a preemptory draft.

The proclamation was in Lincoln's style but was proven to be false. Secretary of War Stanton instantly ordered New York Military Commander, Gen. John Adams Dix, to close the newspaper offices and to arrest the editors and their staffs. Having telegraphed this order "confidentially" to Dix, Stanton proceeded to the White House and asked Lincoln to issue a proclamation authorizing what he himself had already directed to be done.[8]

Lincoln provided the proclamation, but relented a few days later. Stanton's high-handed dealing with the news-

28

papers had cost Lincoln the support of many New England voters.

A knowledgeable politician, Lincoln knew he had to survive back room, powerhouse drives against his nomination during the first week in June. He would have to make some concessions.

The President went to Baltimore to the Republican Convention, a coalition of War Democrats and the majority of Republicans, who could be classed as centralists and conservatives. The Radical Republican group was the smallest in the new party, but it also represented some of the most powerful men in the North.[9]

Although Lincoln had managed to gain considerable support prior to the convention, he knew efforts would be made to force him to step aside in favor of Salmon P. Chase, his Treasury Secretary, or William Seward, his Secretary of State.

On the opening day he learned just how strong that effort would be. A prominent delegate from Philadelphia bluntly told him, "You can't win. The war's going badly. Grant's the sixth general you've tried, and he not only hasn't won any major victories, but he's got more Union men killed in a few weeks than Gen. Lee has in his entire army."

Lincoln was also told, "You've antagonized Congress, especially the Radical Republicans. Nobody thinks you can win in November."[10]

Lincoln listened and considered certain obvious truths.

The Radicals were a powerful minority. The Conservatives stood with the President. The Centralists, middle-of-the-roaders, might shift either way, although they favored Lincoln. The Radicals had much at stake. They would be willing to take big risks to add to their power. They already controlled congressional committees such as the Committee on the Conduct of the War.

Lincoln knew the War Committee members well. Senators Benjamin F. Wade and Zachariah Chandler were men of great influence. George W. Julian was a member, although one not so willing to risk open opposition to the President.[11]

"Lincoln," one of the backroom politicians asked on the first day of the convention, "do you realize the power and popularity behind the other two candidates compared to you?"

"You mean Chase and Seward?" The President managed a wan smile. "I know about those two gentlemen."

Lawyer Chase, a native of New Hampshire, had become famous for defending slaves. He was solidly anti-slavery. Elected to the U.S. Senate in 1849, twice elected Ohio governor, the attorney had risen to prominence in the new Republican Party. In the 1860 Chicago Republican convention, Ohio's favorite son finished fourth in the first balloting. On the fourth ballot, Chase support was thrown to Lincoln.

Lincoln made Chase Secretary of the Treasury, a department in chaotic condition. With the assistance of banking tycoon Jay Cooke, Chase brought order.

Early in 1861, Cooke assisted Chase in getting $50,-000,000 from New York and Philadelphia to fund early war expenses which had jumped from $1 million weekly to $1 million daily.

When banks reached their lending limits, Cooke became the fiscal agent of Lincoln's government and popularized United States bonds, raising nearly $2 billion for the war effort.

In February, 1864, still seeking the elusive presidency Chase had become involved in a confidential paper, "Pomeroy Circular," critical of Lincoln and suggesting Chase as an alternative. The backlash caused Chase to offer his resignation. Lincoln refused it, even though the man was a source of continuing embarrassment.

William Seward, who had practiced law in New York, had been Whig governor of New York twice. In 1849, he had been elected to the U. S. Senate. Re-elected in 1855, he'd made a bid for the presidency in 1860. On the first ballot, Seward handily topped Lincoln, 173½ to 102 votes, but neither man had enough support to win. When Lincoln won the nomination, Seward campaigned for him and was appointed his Secretary of State in 1861.[12]

Powerful New York party boss and Albany publisher, Thurlow Weed, a shrewd lobbyist and distributor of patronage, was a Seward man.[13] At the convention he told the President, "Lincoln, I've come to learn from you about your intentions. You still seeking the nomination in the face of all the opposition?"

"Yes, Thurlow," Lincoln replied evenly. "It is my intention to be re-nominated and win in November."

Weed exploded. "It can't be done! Even if you win the nomination, there's no way you can be chosen in the November canvass."

On a personal matter, Lincoln had turned to Weed in 1863 for help.[14] Mrs. Lincoln had run up a $15,000 dress bill, which the President could not pay. Both Mary Lincoln and the creditors were on Lincoln's back for action. The President called in Weed and gave him a note explaining the reason for needing the $15,000.[15] Weed carried the letter to New York capitalists. In a few hours, the entire amount had been raised and sent to the President.[16]

The publisher of the powerful *Albany Evening Journal* was a political force to be reckoned with, but Lincoln, in answer to his explosion told him, "Thurlow, if you'll walk through this convention and listen well, I think you'll find I am gaining strength. John Nicolay, my secretary, just told me a struggle now's developing among the delegates to see who is going to place my name in nomination. I could be happier if you were behind me, Thurlow."

The visitor shook his head. "When Seward lost to you in 1860, I suffered some power losses at home. But both Seward and I backed you, and you won. Now I'd like you to return the favor and step down in favor of Seward."

"I believe the voters have faith in this administration, Thurlow. I believe they know my goal is right in keeping the Union together and in settling the slavery issue. I believe the voters will support me in November."

"Even if the Democrats nominate McClellan?"

"Even then."

"You'd have to do something about the Radicals. Get

31

Fremont to step aside so the party won't be split, because it will be when this convention names another Republican candidate."

"I have not finished with all possible arrangements, Thurlow."

The old man snorted with a certain grudging admiration.

Officially, Lincoln was neutral about the choice of his running mate.[17] But the incumbent, Hannibal Hamlin of Maine, was now replaced by Andrew Johnson, Military Governor of Tennessee.

While this concession was immediate and obvious, other actions were being plotted which did not publicly take place until later—one as late as September 23 when Postmaster General Montgomery Blair was officially asked to resign.

A lawyer and statesman, Blair had been legal counsel for runaway slave Dred Scott. The case had gone all the way to the U.S. Supreme Court. Blair, a former Democrat who had believed the slavery question could be settled peaceably, had organized the army postal system and introduced compulsory postage payment. A moderate Republican, Blair had antagonized the Radicals, who were determined to unseat him.

Whatever concessions Lincoln made were effective, for on Wednesday, June 8, the convention ballots talllied 484 votes for Lincoln and 22 for Ulysses Grant, a favorite son nomination. The voting was then made unanimous, and Lincoln had the nomination to run for a second term.

His problems were far from over. That same evening, the Union League, a pressure group within the Republican Party, repudiated the President's soft peace platform. The League joined the Radicals in demanding Rebel property be confiscated and proposed that the conquered South should be considered a prize of war.[18]

Pressure would continue to be applied on Lincoln to allow another candidate to run even though the convention had chosen him. Seward's chances were not dead. Chase also seemed a possibility. Three weeks after he failed to unseat Lincoln, the Secretary of the Treasury again tendered his resignation. It was too late for the 1864 convention nomination, but there were other possibilities before the November vote.

This time the President accepted, and in firm terms: "You and I have reached a point of mutual embarrassment in our official relations which it seems cannot be overcome, or longer sustained, consistently with the public service."[19]

The President wanted very intensely now to win victories in the field, and win voter support in November. The Democrats were jubilant that summer. They believed that the election of McClellan was assured.

Nothing seemed to go right for Lincoln. Gen. Grant's assault on Petersburg, southwest of Richmond, had ground to a halt. A long siege could be expected. The Federals, in sight of the Confederate capital, had also been stalled.

On the political front, the first session of the 38th Congress prepared to adjourn by tossing Lincoln one of the hottest possible political potatoes. It was the Wade-Davis Bill, a Radical Republican version of postwar reconstruction diametrically opposed to the President's proposal.[20]

Written by Rep. Henry Winter Davis of Maryland and Sen. Ben Wade of Ohio, it challenged all that Lincoln had done since December 1863, when he had announced his reconstruction plan. His was a "soft" policy designed to bind up the nation's wounds with all possible speed so that the nation could move forward and leave the events of the tragic war behind.

Lincoln reasoned that he should begin to establish a practical and necessary civil government in what had been Rebel territory.[21] He had no historical precedent. The President would have to work without guidelines.

Since the President had the right to pardon, Lincoln reasoned, he could offer a general amnesty to all who would take a loyalty oath to the Union. There were to be no test oaths.

"On principle," the President had explained, "I dislike an oath which requires a man to swear he has not done wrong. It rejects the Christian principle of forgiveness on

33

terms of repentance. I think it is enough if the man does no wrong thereafter."[22]

The oath was to be denied high military and civil leaders of the South, but most of the people of seceded states could take it. In addition, when 10% or more of the people who had voted in 1860 took the oath, they could elect a state government that Lincoln would recognize.

In 1864, Louisiana, Arkansas and Tennessee met the Presidential conditions. The required number of voters had taken the oath, they had abolished slavery, and elected representatives to Congress.

There was one problem. Only the Congress could set qualifications for members; Lincoln could not.[23]

The Radical Republicans persuaded other Congressmen to vote with them to deny recognition of the reconstructed states. They also moved to prevent the ballots of these states from being counted in the November elections.

Under the Radicals' Wade-Davis Bill each seceded state was to be treated as a conquered country. A provisional governor would take a census of all adult white males. A majority (not 10%) was required to swear an oath of allegiance. Only then could a governor call an election for a state constitutional convention.

The only eligible voters, however, were those who would take an "ironclad oath" swearing they had never borne arms against the Union. In the South, almost every able-bodied man had fought for the Confederate States of America (CSA).

The harsh terms provided that a new state constitution must require abolition of slavery. Confederate civil and military leaders would be denied the right to vote. State and CSA war debts would not be forgiven. If all these conditions were met, Congress would admit the state to the Union.[24]

Naturally, the President refused to sign such a measure, and it was automatically killed for that session. The Radicals did not take the rejection of the Wade-Davis Bill without a counterattack, which was planned for early August.

July was a bad month for Lincoln. Gen. Jubal Early,

the hard riding Confederate cavalryman, led his experienced troopers in an invasion of Washington's outskirts. The threat to the capital was so great that the President and his family fled the White House for the safer Old Soldiers Home. Every available fighting man was summoned to defend the capital, and even "invalids" pressed into service.

The Rebel threat was turned aside, but not without more loss of confidence in Lincoln.

That same month the Union dollar's value dropped to 39 cents, the lowest ever. Economically, militarily, politically, the embattled President fought what seemed to be hopeless odds as the election drew near.

His own party again attacked him in August. The first onslaught came on August 5 when the "Wade-Davis Manifesto" was trumpeted in the *New York Tribune*. In defense of the Wade-Davis Bill, the Manifesto was also a slashing attack against Lincoln. He was charged with personal ambition for refusal to sign the bill.[25]

Most of it was rhetoric for the truth was plain. The real struggle was for power. Under Lincoln's "soft" postwar plan, the Southern Democrats would one day join with the already strong Northern Democrats to control Congress. Even though the South could not vote in the 38th Congress, the Northern Democrats alone were sufficiently strong, and if they nominated McClellan for President late in August, they would very likely see him win the November election.

With the nation united, the Democrats could turn the Republicans out of their seats in both houses. The Radical Republicans' power, patronage, and prestige would be lost. Everything this group had, or hoped to have, depended on keeping the South from sending Democratic representatives to Congress after the war.

A week after the Wade-Davis Manifesto, Thurlow Weed and other powerful politicians called on Lincoln.[26] The President took one look at their serious faces and guessed they would ask again that he give up the race in favor of

35

another candidate. Knowing Weed, the candidate would be Seward.

"Since the June convention," Weed began, "the fortunes of this office have steadily gone down hill."

The President wriggled his painful toes and wished he had on his carpet slippers. But these were mighty men of national political strength; Lincoln had decided to wear shoes while listening to them.

Weed waved an impatient hand. "You should have refused the nomination in June. But since you didn't, you can step down now, and we may still be able to put up a winning candidate. There's no way we can win with you at the November canvass."

The President sighed. This was all too familiar ground, and not one inch of it was pleasant. "Thurlow," Lincoln said gravely, "I told you in June I believe I can win in November. I have faith the people will support my policies and return me to office. They know what I'm trying to do and they will back me."

"Then you refuse again?"

The President stood. "I will not quit."

The President had presented a bold front to his detractors, but the melancholy mood that often enveloped him seemed to press harder than ever.

Ward Lamon saw the President preparing for a walk and rightly guessed his deep depression. "Mind if I walk along?"

At 36, Lamon was considered by many to be Lincoln's closest friend. A native of Virginia, he had lived in Kentucky and Illinois, as had Lincoln. In 1852, Lamon had become Lincoln's law partner in Danville, Illinois. He had campaigned for him in 1860 and had accompanied the new President to Washington in 1861. He had been appointed U.S. Marshal for the District of Columbia.

A huge man, handsome and outgoing, something of a swashbuckler, Lamon had an intense dislike of abolitionists. Lincoln was accused of keeping a Southern proslavery man in a position of high authority.

"Where to, Lincoln?" Lamon asked as the President

settled his huge, eight dollar, plug hat upon his head. The President preferred to be called by his last name. He did not like his first name, nor did he favor the use of "Mr. President." He was familiarly known in private as "Old Abe," although he was only 55.

"No place special, Ward," Lincoln replied. "Maybe across the grounds. I need to walk and think."

The two men fell into step, leisurely pacing in silence until Lamon said, "Lincoln, I've heard more rumors about assassination attempts. I'm going to have the grounds patrolled."[27]

The President seemed unconcerned. "Assassination is not an American practice. If anyone was willing to give his own life in the attempt to murder the President, it would be impossible to prevent him."[28]

"I'm just telling you the town is full of rumors, and I want to take some action."

"Properly speaking, Ward, the protection of the President is the responsibility of the Secretary of War."

"I'm not talking responsibility, Lincoln," the marshal replied with some feeling. "I'm talking as a friend. And while we're on the subject, I want to start sleeping outside your bedchamber door again."

The President smiled faintly. "You're a good friend, Ward. Do as you think best." His melancholy seemed to increase with each step. He adjusted his hat, already pressing down upon his large ears. (He was known to have carried a bank book, a large cotton handkerchief, and other items in the hat.)

"Want to talk about anything special?"

"A man's burdens are his own, except what the Almighty carries for him. But thank you."

Lamon seemed slightly hurt. The President said kindly, "I was thinking, not about the scene in my office just now, but about the time when I floated down the river to New Orleans. I was in my early 20s when I first saw a slave auction."

The President lapsed into moody silence. He remembered clearly how it had been. At the auction, he had turned to companions, saying, "Boys, by the Eternal God,

37

if ever I get a chance to hit that thing, I'll hit it hard."[29]

Lincoln's concern for the future of the nation was centered in ending the war, overcoming his own party's detractors, and defeating the November challenge of the Democrats.

His greatest danger, which he could not know, was John Wilkes Booth, a man of many parts. As an actor, he reputedly earned $20,000 annually. He also was a smuggler. With a small band of men, he had obtained quinine, bandages, and other valuable commodities in the North and had slipped them through pickets into the South where they brought a good price.[30]

Between his antagonism toward the Lincoln Administration and the lies he felt Browning had told him about the Dahlgren Raid, Booth was ready for anything new and exciting, perhaps even political intrigues. One came from an unexpected source.

Near Bryantown, Maryland, a group of planters had gathered to discuss ways of ending atrocities committed in the counties of Prince Georges, St. Mary's, and Charles.[31] Among the Maryland planters were Patrick C. Martin, organizer of the project, Dr. William Queen, and Dr. Samuel Mudd, both physicians.

Martin, as spokesman, outlined the grievances.[32] "We've got to put an end to these outrages. Lincoln has promised us redress because he knows the importance of Maryland as a border state. But nothing has been done about thievery by Federal troops, nor about complaints against the Union for seizing of our slaves, our boats, our crops and our livestock."

Dr. Queen added bitterly, "And don't forget how the Maryland legislators awoke one morning to find Federal guns and troops surrounding them! Just because Old Abe heard a rumor that the lawmakers might meet and vote for secession."

The chorus went on. The quiet, soft-spoken Dr. Mudd, who practiced medicine less than he farmed, said little, listening politely. Balding, he wore a sturdy growth of whiskers and a mustache as though in compensation for losing his hair at age 35.

"You know what we should do?" said a young, thin planter with an empty sleeve.

"What's that?" Martin asked.

"We should kidnap Lincoln!"

Someone laughed. "What'd we do with him? Nobody wants him. From what I hear, even the voters don't want him."

Dr. Queen observed wryly, "The only person on this earth who might possibly have an interest in Old Abe is Jeff Davis."

The planters' nervous laughter was cut short by Martin, who jumped up, waving his arms. "Now, wait a minute. Don't laugh! That's not a bad idea! Take Lincoln prisoner and turn him over to the President of the Confederacy. What could be more just than that?"

The planters looked at one another. Maybe kidnapping was just what Lincoln deserved.

Martin said, "If the President could be removed from office for awhile, the country might get back on the right course."

"But kidnapping," Dr. Mudd interjected. "Kidnapping seems like such a criminal thing to do."

"Don't call it 'kidnapping,' Dr. Mudd. This is wartime, when capturing enemy personnel is common practice. Let's just say that someone should 'capture' the President."

The planters looked around the room. Martin was a possibility. He had gone through a brief but stirring time in the Confederate Navy. The strong Federal blockade, which was effectively blocking sea and river traffic in and out of the Confederacy, had inspired him to work on a desperate plan. He had gone to Canada and joined with Alexander Keith of Halifax in blockade-running.

"How about you, Martin?" one of the planters called.

Martin shook his head. "I'm not the right man for you. But I think I know just the man!"

"Who's that?" Dr. Queen asked.

"He's a native of Maryland, intensely loyal to the

South. He's anxious to do something to help. Actor John Wilkes Booth!"[33]

There were exclamations.

"I met Booth in Montreal recently and had many talks with him. He's true blue, the very man we're looking for. If you want me to, I'll talk to him the next visit I make to Canada. Sound him out."

The planters nodded their agreement. Martin would contact Booth during a Canadian theatrical engagement and tell him of the project. If he agreed, he would be brought to Maryland for a meeting with the planters.

The Democratic National Convention had opened in Chicago on August 9, 1864. Confident of victory in the November election, the delegates adopted a strong peace platform, attacked Lincoln's administration, and prepared to nominate Gen. George McClellan for President.

By that time the planters' kidnap plan was under way. Booth, following the convention closely, wrote in his diary: "I have heard that George McClellan may be nominated with George Pendleton as Vice President.

"If that is so, it may be possible to bring this futile, stupid war to an end. If McClellan is elected, it portends favorably for the South where he has always enjoyed a favored status. With McClellan as President, it might still be possible to reconcile the North and South. I pray that this is possible."[34]

The first day's work of the Democratic Convention was proclaimed in the press and loudly discussed in saloons and other gathering places.[35]

"The Lincoln Administration has failed to restore the Union by the experiment of war," was a popular and quotable plank from the Party's peace platform.

"The Administration has disregarded the Constitution. Private rights and public liberty have been trampled underfoot!"

"Arbitrary arrests, subversion, replacement of civil law by military tribunals—and that's just a beginning."

Convention speakers zeroed in on the voters' soft spot:

war weariness. The Democrats were the peace party. Their highly popular platform demanded immediate efforts for cessation of hostilities on the grounds that justice, humanity, liberty, and public welfare demanded such endeavor.

On August 31, the convention chose McClellan as the standard bearer. He received 174 votes, to 38 for Thomas Seymour, on the first balloting. A delegate moved that the vote be made unanimous. McClellan and Rep. George H. Pendleton of Ohio became the Democratic running mates who would defeat Lincoln and Johnson.[36]

"Elect McClellan and put an end to administrative usurpation of extraordinary and dangerous powers not granted by the Constitution," shouted Democrats. "Elect Little Mac and there will be a negotiated peace, an end to the war!"

Chapter 3

TWO MORE KIDNAP PLOTS

Near the end of September 1864, Patrick Martin met with John Wilkes Booth.[1]

At Martin's mention of "capturing" the President, Booth's dark, oriental-like eyes sparkled. The proposal had its irony. Lincoln had sent Dahlgren to capture Jeff Davis; out of that fiasco had come the idea to capture Lincoln.

"The right man," Martin said smoothly, "could succeed where Dahlgren failed."

"It would be a hazardous venture," the actor said in his rich voice.

"There'll be adequate compensation for the risks, especially to the leader of such a bold and daring campaign. And, of course, all expenses will be covered. Gold will be available for recruitment."

Booth's ivory pale hands smoothed his black mustache.

"Why do you tell me these highly confidential matters?"

Martin smiled. "I'm sure you must have already determined that, Wilkes, since you are known as an astute man whose loyalties to the South have not detracted from your duties to theatre-goers in the North. A man who can keep his eyes and ears open and mouth shut is always welcomed by the Confederacy."

The actor bowed his head at the compliment. "I would have to think long and hard about an involvement in such a venture, Patrick."

The Confederate agent spread both hands. "Of course, I would like to suggest you take all the time you want. But there is a certain urgency. Grant has advanced to within seven miles of Richmond, you know. He's been laying seige to Petersburg since mid-June."

Booth sighed. "If Richmond falls, God only knows how it will effect the war's outcome." He smashed his hand into his palm. "If McClellan is elected, this stupid war may be brought to an end. The South likes McClellan. He might be able to reconcile both sides."[2]

Martin nodded. "But if McClellan is elected, he will still have the Radical Republicans in the Northern Congress to contend with. If they have their way, the Confederacy will be stripped and plundered without mercy."

Booth's dark eyes glowed. "On the other hand, if that old tyrant, Lincoln, is re-elected, we know he'll continue to push until the rights of the states are overridden and the Confederacy will be denied her right to freedom."

"The American colonies threw off the yoke of tyranny to be free. And yet the Union now denies that very same right to the Confederacy. It doesn't seem fair, does it, Wilkes?"

The actor changed the subject. "If I accepted this responsibility, what are the terms and conditions?"

"First, of course, I can assure you of the cooperation of Richmond."

"That would be essential."

"You're already well-known in the South because of your efforts as a peace negotiator, plus your fine acting.

I have heard that you have befriended the Confederacy in other ways, too."

Booth's eyes locked onto Martin's. If the agent was indicating he had heard Booth smuggled medicines and other contraband into the South, the actor would give no sign.[3]

Martin broke an awkward silence. "You will be well paid, Wilkes."

The actor smoothed the locks that so enthralled women. "I'd need letters of introduction to your planter friends."

"I can arrange those."

Booth offered his hand. "I'll think about it."

"When will you decide?" Martin held the actor's hand in a firm grip.

"After I've considered the situation from every angle. Perhaps I'll send a letter to Jefferson Davis.[4] I have a friend who could deliver such a message. We'll see if Davis answers."

"He'll answer," Martin said, opening the door. "I'll await your decision."

While Booth debated his decision, the Chaffey Company at 178½ Water Street in New York was doing a brisk business of a highly questionable nature.[5]

The Chaffey Company was located in a former sail maker's loft. When steam replaced sails, the loft had been converted into several small offices. A number of smugglers and speculators, including Booth, Confederate courier John Surratt, and Michael O'Laughlin, a childhood friend of Booth and involved with him in a smuggling operation, used the Chaffey address.[6] Another customer was Lafayette Baker who began using Chaffey's in July.

Baker had been transferred to New York early in 1864 after a dispute with Stanton which had lost him the title of Special Provost Marshal of the War Department. It seems that Lafe had been tapping telegraph lines between Nashville and Stanton's office.[7] When Stanton found out, Baker was put out in the field. He was now a "special agent" in New York.

Baker's demotion was simply a hand slapping by Stanton to let him know who was the real boss. His power was not curtailed, even though Stanton's aide, Charles Dana, was appointed Washington operational head of the NDP. Dana had little interest in the post and no time to oversee it.[8] The detectives at the NDP were all loyal to Baker. They not only continued to keep in constant touch with him, they took their orders from him.

The Chaffey Company and Baker had mutual business interests. On July 20, $35,124 was credited to Baker's account there. On August 30, $36,520 more went on the books, and another $21,500 was added at the end of September.[9]

It had been Baker's practice to turn in confiscated contraband to the military commissary. When Stanton replaced him, Baker had changed tactics. He still turned in eggs, pork and other less valuable commodities, but sold seized cotton through the Chaffey Company and deposited the cash in his own personal account.[10]

The South was desperate for meat. If Gen. Robert E. Lee's command was to continue the war effort, many barrels of pork were essential. Baker had no interest in selling pork. It was cotton that could make a man rich in a hurry. At the beginning of the war, cotton had sold for 10 cents a pound. Three years later, after Lincoln instituted a military blockade of southern ports, it was valued at a dollar per pound. A single bale was now worth more than a $1,000, and a seized shipment of several bales could be quietly sold for a tidy sum. At the rate Baker was making deposits, his account would hit $150,000 by the end of the year.[11]

When Booth decided to contact Confederate President Davis, he entrusted the message to a Confederate courier friend. While awaiting a reply in Washington, he obtained 1,000 ounces of valuable quinine, hid the contraband medicine in a trunk, and sent it by blockade runner to Richmond as proof of his sincerity.[12]

Booth received instructions to meet Clement Clay and Jacob Thompson in Montreal.[13] The actor proceeded at once to Canada and on October 17 or 18, checked into the St. Lawrence Hall.[14]

The five-story hotel covered an entire block on St. James Street. Only the best people stayed at the Hall, including English diplomats concerned over the Union naval blockade which denied cotton to English mills.

Sir Fenwick Williams, General in Chief of British forces in Canada, was quartered at the hotel. Canadian and British officers came and went since Canada held a strong belief that the North was trying to involve her in the war.

That the Confederacy's "second Richmond" was in the Hall Hotel was obvious. Confederate diplomats and agents roamed every floor.[15] Jacob Thompson, the 54 year old former Secretary of the Interior under President James Buchanan, had his Rebel Secret Service headquarters at the St. Lawrence. Other Confederate officials at the hotel included 48 year old Clement Clay, former Alabama senator and now Confederate diplomat working on peace feelers. The Hall provided unblockaded access to the Atlantic and a neutral ground for initiating peace talks with the Union.

Booth had scarcely settled into his luxurious quarters when the city was electrified by news of a bold rebel raid launched from Canada which struck three banks across the border in St. Albans, Vermont, on October 19. One villager was killed and several wounded before the raiders escaped with nearly $200,000. The raiding party was pursued across the border into Canada.[16]

Booth heard the news in the hotel's ornate dining room where he waited to keep a breakfast appointment with Jacob Thompson. The Confederate Secret Service Chief in Canada sat down promptly at Booth's table.[17] They were soon joined by the tall, thin Clement Clay.

When pre-war cigars were finally lit, the agents leaned across the table and spoke in low tones. "If you're willing to undertake a mission for the Confederacy as I understand you are," Thompson began, "we can use your services."[18]

"That's why I'm here," Booth replied.

45

Clay regarded the tip of his cigar. "If the services are properly rendered, a great deal of pressure can be removed from Confederate armies in the field."

Booth asked, "What are your suggestions, gentlemen?"

"For the service we require," Thompson said, "about 15 men would be necessary. They must be hand-picked by you, Mr. Booth, and must be men you absolutely trust."[19]

"That can be managed."

"Certain expenses and compensation will be required for recruitment," Clay put in. "About $20,000 in gold should cover that expenditure, I should think. Do you agree, Mr. Booth?"

"That would be adequate for recruiting," Booth said with a smile.

Thompson blew cigar smoke, "Of course, there will be additional compensation for you, as leader, above expenses and recruitment. I have an account at the Ontario Bank. The necessary money has been put aside."

Booth nodded and pulled on his cigar.

"You'll need to hire certain services along the way, plus transportation and lodging. The first step, I suppose, is to put you in touch with a reliable man to help in recruitment."

John H. Surratt, Jr. was suggested.[20] Surratt, Thompson said, was the 20 year old son of Mary Eugenia Jenkins and the late John Harrison Surratt. He had once thought of entering the priesthood. Instead he had become a Confederate courier passing through Union lines around Washington to Confederate boats on the Potomac, and sometimes riding on into Richmond.

"I have met Surratt," said Booth.

"As you can well understand," Clay said, "absolute secrecy will be required at all times. A secret cipher-code will be used and decoded in Richmond or Montreal."

Thompson added, "Messages can be gotten to the War Department in Richmond through the pages of the *New York News* if you're in a hurry. Use the 'personals column.' The *News* is friendly to our cause.[21] You will accept the assignment?"

Booth put out his hand. "I accept. It is a way I can serve my country without wearing a uniform."

When the handshaking was over, Thompson said, "You could have a uniform, Mr. Booth, by becoming part of our detached service."

"You mean, 'secret service?' " Booth asked.

Thompson smiled. "We prefer the term 'detached service.' It allows us to operate in mufti, yet we're entitled to wear a uniform if we wish."[22]

Booth's eyes shone.

"I have heard," Thompson continued, "that you are considered the handsomest man in Washington, and I concur. Think how you'd look in a uniform, if you wanted to wear one."

Clay understood what was happening. "You could keep your uniform in your theatrical wardrobe trunk. If someone saw it, he would assume it to be just one of your costumes."

Booth regarded his cigar. "What rank did you have in mind?"

"For the service you're about to render to the Confederacy," Thompson replied, "I should think a colonel's rank proper."

Booth smiled broadly. "Gentlemen," he said, "I am pleased to become part of our country's detached service."

When Booth left Montreal, a dashing Confederate colonel's uniform was in his trunk. His theatrical baggage was to be shipped by schooner to Nassau, the Bahamas. Martin, who had also met Booth in Montreal to give him letters of introduction to the Maryland planters, told Booth the North's patrol boats were not likely to apprehend the schooner. From Nassau, the baggage would be shipped into the Confederacy where Booth could reclaim it.[23]

Considerably better off than he had been in September, Booth returned to Washington. He had deposited $455 into a newly opened account at Montreal's Ontario Bank and had purchased some British currency.[24] Also $12,-499.28 had been transferred from the Bank of Montreal to Booth's account at the Chaffey Company in New

47

York.[25] This was, to the penny, what Daniel Watson, a Tennessee cotton speculator, had deposited in the Bank of Montreal on July 4 for some unknown reason.[26]

Booth wrote in his diary, "I am to find and send North 15 men whom I trust. The messenger brings me $20,000 in gold to recruit them. I'm to start at once."[27]

The messenger who brought the gold was connected with the Union's Judge Advocate General's Office—an indication that others besides Southerners may have had an interest in Lincoln's removal.[28] Or was there one huge plot, masterminded by a single individual who controlled all the players like puppets on strings? Booth didn't take time to think about such possibilities. He had a kidnapping to arrange.

As Booth prepared for his starring role, another highly secret plot was developing inside the government in Washington. Its aim was the same as the planters' and the Confederacy's: abduction of the President. But the Northern conspiracy was for entirely different purposes.

A hint of the Northern plot was turned up by NDP operatives.[29] The secret Tenth Street workshop detectives sent a coded message to Lafe Baker urging him to see them. Baker arranged a meeting in New York.

"It was too risky to send the whole story by cipher," Earl Potter said as he and Andrew sat down at a quiet restaurant table with their boss.

Andrew whispered, "There's a plan under way to kidnap the President, Vice President and Secretary of State."

Baker let out a startled exclamation.

"Lincoln has completely refused to step aside in favor of another Republican who could win in November, and that's where the plot begins," Andrew said.[30]

"Members of Lincoln' own party are going to have him kidnapped and kept out of sight until fake charges are arranged to impeach him. Meantime, the Radicals will set up a system to run the executive branch. We know they're going to hide their prisoners in Washington."

"Where?"

"You remember when Stanton planted Alfred Cridge

inside the White House in '63 to spy on Lincoln, and the wife and sons?"

"Of course."

"And Cridge learned something strange was going on at the Thomas Green home at the foot of Tenth and Seventeenth Streets?"

"Yes, yes. I ordered the house kept under surveillance."

"We've learned that Mrs. Thomas Green is the sister of L. L. Lomax, the Rebel general. The Green mansion is fixed up in the basement with cells and shackles. That's where the Rebels were planning to hold Lincoln instead of trying to sneak him out of town after they grabbed him."

"But nothing ever came of that," Baker reminded the brothers. "I thought that was a dead issue."

"So far as the Rebels are concerned, it is. But the Radicals apparently know about the cells. Now they're planning to snatch the President and the other two and hold them in the Green's basement."

Baker slapped the table. "Then if somebody should find Lincoln, Johnson and Seward, the Rebs will be blamed!"

Earl leaned nearer. "And if they're not discovered, the power-grabbers will keep Lincoln out of sight long enough to frame him, and seize power."

His brother muttered, "Shouldn't be difficult! Mrs. Lincoln is known to have four brothers and four brothers-in-laws fighting for the Confederacy."

Baker put in. "Lincoln will have to disappear long enough for public opinion to be built up against him. They'll charge him with treason."

Earl said, "Or, he might just permanently disappear somehow!"

"Why Johnson and Seward?" Andrew asked.

"That's a tough one. The order of succession to the presidency's involved, I guess."

"If the President, Vice President, or Secretary of State can't serve, who's next in line?" Andrew asked.

"I'm not sure," Earl replied. "But I don't think it matters in this case, because they're not going to be taken

49

prisoner until after the election—when McClellan is elected."

"Lincoln would continue as President only until March, when McClellan would be seated?"

"Right. Then there's going to be, or maybe already is, a Committee of Twelve," Earl said. "But we don't know who they are. They'll appoint an interim President, probably one of the conspirators. He'd serve until about March, when it would be announced that McClellan wouldn't be seated because he was a Southern sympathizer."

Baker whistled. "That's quite a plot."

"The biggest problem," Andrew said, "is, we haven't found out who all is behind it. We know Stanton knows about it. We don't have any evidence he's the mastermind."

"It could be the bankers-cotton-and-gold speculators. The blockade's really hurting them. The entire Committee on the Conduct of the War may have a hand in it," Earl said. "But the Radicals on the committee are the only ones we actually know are involved."

"Find out who's the leader, or leaders."

Earl shook his head. "Not easy, Chief. Whoever's masterminding this is smart enough to keep his name off people's tongues. It looks like he has in mind to set up a dictatorship over the entire country, both for now and after Reconstruction begins."

"One man's behind this," Baker declared. "One man. He's got to be setting up machinery to carry out this plan. We've got to find him. We start by looking for unusual movements of the North's Rebel prisoners."

"Why so?" Earl asked.

"Union men cannot do it. They've got to have a cover of Rebs, so if they're caught, it'll look like a Rebel plot."

Earl asked, "What happens when we discover the leader?"

"We'll decide that later." Baker ordered, "Get every NDP man we can trust onto trying to find out names behind the plot."

Some of the questions facing the detectives seemed unanswerable. Why kidnap Seward? He was not third in succession.[31] The Founding Fathers had seen a time when two vacancies in the executive branch might occur. If the President and Vice President could not serve, the President Pro Tempore of the Senate was next in line.

That Northern conspirators didn't know the Secretary of State wasn't third in line to the presidency was totally unlikely. Perhaps Seward was to be snatched because he favored too many of Lincoln's "soft" reconstruction plans. Or perhaps, whoever was behind the triple kidnapping plot simply hated Seward.

No legal precedent existed for the action planned. The Constitution contained no provision for a committee to run the country, to appoint an interim president, or to declare that a legally elected President could not be inaugurated. The whole American system of government was to be disrupted in a game of politics without equal in history. Kidnapping, possible murder, and the circumvention of the people's will were all in the plan.

Oblivious of the conspiracy inside Washington, John Wilkes Booth set up his plans to kidnap the President for the South.

At the White House, Lincoln moodily waited for the November 8 general election.

Chapter 4

THE MONEYMEN CONSPIRE

On November 8, 1864, the voters gave Abraham Lincoln a 55 percent popular vote and returned him to office for another term.

How had he carried this off? There were numerous explanations. Arguments could be heard in every bar and restaurant in the North. How could a man come from so far behind and roll up 2,330,552 popular votes to 1,835,-

985 for McClellan? How could "Old Abe" pick up 212 electoral votes to 21 for McClellan?[1]

John Wilkes Booth, brooding over a brandy at Peter Taltavul's Star Saloon, heard explanations and gossip at a nearby table of Washington diners.

"It was the military vote! He got those 116,887 military ballots to Little Mac's 33,748 because Old Abe was smart enough to send the troops home to vote. He knew he could count on the soldier boys to back him."[2]

Lincoln had pressured commanders to furlough soldiers home in time for the election. The President received a better than three-to-one military vote.[3]

"It was the military victories! Sherman taking Atlanta, Sheridan clearing out Jubal Early's troops from the Shenandoah, Farragut in Mobile Bay!"

"Chief Justice Roger Brooke Taney couldn't have died at a better time."

Booth, still listening, knew Taney had taken a lot of criticism for his decisions, especially in the Dred Scott case.

Dred Scott, a slave from Missouri, had been taken by his master to Illinois and Minnesota territory, which were free. Scott had returned to Missouri, his master had died, and the slave had asked to be legally declared free. In 1857, his case reached the U.S. Supreme Court where it was held that Scott was still a slave. In addition, the decision challenged the right of anyone of African descent to claim U.S. citizenship. Chief Justice Taney's opinion, speaking for the court, said no Negro could be a citizen under the Constitution. Voluntary return from the free state of Illinois had made Scott subject to the Missouri's slave laws, Taney wrote.[4]

"What a beautiful opening the death left for Old Abe to fill with that eternal presidential candidate, Salmon Chase."

"I didn't know Lincoln had offered Chase the chief justice position."

"He hasn't. Not yet, but you wait and see. Old Abe's going to get Chase out of the notion of ever running for President again, and the top spot on the Supreme Court

52

is the safest, most comfortable place for a politician to be, especially if he's lost out on the presidency enough times."

"Speaking of Supreme Court cases, Lincoln's going to have trouble with the Milligan case when it comes up."

Lambdin P. Milligan, a Copperhead, had been arrested by Indiana military authorities in October.[5] Copperhead was a reproachful term for Northern Democrats who opposed the Lincoln Administration. They were "Peace Democrats" who urged negotiation as a way to end the war and unite North and South.[6]

Charged with conspiring against the United States, helping Rebels, and inciting to insurrection, Milligan had faced a military trial. If he were sentenced to be executed, as seemed likely, he would surely appeal to the nation's highest court on grounds the military had no authority to try a civilian when the courts were still operating.

There had been much talk about the long practice of military trials for civilians. Secretly, most people were glad someone was finally going to take it to the Supreme Court.

The Washington diners talked on. No matter how Lincoln had managed to win the canvass, he now had another four years to try to implement his Reconstruction plans.

Booth rose and walked out. So much for the public's opinion.

By early November, the NDP had made progress in its investigation into the rumors that Lincoln was to be spirited away. The secret police had also discovered Booth's involvement.

Earl and Andrew Potter discussed the plot with Lafe Baker.[7] "How'd you find out about Booth's kidnap plans?" Earl asked.

"Through Ohue Rice," Baker replied.

"Code name for Marsh Frye, major in the Rebel secret service," Andrew said.

"Right. I'm paying him $1,500 a month for information and he's well worth it."

Earl knew the double agent who had come from Georgia to live in Philadelphia. "What's the story?"

"Booth's wife's been working with Frye as a spy and courier. She makes frequent trips to Canada and the midwest. The Booth home near Harpers Ferry is used as a way station for the spy route into the Shenandoah Valley by way of the Appalachian Trail. She doesn't even know Frye is a northern agent, too."

"What's our next step?" Earl inquired.

Baker rubbed the tip of his nose. "We're just going to a wait until the right moment and catch Booth in the act."

"Isn't that risky?" Andrew asked. "I mean, giving a kidnapper time to set his plan in motion and then trying to grab him in the act? What if you're too late?"

"It's not just Booth," Baker said soberly. "Several high ranking army officers are treasonously helping him with his plot."

"We're going to grab them when we pick up Booth?" Andrew asked.

Baker smiled. "What do you think?"

Andrew had to admit such arrests would cause tremendous military and political eruptions. "McClellan's defeat must have thrown a clinker into the Radical Republicans' kidnap plan."

"I'm not sure it's a dead issue. We've picked up something curious from one of our informants," Baker said. "You remember James William Boyd, prisoner of war who'd been a captain in the Rebel secret service?"

"I'm not sure," Andrew said. "There've been so many."

"Well, Boyd was captured in '63. We made an agreement with him and he's an informant inside our prisons. He's been getting word to us on what the Rebs are up to. Suddenly, he's transferred to Old Capitol Prison from Hilton Head in South Carolina. And I didn't request his transfer! Remember I told you boys to look for unusual movements of Reb prisoners?"

"Several Reb officers are being transferred to Old Capitol. Did we request those transfers?" Andrew asked.

"I don't know about it," Earl answered.

"Any chance they're part of Booth's project?"

Baker shook his head. "No, I don't think so. We know pretty much all there is to know about Booth's plans.

This one involving Rebel officers could be part of the Northern plot. Let's see what else we can turn up. Find out more about Boyd."

Earl made a note on a small pad. "That's interesting," he said.

"What is?" Baker asked.

The detective held up the notepad. "J.W.B. See? James William Boyd has the same initials as John Wilkes Booth."

John Wilkes Booth recorded an apparent chance meeting in his diary, "I ran into John Surratt the other day and in a by-the-way conversation, he told me that he was now serving the Confederacy as a courier between Washington, Richmond and Canada."[8]

Booth had told Surratt, "Yes, I already know you're a courier. Jacob Thompson and Clement Clay in Montreal told me and suggested I look you up. Let's have a talk, John."

Booth and the tall, slender boy had met in 1861 when Booth's boyhood friend, Michael O'Laughlin, had introduced them.[9] Surratt had also been postmaster in Surrattsville, Maryland, where his family owned a small farm, tavern, and store. But someone had suspected the youth of Southern sympathies, and he had lost the postmaster's job.

Surratt would later tell a different version of his involvement, but Booth's diary claimed they joined together and began recruiting men for the kidnapping. The actor wrote in his diary about Surratt: "He comes tonight bringing with him four trusted men he swears by. We are to meet at Ella Washington's boarding house in Georgetown."[10] Ella B. Washington had been the wife of a Rebel colonel who had died in 1863. Baker's detectives knew her as a great favorite at the White House and the Treasury Department.[11]

"Being a woman of more than ordinary attractions," as Baker expressed it, "her influence at the departments had become very great." She gave soirées at the boarding house, sending invitations to heads of the different departments and bureaus. One of her frequently invited guests was Col. William Browning, private secretary to Andrew Johnson.

John Wilkes Booth moved easily through Washington social circles. He was among the guests at a party given in mid-December at the home of the parents of Eva Grey, a Washington socialite.[12] There the actor met John Conness, a handsome senator from California.[13]

"I knew your brother, Edwin, in California," the Democrat turned Union Republican began.

"You knew Eddie?"

"We're old friends from the days of '55 and '56, when he was touring my state."

Conness had been born in Ireland in 1821. He had been miner, merchant, and politician, had served two terms as a California State Assemblyman, and had been elected to the U.S. Senate in March, 1863.

"If we may, I'd appreciate meeting privately with you," the Californian suggested. "If you can slip away from this rather boisterous crowd, I'd like to talk to you about some confidential matters."

Booth raised his eyebrows. The senator, he knew, was friendly to the Radical Republicans, whose anti-South and anti-Lincoln attitudes were the talk of Washington. What could this highly placed man want with a Southern patriot?

The two met in a corner of the Grey's library for cigars and brandy.[14]

"I could render some service to the South," the senator began. "I have a friend who's in the weaving business in the northeast. He could supply a large amount of bandages. Naturally," Conness said, blowing cigar smoke expansively toward the high ceiling, "I'm offering these for a price."

"Why tell me, Senator?"

Conness puffed on his cigar. He regarded Booth with a knowing look. "Why not call on me tomorrow? We may have some common interests."

When Booth met Conness as agreed, the senator produced several documents. "These should prove I'm not an enemy spy,"[15] he observed wryly.

Booth looked them over and nodded.

"I'm going to give you the name of a wholesale druggist. He can be trusted; take my word for it. He'll supply you with 5,000 to 25,000 ounces of quinine and a supply of bandages."

"For a price?" Booth asked with a hint of a smile.

"It's almost Christmas," the senator said, grinning broadly.

Booth nodded.

"Perhaps you might find it expedient to know of an easier way to move along the post roads?"

The actor's dark eyes glinted. The senator had access to many vital items and was willing to exchange them for cash.

"There is no easy way to move along the post roads without knowing the passwords," Booth said. "They're changed daily, as you surely know, since you're on the post office and post roads committee."

"You could purchase a six week list of all the passwords—in advance—for a very nominal sum."

"How much?"

"Oh, $3,000."

Booth frowned. "For how long?"

"As long as you wish, Mr. Booth," Sen. Conness paused, adding with a smile, "providing, of course, there is always another $3,000 forthcoming for each list.[16]

"Why are you so interested in helping to save the Confederacy?" Booth asked bluntly.

The senator was equally as blunt. "Oh, I don't care who wins this war. But the war will end—and before too long, I think. And with it will end these golden opportunities."

"Money? That is your only interest?"

"Mr. Booth, I am not a patriot for either the North or the South, but rather a man with a small pocket and a large need![17] And you, I take it, you consider yourself a Rebel patriot?"

"I shall serve the South to my dying breath," declared Booth.

"I shall regret to see you die so young. The South is passing, Mr. Booth. Soon it shall be gone, like last night's dream."

"I do not accept your opinion, Sen. Conness. The South is far from lost. I tell you, great and unexpected events may yet happen—events that overnight can change the entire course of the war. In fact, I'll wager on it!"

"Well, I hope you're right, Mr. Booth. Goodnight!"

Booth made another trip to Richmond to see Judah Benjamin, English lawyer and statesman who had served as a U.S. senator from Louisiana from 1852-61.[18] He had held three posts in the Confederacy: Attorney General, Secretary of War and Secretary of State.

Benjamin seemed to have a perpetual small smile tugging at the corners of his mouth. "Mr. Booth," the wily lawyer said, when Booth was ushered into his office, "I'd like to take you to meet Alexander Stephens."

The Confederate Vice President was a sharp contrast to Benjamin. At 52, he was cadaverous, a man in poor health.

After the visit with Benjamin and Stephens, Booth was able to write in his diary, "The two of them and I went to see Jefferson Davis."[19]

Over six feet tall, the strong-jawed, 56 year old President of the Confederacy was a distinguished looking man. Thin from health problems and worry, blind in one eye, Davis had been President of the Confederacy since it had been formed.

Out of this meeting came detailed instructions for Booth. An order for $70,000, "drawn on a friendly bank," was also handed the actor.[20]

Benjamin said he would arrange for Booth to meet some very prominent Northern speculators.[21]

Though on opposite sides of a civil war, the Northern speculators and the Confederate politicians had a common commodity problem. The speculators needed cotton.

58

The South needed meat. The Union's blockade prevented cotton from leaving the South.

Lincoln had softened the rules before the 1864 election by providing "cotton passes" to a limited number of people.[22] These passes allowed the valuable cotton to move by private means through the lines to European markets, provided it was purchased with Union "greenback" dollars and certain other tradeables such as meat. Gold was not to be a part of the exchange.

After the 1864 election, the increase of NDP seizures of commodities as Rebel contraband prevented such deals. Millions of dollars of meat and other goods were tied up in warehouses guarded by Baker's secret police. Since Northerners couldn't deliver on their part of the bargain, millions of bales of cotton were not allowed to move out of the South.[23]

The complications would be explained to Booth when Benjamin arranged a meeting with a top authority.

"In Philadelphia today," Booth confided in his journal, "I met with Jay Cooke."[24]

The banker-financier told Booth, "I'll be frank. The plans I'd like to discuss with you are sensitive in the extreme. I'm concerned about being compromised."[25]

"I am sure you've already investigated me," Booth replied, "and you have been assured I am totally trustworthy and discreet."

"Yes, well. To be blunt, Mr. Booth, I would like to arrange for you to meet a number of people who are interested in your . . . uh . . . plans. Would you be able to meet with me at the Astor House in New York on Friday next?"

At the Astor House, Jay Cooke introduced Booth to his 39 year old brother, Henry.[26]

"What a pleasure to meet you, Mr. Booth," Henry cried warmly as he pumped the actor's hand. "I have seen you upon the stage so many times, and always admired your many talents!"

Henry, head of his brother's Washington office, was also lobbyist for the capital's first street railway and president of his brother's Washington-Georgetown Street Railway Company. He had organized the First National Bank and, later, the National Life Insurance Company.

"To be quite honest with you, Mr. Booth," Henry Cooke boomed, "I think most highly of . . ." He lowered his voice and glanced around the lobby. ". . . I think most highly of Judah Benjamin. And I must acknowledge that anyone the old fox should send would be the best man available."[27]

Booth bowed his dark head slightly. It was curious; one of the top men in the Confederacy's cabinet had sent him to meet the very bankers who financed Lincoln's war.

The two brothers led the way to a large private room where a number of speculators in cotton and gold waited. Booth acknowledged introductions. Bankers, industrialists, and politicians were also on hand.[28]

Booth met political boss, Thurlow Weed, Samuel Noble, a New York Cotton broker, and Radical Republican Zachariah Chandler, Michigan senator.

"Mr. Bell?" Booth repeated to the next man. "It's a pleasure to make your acquaintance, sir."

"I'm a friend of John Conness," the 32 year old lawyer, Clark Bell, told the actor. Bell was associated with promoters of the Union Pacific Railroad and Telegraph Company. When it had been unable to proceed with construction, he had helped reorganize what amounted to a conspiracy, and drafted an act which Congress approved on July 2, 1864, under which the firm received federal funds.

When the introductions were completed, Jay Cooke declared, "Lincoln's friends and former law partners, Ward Lamon and Leonard Swett, are speculating heavily in cotton and gold."[29]

Booth sensed the direction the talk would take.

Lincoln and Swett, as lawyers, went back to Illinois days when they practiced before the bench in the eighth judicial circuit. Lamon was one of the very few men in Washington identified as a close friend of the President.

"Lamon is the key," Cooke told the group. He could get cotton passes signed by the President. The way it was explained to Booth, the U.S. Marshal of Washington, D.C., would go to the Treasury Department and obtain a pass from Treasury official Hansen Risley.[30]

Lamon would then walk up to his friend, the President, and say, "Here, Lincoln, sign this for me, please."

The Chief Executive would scribble, "A. Lincoln", and Lamon would go out to make himself a fortune through friends who had arranged for the cotton to move.

Unfortunately, some speculators, after arranging cotton deals with the South via the passes—but before they could make the cash-commodities exchange—had suffered secret service raids in which millions of dollars worth of meat were seized as contraband. The speculators were also troubled by provost marshals seizing supplies that could be traded.

"This means brokers can't deliver the meat to the Confederacy, as per contract. There's not only the financial loss of the meat, but the brokers are in arrears with their contracts to foreign governments."[31]

Noble observed, "It seems to me that the government is planning all this to deliberately force default. You can be sure we're not the only ones unhappy about it. England's really upset."

"It seems to me," Sen. Chandler said savagely, "Lincoln made a deal before the election to help him win in November. Now he's got what he wants, and he's disclaiming those agreements; he's not beholden to anyone."

Jay Cooke declared, "I will continue to have dealings with the Confederacy. Not out of fear of betrayal, but because, in peace and in war, a businessman must do business, whatever the stakes." (In his diary Booth later recorded, "Each and every one asserted that he had dealings with the Confederate States and would continue to whenever possible.")[32]

The financier turned to the actor. "That's why we think you can render us some service. At the same time, you can be of service to the Confederacy. You may already know some of our problems, but let me review them for you. Then these gentlemen may have some questions, or you may want to ask them something."

61

Cooke reminded Booth that in the national Union blockade, the rivers and the Atlantic seaboard were patrolled by Federal gunboats.[33] The general blockade was tremendously effective.

"Everyone is hurting," thundered Cooke. "French and English mills are shut down. In fact, there's speculation England will enter the war on the side of the South.[11]

Booth's smooth, vibrant voice filled the room. "I have been wondering what would happen if a British man-o'-war accompanied an English merchant ship through the blockade."[34]

"A lot of people have been wondering that," Jay Cooke replied. "An international incident like that could bring England into the war against the Union."

Booth's forefinger brushed his mustache. "So much of the problem you gentlemen face has grown out of the new Treasury system."

"I wish I'd never heard of the Commercial Intercourse Act with Insurrectionary States," Noble said bitterly, referring to the formal name of the act that had led to "cotton passes."

At meeting's end, Jay Cooke slapped the actor on the shoulder. "There are millions of dollars in profits to be made, and we're being denied our share. We'll be ruined if Lincoln's policies are continued."

Booth suspected that, since 90 percent of the world's cotton had passed through the hands of these speculators before the war, they were still thinking selfishly.[35] He found it difficult to keep his anger from showing. Men were fighting and dying on both sides because they believed in certain principles. Yet here was a room full of rich men planning ways to get even richer, and complaining because their road to more wealth was blocked.

"Gentlemen," Booth said, managing to remain poised, "how may I be of service to you?"

"Cooke gave me two letters," Booth wrote that evening in his diary, "one to Beverly Tucker and the other to Jacob Thompson." Both letters were in cipher code.[36]

Booth pocketed the letters to the Confederate agents and again departed for Montreal.

Chapter 5

THE RADICALS PLOT THICKENS

John Wilkes Booth was jolted by a disconcerting surprise in Montreal. As he entered St. Lawrence Hall, he recognized two men just leaving. The first was Confederate agent Nathaniel Beverly Tucker.[1]

The 44 year old Tucker, a driver of hard bargains, was in Canada on a delicate North-South mission to exchange cotton for bacon. The Confederate agent was also on some kind of secret diplomatic mission to see certain influential Union men.

It was the man with him who had given Booth such a start. The actor turned aside quickly and made his way to the room of George Nicholas Sanders, a Confederate agent whom the actor knew.[2] Booth knocked nervously.

Sanders, 52, was a revolutionist. Always in debt, he had tried magazine publishing, then had gone to London, where he had written letters to newspapers advocating the assassination of Napoleon III. Because of his wild imagination and grandiose ideas, he had many enemies at home and abroad.

Sanders was in. "Booth! Come in!"

The actor shut the door quickly, stepped to the window, and motioned for the agent to look. "You see that man with Tucker?"

"Of course, but why're you so agitated? Who is he?"

"Lafayette Baker!"[3]

"The North's secret service chief?"

"He was, and I think he still is," said Booth. "Why's

63

Tucker talking to him? Doesn't Tucker know who Baker is?"

"He must not. I'll go see if I can warn Tucker." Sanders rushed from the room. Booth paced the floor until Sanders returned.

Booth was still in the room an hour later when Tucker knocked. The two Confederates held a conference outside the door before Tucker came in and greeted Booth.

Small talk took up an uncomfortable half-hour. Booth was given no explanation why Tucker had been talking to the head of the NDP. He kept his coded letters in his pocket.

Then, Jacob Thompson, Canadian Confederate secret service chief, arrived, and Booth pulled out the letters, handed one to Thompson, the other to Tucker.[4] The men decoded the messages and read them in silence.

"Let's have dinner," Thompson suggested.

After dining in the hotel, Thompson handed Booth the satchel he'd been carrying. "Guard it well." Thompson leaned forward. "It contains $50,000 in bank notes."[5]

Booth glanced around the dining room. The usual waiters, military men, and important civilians in expensively tailored suits—none seemed to be watching the four men in the corner.

"Instructions are inside. Fifteen thousand goes to Conness. Leave the sealed envelope at the home of Senator Wade."[6]

"Benjamin Wade?"

"Yes. There's $20,000 in notes in his envelope."

Wade, of the Wade-Davis Bill and the Radicals' Manifesto, chairman of the powerful Committee on the Conduct of the War, one of the most belligerent men in Congress, bitter critic of General McClellan and of Lincoln, close associate of War Secretary Stanton!

Booth ran nervous fingers along his mustache. Wade was the third Radical Republican he had recently met. Conness at the Grey's party, Sen. Chandler at the speculators' meeting. Now Wade. Why was he getting $20,000?

"The balance of the money is to be used for recruitment," Thompson said. "Now, let's get on with our plans."[7]

Booth was uneasy when he returned to Washington. The end of the year was near. Much remained to be done. And he couldn't get over seeing Lafe Baker with a Confederate agent in Canada, nor Ohio Sen. Wade's payoff. He had a feeling he knew very little of what was simmering beneath the surface.

Washington was reeling with rumors about plans to kidnap the President. Everyone seemed to have heard about a December 1 classified ad that ran in the *Selma* (Alabama) *Dispatch:* "One million dollars wanted to have peace here by the first of March. If the citizens of the Southern Confederacy will furnish me with the cash, or good securities, for the sum of $1 million, I will cause the life of Abraham Lincoln, William Seward and Andrew Johnson to be taken by the first of March next."

The ad went on to say that the death of those three would give peace and "satisfy the world that cruel tyrants cannot live in a land of liberty."[8]

Only $50,000 in advance was demanded.

Ten days later, Ward Lamon sat down at his desk at 1:30 in the morning to warn Lincoln, "You are in danger." He regretted that the President did not appreciate what "I have repeatedly said to you in regard to the proper police arrangements connected with your household and your own personal safety."[9]

The President had again gone unattended to the theatre, taking with him a senator and a foreign minister. "Neither could defend himself against an assault from any able-bodied woman in the city," Lamon went on.

He tendered his resignation (which wasn't accepted), stating that the President's life "will be taken" unless Lincoln was more cautious.[10]

The NDP had picked up more kidnap information. William R. Bernard, NDP adjutant, was in Montreal when he came across details of Booth's kidnap plan.[11]

Bernard had been searching for Confederate agent Thomas Henry Hines, who looked like Booth. The adjutant wrote Baker saying that he had found Hines and that he was up to something. A week later the detective again wrote. It wasn't Hines, he'd found, but John Wilkes Booth, and he was involved in a plot to kidnap Lincoln.

Twice the NDP notified Secretary of War Stanton that a plan was under way to kidnap Lincoln. After he'd heard of the plot from the double agent, Marsh Frye, Baker had sent word to Stanton. Now after receiving the Bernard letters, he again warned the Secretary.[12]

At least one person inside Edwin Stanton's office had specific knowledge of the proposed kidnapping of the President. In November, Major Thomas Eckert, head of the military telegraph and Stanton's most trusted aide, was sent to New York to investigate several big fires the Confederates were suspected of setting.[13]

Eckert claimed he had picked up a letter on a streetcar which named Booth as a prospective kidnapper. At about the same time, a woman also claimed to have found a letter on a streetcar linking Booth to a kidnap plot.

The only action taken to protect the President was the appointment of a cavalry escort for trips and naming a four man White House police force.[14] William B. Webb, Washington Chief of Police, detailed the four officers and gave them general instructions.

"Alphonso Dunn, John Parker, Alexander Smith, and Thomas Pendel will guard all approaches to the President, whether in his office or elsewhere in the building. Whichever one of you is on duty will accompany the President on any walks he might take. In general, you are to stand between him and possible danger."[15]

The night guards were to protect the President on trips to and from the War Department, where he visited the telegraph office, to guard Lincoln at any place of amusement, and to patrol the corridor outside his room as he slept.

"Your only arms," the chief added, "will be revolvers."

Officer John Parker was not a bit happy. The job would

interfere with his personal ideas of police activity. Parker had a long record as a troublemaker. A year after joining the Washington force, he had been charged with conduct unbecoming an officer, and the use of violent and insolent language.[16]

A short time later, he had been charged with willful violation of police regulations. The charge of conduct unbecoming an officer was repeated. Parker was accused of using highly offensive language toward Officer Humphrey and visiting a house of prostitution. The report added, "Parker was intoxicated and had been put to bed, but fired a pistol through the window."

The next month, Parker faced charges of sleeping on a streetcar while on duty. Three months later, he was brought before the police board again, for refusing to restrain some disorderly Negroes, and had used insulting language to the woman making the complaint.[17]

This was the type of policeman assigned to guard President Lincoln in November, 1864. If Lincoln knew of Parker's background, he did nothing about it.

In Washington, Booth met with Sen. John Conness at the National Hotel where Conness was having coffee.[18] He motioned for Booth to join him. "You've been to Montreal again, I believe?"

Booth thought, "He really means, 'Do you have some money for a man who is neither a patriot for the North or South, but one with a small pocket and a large need?'" Aloud, Booth said, "I have a package for you."

The senator took the packet of money and slipped it, uncounted, into an inside pocket. "My thanks." He reached for his coffee cup. "I welcome your visits when they are so profitable."

"I'm pleased to be of some service."

"Did you also have a package for Sen. Wade?"

"I left a sealed envelope at his home."

"I understand you have also made the acquaintance of Sen. Chandler?"

"I have had the privilege."

"In the future, I will work with you in matters pertaining to these gentlemen."

Booth frowned. John Conness was to be the contact for the Radical Republicans who strongly opposed Lincoln?

"You are undoubtedly wondering when you will be given details of what's going on."

"Yes, I have wondered when information would be given me and what your connection is in all this."

"I'll make it brief, Mr. Booth. I know of your kidnap plans."

Booth flushed a telltale red.

"Don't be alarmed, Booth. I represent people who are interested in helping you."

"Senator, I can't see you, a Radical Republican, helping the South. What's your motive?"

"Let's just say my motives are not important to your involvement."

Booth shrugged. "If you don't want to tell me, I suppose it doesn't matter. But I can guess."

"Guess all you want, but don't forget the basic problem. He must be removed from office."

"He?"

"Yes. If you undertake to carry out the abduction, a place will be provided for them to be kept."

"Them? I thought you said 'he'."

"I did." The senator grinned. "There will be three." He leaned forward, "We want the President, Vice President, and Secretary of State taken."[19]

Booth suppressed a low whistle. "What!"

"You understood me correctly, Mr. Booth."

"But why? Why those three?"

"My apologies, Mr. Booth, but that is confidential. All we're asking you to do is to abduct three people. Will you do it?"

Booth thought quickly: Conness is allied with the Radical Republicans who want to control the government and ravage the South. Still, the Rebel Thompson had given him $15,000 for Conness. There had to be some mutual aim between the Confederacy and this California senator.

Booth's fingers tapped on the tablecloth. The Maryland

planters had only wanted him to capture Lincoln and spirit him to Richmond. The Confederacy had provided the money to augment the Maryland plan.[20] But now the mystery began. Rebel Judah Benjamin had set up a meeting between him and the Northern financiers and speculators.[21]

Booth hated the speculators. They were leeches and profiteers, but didn't they serve a purpose for the South? If the Confederacy could get its cotton out, cash and pork could be gotten in for Lee's army. Booth could support the results if not the reasons.

Now, here was Conness, representing a fourth group whose politics Booth loathed. Why did his group want Lincoln out? Why Johnson and Seward? He turned at last to the Californian. "I do have some questions, Senator."

"I thought you might, Mr. Booth."

"Let's start with the question of 'When?' "

"We'd like this to take place sometime after the inauguration but before the cessation of hostilities."[22]

Were they so sure the South would soon lose? Still, the President's abduction by any group could accomplish his goal: to be in a position to bargain for the release of Confederate prisoners, to gain advantage for the Confederate war effort.

"How does your group propose to help me carry out this—uh—enlarged plan?"

"My group knows the movements of all three men. I'll be able to tell you when to strike."

"And what if I fail to capture all three?"

"Remember, Mr. Booth, if all three cannot be captured at the same time, Lincoln must be the first. Let there be no mistake on that point."

Booth had not known of the original Radicals' plan to appoint an interim Radical Republican to run the executive branch and to deny inauguration to Southern-leaning McClellan who they had assumed would beat Lincoln in November.[23]

Nor did he know that with Lincoln's re-election, the Radicals' plot had simply changed.[24] Now they would kidnap the President, Vice President, and Secretary of State and seize control of the executive branch, control reconstruction, and prevent Democrats from dominating Congress.

Lafe Baker and Earl Potter met to update their findings. "Anything new on Boyd?" Baker asked.

"We found the transfer order. Thought you'd like to see a copy."

Dated October 5, 1864, on the letterhead of the Office of the Commissary General of Prisoners in Washington, D.C., the special order was addressed to Major General John G. Foster, commanding the Department of the South, Hilton Head, South Carolina:[25]

"By direction of the Secretary of War, I have the honor to request you will order Captain J. W. Boyd, Co. 'F', 6th Tenn. Rebel Army, a prisoner of war recently transferred from Fort Delaware to Hilton Head, S.C., to be delivered to the Provost Marshal in this city with as little delay as practicable."[26]

"Stanton personally ordered the transfer." Earl Potter pointed to the document. " 'By direction of the Secretary of War.' But it was signed by Colonel William Hoffman. Does this mean Stanton's the mastermind?"

"I don't know. I hate that man; I admit it. But I've got to give him his due. He may or may not be involved in whatever this Boyd transfer means. Did somebody instruct Stanton to do that? Who knows?"

"All Boyd does is sit there in his cell like he's waiting a call," Potter said. "Same with some other transferred Reb officers. Boyd is apparently the one who's likely going to be in charge. He was one smart agent."

Baker smiled. "And smart Rebel agents are expendable."[27]

"If he gets caught, the South will be blamed."

Baker said, "I've made sure Stanton knows we're investigating all kidnap rumors. I've sent him several memos on the Booth plot; now I'll send a note warning him of another known plot to kidnap the President. Then we've protected ourselves. Our job is to learn things; his job is to protect the President."

A newspaper story near the end of the year didn't cause too much excitement, but it had significance for Booth. A ship, bound from Canada for Nassau, had exploded and sunk in the lower St. Lawrence. It was suspected that the blast was planned.[28]

On board was the theatrical trunk containing the Confederate colonel's uniform given Booth. The trunk was later recovered and sold at auction.[29] But the body of Patrick Martin, who had brought Booth and the Maryland planters together, was not recovered. A few men wondered if the ship had been destroyed because Martin was aboard.[30]

Chapter 6

FIRST KIDNAP TRY A FIASCO

Not everyone Booth approached agreed to help him, and to find qualified men took time. Among the earliest recruits were Samuel Bland Arnold and Michael O'Laughlin, both of Baltimore.

Arnold, 28, had been a schoolmate of the actor at St. Timothy's Hall in Maryland. He had not seen Booth since 1852. Then a note arrived inviting him to meet Booth at Barnum's Hotel in Baltimore, where the actor was stopping enroute to Washington.[1]

Booth ushered his old school chum into his hotel room. "Sam! I'm delighted you were able to join me. Come in! Sit down! I've ordered wine and cigars. They should be up any moment. Well, tell me all that you've been doing since we last met."

Arnold, warmed by Booth's greeting, sat down in a comfortable chair and began talking. He had served two

71

years as a Confederate soldier, he told Booth.[2] "But I recently took the Union oath," he added.

A knock at the door interrupted. The actor opened the door to see another old friend. "Michael O'Laughlin! Come in! I've an old friend I want you to meet."

Booth and O'Laughlin had not only kept in touch over the years, they had been in a smuggling ring together, shipping contraband quinine, morphia, and other medicines to the South. O'Laughlin believed Booth had been in charge of the operation but knew the actor had had the help of men in government. Booth had "passes" down through the lines of Ohio, Illinois, Indiana, Kentucky, and Tennessee.[3] As an actor, Booth had obtained a pass signed by General Grant.

O'Laughlin had been receiving drugs in Baltimore from ship captains. From there, his shipments moved south and west. For about a year, he'd been going regularly to New York to the Chaffey Company on Water Street. One of the company's many activities was as a shipping agency where arrangements could be made for ships and shipments of all types of cargo, including contraband.[4]

Booth opened one of the bottles brought by a steward.

Sipping his wine, Arnold turned to O'Laughlin. "How long have you known Wilkes?"

"All my life. We grew up together. We're boyhood friends, went to school together."[5]

"Really? So did I! Wilkes and I attended St. Timothy's Hall.[6] What school were you and Wilkes at?"

"Primary school in Bel Air."

The talk turned to the war. O'Laughlin said he had been in the Confederate Army but had taken the Union oath just as Arnold had done.[7]

Booth skillfully turned the talk to politics. He spoke in glowing terms of the Confederacy and dwelt upon the large numbers of Confederate prisoners held by the Union.*

Arnold was surprised to find that his host knew some-

*Gen. Grant had steadfastly refused to exchange prisoners of war. He was willing to let captured Union soldiers sit out the conflict in the Confederacy so he did not have to give back captured rebels.

thing of his political feelings although they had not seen each other in 12 years.

"We could help free those wretched prisoners held in such deplorable conditions by Union guards." Booth let the words sink in.

"How could we do anything?" Arnold asked.

"We would need something so valuable that the North would gladly exchange Confederate prisoners."

His visitors looked expectantly at their host.

"You're wondering what could be that valuable as an exchange commodity, are you? Well, I have the answer. We capture the President and use him as hostage until our prisoners are exchanged; ours for him."

Booth quickly sketched in the details. "The old scoundrel frequently goes unguarded from the White House to the Soldiers Home.[8] We can pick him up on the road, or we can capture him at the theatre and carry him off to Richmond. Then we negotiate exchanging him for all Confederate prisoners in Federal hands."

Booth painted such glowing pictures of success that by the time their glasses were empty, the two men began to share his belief in the plot. When Booth saw them to the door, he murmured, "Remember, you're bound not to divulge this plan to a living soul."

Later, Sam Arnold told Booth he would join. "I think O'Laughlin will, too. But he needs a week in time and a hundred dollars in cash."[9]

Booth counted out the money. "Give this to him," he said, "and tell him he also has the time he needs."[10]

The two recruits began arranging what Arnold called "a blind"—they were to be in the "oil speculating business."[11]

The first Sunday in November, Booth traveled by stagecoach from Washington to Bryantown, Maryland. He had letters of introduction from Patrick Martin in Canada. Booth's first stop was at the home of Dr. William Queen who invited him to attend mass at St. Mary's church.[12] Booth was introduced to many of the more esteemed members of the congregation before services began.

The handsome stranger with the famous name attracted general attention. It was already said that he had come down from Washington to buy land for improvement.[13]

One man attending church that morning was David Herold, an apothecary's clerk in Washington. His passion for hunting partridge had caused his frequent discharge by a succession of employers. He loved the vicinity of the old academy he had attended at Charlotte Hall, six miles from Bryantown church. He came up to the distinguished guest to say, "Mr. Booth, I met you at Harpers Ferry in the time of John Brown."[14]

Booth's eyes flashed in recollection. For a short time, in 1859, he had been a member of Militia Company F, Richmond Volunteers.[15] With a borrowed uniform, Booth had proceeded with the fashionable company to Charlestown to see the execution of abolitionist John Brown. Booth had watched as the noose was adjusted. The then colonel, Robert E. Lee, leading American forces that had captured the bearded prophet at Harpers Ferry, gave the command. John Brown's body plunged into death and his spirit into immortality.[16]

The actor remembered David Herold's little, simpering face. The eyes seemed even more close-set and furtive than he remembered. "Why, Dave, how queer that I should see you here! Where's George Atzerodt?"[17]

"Down to Port Tobacco, making carriages and running the blockade."

"Dave, are you very busy now? Could you take me to see Atzerodt?"

"Oh, yes, Mr. Booth. I can always borrow a horse down in Charles, and I like to hunt and ride. Don't you want to shoot some partridges?"

"That's just it," Booth replied. "Don't tell anybody we are going, but meet me tomorrow noon at Bryantown tavern."[18]

At church services Booth sat in the family pew of Dr. Queen. In a neighboring pew sat Dr. Samuel Mudd. After the service, Booth presented a letter of introduction. Mudd owned seven slaves.[19] He considered his family's grievances on a par with other Marylanders; all were highly disturbed that Union General Winfield Scott had ordered the wholesale arrest, without formal charges, of Maryland citizens suspected of disloyalty. More than 20,000 Federal troops were stationed in Charles County alone.[20]

Booth distinguished the good doctor by accepting an invitation to his home for dinner and to spend the night.

David Herold and Booth went the next day to Port Tobacco. They found Atzerodt in his wheelwright's shed, asleep in an old family carriage.[21] His business had been neglected for blockade-running.

"By jing," he cried when Booth's proposal was made to him. "I know just the boat. I can make a wagon to run like a streak of greased lightnin', and I want money bad."

The three men rode together down the west side of Port Tobacco River. On the way, Atzerodt fell behind, saying, "There's a dog here at Carpenter's that I believe knows a Rebel from a Union man. He comes for me every time, though I sold him to this feller."

As they spoke, a large, fierce dog bounded down the road, looked at the horsemen, and leapt the fence. The dog snapped at Booth's knee and rushed his stirrup for a distance.

Three or four miles below Port Tobacco, in a woodsy ravine, Atzerodt uncovered a large boat on low wheels and axles.[22]

"I made these wheels," he said. "The Yankee navy has broke every boat afloat to stop the running of the blockade. So we haul this one up an' hide it. Abe Lincoln will get to Virginia so soon in that boat he won't know it from Maryland."

"How far to Washington from this spot?"

"Thirty-six miles. If you get Old Abe at 4 o'clock in the afternoon, you can make this boat landing at half-past 8, and have him in Virginia by 10."

As they rode back to Port Tobacco, the dog bounded up and lunged again at the three horsemen. Booth said between clenched teeth, "I'll settle with him now." He stopped, balanced his derringer, and fired.

"So Abe Lincoln shall die by this pistol!" Booth exclaimed. "If other measures fail to bring him. And now, both of you," Booth said, reloading, "raise up your hands and swear to what I say. If you refuse, you die like that dog, for I'll have your lives later if you dare disobey me or betray me. You both possess my secret."[23]

The German's stomach felt heavy as he slowly raised his hand. Herold, filled with admiration for Booth, held his up quickly.

Booth's vibrant voice, along with the death of the dog, gave him complete mastery. They swore, and were silent all the way back to Port Tobacco.[24] There the actor instructed them when to call on him in Washington at the National Hotel.

For the next several days, Booth scoured the countryside and surveyed the roads, planning a kidnap route southward. He met with Maryland planters Dr. William T. Bowman, John C. Thompson, Samuel Cox, and Thomas Jones. Jones said of his brother-in-law, "Thomas Harbin could be enlisted, but he has a family to support and would require $100 a month."[25] Harbin had been a Confederate signal officer in lower Maryland. Arrangements were made to take care of him.

When Booth found those he felt he could trust, he enlisted their help in working out escape routes and arranging for trusted men to help hide Lincoln along the route to Richmond.

From Dr. Mudd's neighbor, Booth purchased a bay horse, blind in one eye, to take back to Washington for use in the kidnapping.[26]

Back in the capital, he debated which of the possible exits from the city would be best to use. Georgetown Aqueduct was farthest from the White House. It was a mile and half ride through the city. Once over the aqueduct, they would be northwest of Washington in Virginia. Hard riding Federal patrols might cut off the escape. Booth rejected this possibility.[27]

Even considering the second possibility seemed useless. Bennings Bridge lay beyond the poorhouse to the east. This would take them across the east branch (Anacostia) of the Potomac River into Maryland. The problem then would be that the party would not be heading south toward Virginia, but southeasterly toward Annapolis.[28] Booth knew that wouldn't work.

Long Bridge, just blocks south of the White House, was a third possibility. Once over the bridge, the road ran straight to Richmond 100 miles away. The problem was that the Union had command of parts of the adjacent area, and troops going to and from the front used the road.[29]

The fourth route lay across the Navy Yard Bridge at the foot of Eleventh Street. Maryland was just across the river, and here were likely to be found many secessionists to help in the escape. No armies were in the area and never had been.[30] For racing out of Washington with the captured President, Booth was satisfied that the Navy Yard Bridge was the best route.

But alternate routes must be planned. Four would be best. If something happened to close one, or two, or even three, there would be one more choice.

Booth turned to further recruitment. He also rented a stable in the alley behind Ford's Theatre, where Edward "Ned" Spangler, a journeyman carpenter from Pennsylvania and stagehand, groomed Booth's horse.[31]

To Spangler, Booth was an educated gentleman. He liked the connection with such an important person and became the actor's faithful dog, ready to do anything for him without asking questions.

Spangler would be able to turn off the gas lights through a master control. He was familiar with the stage and would have no trouble moving about in the dark, helping with the long, lanky body when it was lowered from the presidential box.

For Booth had determined that only the most dramatic, the most bold and daring capture would do. There would be no stealthy strike in a dark alley. No, sir! John Wilkes Booth's name would be on every lip; his brain and his planning would make the capture the most talked about event in years. Best of all, he and his band would be heroes when the Confederate soldiers were released from Union prisons. It was a project to make the chest of an egotist swell with pride.

Booth hoped to recruit an actor to help and tried to persuade two friends. Samuel Knapp Chester, a character actor, refused hands down.[82] Booth then tried John Matthews whom he told, "If I capture the President and carry him within the Confederacy, we could hold him for ransom. That would compel the exchange of prisoners, man for man."[33]

Matthews would not go along with the plan. Still, Booth kept trying. Matthews was in Washington, studying for a new role, when he and two friends entered his rented room at William Petersen's house across the street from Ford's to find Booth sprawled upon the bed.

Matthews' friends began talking with Booth about the war. They had just visited some soldiers' hospitals and were stirred by what they had seen. They had decided to give a benefit for the Soldiers Home. Booth said he'd be a member of the audience. The play, *Still Waters Run Deep*, was one Matthews thought the President would likely come to see.

Just before the scheduled performance, Booth asked Matthews to deliver a trunk to Baltimore. He did, leaving the trunk, as Matthews later claimed, "filled with potted meats, sardines" and other items, even toilet articles, intended for "the comfort of President Lincoln on his journey to the Confederate's lines."[34]

Lewis Payne, 20, the last man to join the conspiracy, was a handsome giant from Florida. In 1861, he had attended his first stage play, in which Booth appeared. The deep, rich voice and graceful performance had so fascinated the young Confederate irregular that he had gone backstage to introduce himself.[35]

Now down and out, Payne was in Baltimore when he happened to pass Barnum's Hotel and was hailed by Booth.[36]

"Booth!" the young giant was delighted.

Booth took the soldier to eat, the actor's shrewd look assessing the powerful physique. Such a man could help handle the lanky Lincoln. When Booth told him his plan, Payne was enthusiastic.

Shortly before the middle of January, Booth had stopped by the Philadelphia home of his sister, Asia, now the wife of comedian John Sleeper Clarke.

"You have that letter I left with you last autumn and asked to keep for me?"

"The one you said was not be opened unless something happened to you? Here it is."

"Don't release it unless I'm captured or killed."[37] Her brother opened the letter.

"What does that mean?" Asia demanded in alarm.

Booth ignored his sister's concern. He hurriedly glanced at what he'd written months before: "Right or wrong, God judge me, not man. For by my motive good or bad, of one thing I am sure, the lasting condemnation of the North. I love peace more than life. Have loved the Union beyond expression."

The letter was long. Booth skimmed it, catching a line or two: "The country was formed for the white man and not the black.

"I have also studied hard to discover upon what grounds the right of a state to secede has been denied, when our name, United States, and Declaration of Independence both provide for secession. All my hope for peace is dead. My prayers have proved as idle as my hopes. God's will be done. I go to see and share the bitter end."

There was more. Booth's love today was for the South. He would "make for her a prisoner of this man, to whom she owes so much misery. If success attend me, I go penniless to her side."

He glanced at the closing line. "A Confederate doing duty upon his own responsibility."[38] That was good. No changes.

In the autumn of 1864, Mary E. Surratt bought a substantial, three-story, brick boarding house at 541 H Street, Washington. Mrs. Surratt could not move in until December, when she completed arrangements to lease her Maryland property, a tavern, to John M. Lloyd for $500 annually. He wasn't a very likely tenant, for he drank too much and didn't enjoy the best reputation, but his tenancy would permit Mrs. Surratt to make the move.[39]

The boarding house was a paying proposition, the boarders unpretentious, but reliable.

Louis J. Weichmann, 22, lived in the third story bedroom for which he paid $35 a month and shared the room with John Surratt when he was in town. They had known each other since 1859, when both were studying for the priesthood at St. Charles College. Weichmann had failed, turned to teaching, but had not done well. He was now a clerk in the Office of the Commissioner of Prisons, a branch of the War Department.[40] He was a large, soft youth, with a sneaking, gossipy nature wrapped up in an almost saintly manner.

Honora Fitzpatrick, 17, roomed with Anna, the 18 year old daughter of Mrs. Surratt. John T. Holohan, a tombstone cutter, his wife, Eliza, and their two children also roomed at Surratt's. Apollonia Dean, a nine year old whose mother boarded her out, completed the roster of tenants.

The widow had known a hard life. She had never enjoyed much of the world's finer things, but she was not a complainer. Quietly she had borne the problems of an alcoholic husband until he had died in 1862. She was a convert to Catholicism.

At 45, she was nearsighted, but hated to admit the need for glasses, and she suffered periodic physical illness due to menopause. She seemed worried about her son, John, who had left school to participate in the "exciting times," as he put it.[41]

On February 25, Payne rang the bell at the Surratt boarding house in Washington. Louis Weichmann answered the door. The handsome stranger said he'd come to see John Surratt. John wasn't home, but Mrs. Surratt gave Payne a meal because he admitted he hadn't eaten that day. He also stayed the night. He told Weichmann he was a clerk in a Baltimore china store.[42]

Booth began rehearsals for the abduction from Ford's Theatre.[43] Although the conspirators would try to capture the President in other opportune places, such as on one of his rides between the White House and the Soldiers Home, the drama demanded the kidnapping take place in the theatre, if possible.

Booth was, of course, familiar with Ford's. He had played there often; now he began spending afternoons studying the layout with a different eye.

The lighting apparatus would need to be lowered at just the right time. In the darkness and confusion, he and his band alone would know where everything was and what to do. They would seize Lincoln in his box, handcuff him securely, lower him to the stage, carry him to the alley where doors would be opened at the right time. They would shove him into a closed carriage, drive off swiftly, heading for the Navy Yard Bridge. The plan's very audacity would never be forgotten.

It was rumored that Lincoln and two guests would attend Ford's Theatre to see Edwin Forrest in *Jack Cade*. Booth's well oiled communications machinery went into action. Word went out through code signs, passwords, and secret orders.[44]

Herold rushed to Prince Georges County, Maryland, to get a team of horses. He was to have them ready for relay on the southern branch of the Anacostia near the Navy Yard Bridge.

His employer at the Adams Express Company refused to give Surratt time off, so he quit his new job and galloped south, spurring his horse to Port Tobacco to tell the Dutchman to have a flatboat ready to receive a carriage. He figured 15 men to the boat.

Arnold and O'Laughlin didn't show up at Ford's. Booth was furious, but he proceeded with plans. Everything was ready—two sets of handcuffs, gags and ropes. The stage lights were to be killed on cue. A vehicle with side curtains was stationed in the alley behind the theatre. At a signal, this delivery cart would pull up to the stage door.

Surratt and Booth were ready to enter the presidential box, seize Lincoln, bind him, and lower him in the darkened house over the front of the box.

They waited.

The elaborate plot was a stunning flop!

The night of January 18, 1865, was stormy, and the President stayed at home.

Chapter 7

BOOTH OUT, "CAPT. B" IN

On February 14, 1865, Confederate prisoner of war Captain James William Boyd sat in Old Capitol Prison and wrote a letter.[1] The former head of the Rebel military secret service in Virginia had already written two letters, but this one was special.

Of slightly above average height, with wavy, reddish brown hair and scraggly mustache of the same color, Boyd nevertheless bore a resemblance to John Wilkes Booth, whose initials he shared.[2] Boyd was in his 40s and Booth was 27, but pictures of the two showed similarities.

Addressed to Secretary of War Edwin Stanton, Boyd's letter began by noting that he had already written Col. William P. Wood, in charge of Union prisons, and Charles A. Dana, Assistant Secretary of War.[3]

Boyd introduced his subject by saying that he knew about the treachery of a Union officer that had resulted in losses of military stores and the garrison at Holly Springs, Maryland. But Boyd was writing Stanton for a personal interview in the hope of a transfer from the Union prison to do Union detective work in Tennessee. "I know every prominent man in West Tennessee and North Mississippi," he wrote.[4] "I know every hog path from Corinth to Paducah. I know who has been smuggling and who gives information and how it is all done."[5]

Some matters Boyd could not write about.

He had enlisted in the Confederate States Army and had been made head of the secret service in West Tennessee. When Col. (now Gen.) Lunsford L. Lomax was transferred from West Tennessee to Virginia, Lomax had Boyd moved to the Shenandoah. Boyd's job was to check out secret service arrangements with local partisans.

Boyd could write that he knew where cattle, sheep, and grain were hidden in Tennessee. "In fact," he scribbled, "everything connected with the army. Also the cotton dealers and how they pay for it. And how goods get in and out in large quantities."[6]

The captain chewed his pencil. Had he established his worth enough in the letter to get to the point? He considered that and thought back to how he'd arrived at Old Capitol.

Boyd had been with two other Confederate agents when captured in August 1863, by the NDP. Harry D'Arcy and James E. Watson had been promptly executed as spies.[7] Detective Pappy Walker had demanded of Boyd, "Where's those dispatches you're carrying?"[8]

"My name is James William Boyd, Captain, Sixth Regiment, Tennessee Volunteers, Confederate States Army," was Boyd's only answer.

The NDP operative already knew who he was; it was information he was after.

At headquarters, Walker discussed the prisoner with the Potters. When Boyd was told that D'Arcy and Watson had been executed, "he was visibly shaken," Andrew Potter said. "But he controlled himself. He knows he can't legally be killed and he's sure he won't be because he knows the whereabouts of those dispatches."[9]

Walker sent Boyd to the provost marshal's stockade in Memphis.

"The stockade at Memphis isn't the worst the Union Army has," Walker said, "but it's far from the best. Hot in summer, cold in winter, full of vermin and rats, food barely edible."

From early August until near mid-September 1863, NDP men questioned Boyd daily. They brought all the pressure to bear on him that they could. Finally, he agreed to work for the NDP if he could get a temporary release to visit his dying wife.[10]

83

For this favor, the Captain became a Rebel turncoat. He was paid $90 a month and, in return, reported on prisoners' activities and plans, as well as informing on crooked prison guards.

The life of a snitch is always in danger. The NDP kept Boyd moving. He was at Johnson's Island north of Sandusky, Ohio, on October 1. Using contacts set up inside the Federal prison, Boyd was assigned to discover Confederate prisoners' escape plans.[11] As a captured captain and secret service agent for the South, Boyd was accepted and was told of a planned mass escape. Complaining of chronic diarrhea, a common ailment in prisoner of war compounds, he contacted the infirmary doctor and gave him news of the plan.

The escape committee had not completely trusted Boyd. Some of the information he'd been given was false. Only Boyd could have been guilty of revealing it to the Federals. He managed to talk the Rebels out of harming him, perhaps by engineering an escape for several important Confederate officers.[12] Boyd had the permission and help of the NDP in the escape effort. The Potters reasoned it was necessary to cover their agent. The escapees were recaptured and taken to another camp, but Boyd was off the hook.

By April 1864, Boyd's life was again in danger. An NDP agent in the prison at Johnson's Island reported Boyd was marked for elimination.[13] The detectives first thought about "letting the Confederate prisoners do away with him rather than go to the trouble of transferring him." But they decided he might be useful at Point Lookout, Maryland. On May 20, Boyd was transferred to Hammond General Hospital so the NDP could be sure of his safety and to receive treatment for an old wound.[14] Boyd's leg near his ankle had continued to give him trouble. A bone and muscle infection had developed from the wound that had never healed properly. It periodically drained and caused him great pain.

On October 5, by order of the Secretary of War, Boyd was transferred to Old Capitol Prison in Washington[15]—

just about the time the bankers and speculators were going ahead with kidnap plans with Booth.

Now in his letter to Stanton, Boyd tried to convince the Secretary that he had good reason for offering to be a Union detective in Tennessee. His wife was dead, and his seven children were living on charity. ". . . A fine excuse for me to remain at home, and I could travel over the county without a question being asked."[16]

Within 24 hours, Boyd had an interview with Stanton or Maj. Thomas Eckert. He'd taken the oath of allegiance and was a free man.[17] He stood blinking outside the Federal prison gates, surprised at his assignment. He was not going to Tennessee, but on a mysterious mission that would take him to Canada, then Mexico.[18] He wrote Moe Stevens, a friend from Tennessee who had moved to Missouri, "I have taken a job with the government."[19]

Boyd's letter to Stevens explained his rationale for his actions. "I know that there are those who will condemn me for what I am doing. But they just can't know how I feel. From the day the Confederacy was formed, there were those who began to sell out. I never did that and never will, but it is a smart Rebel who knows when he is licked and a dumb one who keeps on fighting when he has his brains beat out. I hope you understand. I'll write you after my assignment from Mexico."[20]

John Wilkes Booth was furious over the jolting news that he had been fired as leader of the bankers and speculators' kidnap plan.

Before the first of March 1865, James V. Barnes, a Wall Street cotton broker, returned from Canada through Bellevue, Maryland, where he talked with Booth. Barnes was involved in a multimillion dollar cotton speculation transaction with R. D. Watson and other New York cotton brokers. [21]

"They've replaced me!"[22] Booth cried in his deep, musical voice. "Me! It was my idea. I originated it. I planned it. Now they've decided to put a military man in because they think a civilian can't handle it."

"The situation changed," Barnes replied. He knew the whole plot. "It's no longer a question of what you would do, but rather what you are able to do." Booth was being melodramatic, Barnes thought.

Booth exploded, "I tell you, I will not be replaced! It was my idea! I'm the originator of the plot, and I won't relinquish leadership, especially to some Reb captain."

"Is that who they got? A Rebel officer?"

"Captain B." Booth threw up his hands in a sweeping gesture. "Captain B. I'll find out his name. But it doesn't matter. I'm still going ahead with my plans."

Barnes tried to calm the actor. Booth strode angrily about, striking his riding boots with his riding crop.

Barnes studied the pacing Booth. The actor didn't know the true motive behind the triple kidnapping plot. The new government-to-be, the Radical Republicans, had indicated it would honor cotton contracts in which Barnes was greatly interested.

"The Confederate States Army is dead, they cannot help you now," Barnes told the actor.

"Don't say that, Barnes! Don't say that!" Booth's anguish was sincere.

"It's a reality. I'd be surprised if Gen. Lee's forces can hang on another six weeks."

The actor struck his high boot a furious slash. "It's all his fault! It's all his fault. The old tyrant!"

Barnes watched the agitated conspirator stride across the room, bringing his arms up in sweeping motions. "The old scoundrel! They can't replace me!" Booth cried out.

Barnes shook his head. The scene was what seemed to matter to Booth, both on and off the stage.

As soon as was possible, Barnes addressed a letter to R. D. Watson.[23] Under the date March 2, 1865, he wrote, "I was much dismayed by what I found on return from Canada. You were gone but four days when I arrived, but a great amount had transpired in the interim. The provost marshal has seized much of our pork supply and has placed the rest beyond our power to deliver it in compliance with our contracts."[24]

Barnes hesitated; it was risky to say too much in a letter, but the time for hesitancy was past. Barnes listed the number of pork barrels and locations, wrote of acute financial loss, and what he thought of the government deliberately confiscating the pork—part of their transaction with the Confederacy.

The cotton merchant paused again, then wrote, "Whatever is done must be done at once, no later than May 1.[25]

"It is essential that the President, Vice President, and Secretary be not harmed, but if they could be deposed for a fortnight. . . .[26]

"I do not—I am sure—need to point out that all we have rests with decisive action; the time for caution in the extreme is long past."[27]

He saw little chance of filling contracts by June 1, but "Stringer" had assured Barnes he could have five million pounds of pork at Wilmington or Charlestown by July 1, for transaction.

Barnes wrote, "Contact S. and have him get in connection with W. H. Lamon and see if the change can be made. Be positive and prompt—all else is useless."[28]

Barnes added another note about his talk with Booth: "J. W. was greatly annoyed at being replaced by 'your Northern speculators' friend, Captain B.' "

Other significant letters were being written.

In early March, a letter from the Chaffey Company's manager-agent, Thomas Caldwell, gave instructions to Captain John Scott, master of a sailing vessel flying the Canadian flag but under British registry:[29] "You will proceed in the brig, *Indian Prince,* to the city of Baltimore, Maryland, with a cargo of planks and shingles . . . Have your ship ready for taking on cargo no later than the 10th instant next.

"Cargo will be taken about the 12th at Benedict's, south of Washington, depending on the tides and other circumstances.

"Familiarize yourself with Okahanikan Cove and the currents in advance. You will receive instruction from a man named Stevenson in Baltimore. Proceed with caution."[30]

Okahanikan Cove was on Bloodsworth Island in the Chesapeake Bay about 70 miles from Washington. A swampy, desolate island, it had been chosen as an alternative to the Green mansion for holding the captives.

A few days later, Joao Celestino with the brig *Indian Queen* was ordered to Nanjemoy Creek near Port Tobacco, Maryland, less than 20 miles from Benedict's Landing. In October as the Northern speculators' plot moved toward its climax, the owners of these two ships under British registry had accepted $10,000 "for advanced payment for services" from Booth.[31]

Booth had arranged four abduction routes for bringing the President to Richmond.[32] One route was east of Washington to Upper Marlboro and down the Patuxent River. The second route was entirely by land, using loyal Maryland and Virginia planters to help move and hide the President en route to Richmond.

A third route was to move the President by land to the waiting *Indian Queen,* then sail south down the Potomac River. If that failed, the fourth route called for moving Lincoln overland from Washington to Benedict's Landing to the waiting *Indian Prince,* which would sail down the Patuxent River into the Chesapeake Bay and on to a Southern destination.

Once under sail, the ships, under British registry and manned by foreign crews, had no fear of search by federal patrol boats. The Union forbid encounters with British ships to avoid provoking Britain into the war on the side of the South.

At the National Hotel in Washington, Booth gave the appearance of taking his dismissal by the speculators rather lightly.[33] "What does it matter if the speculators have replaced me? I'm still leader of the three other groups—the Maryland planters, Confederacy leaders and Radical Republicans," he said.

However, a disturbing element needed to be considered. The speculators, with Captain Boyd as their leader, appeared to have a new strategy and Booth suspected what it was. They were not going to take Lincoln to Richmond, but to Bloodsworth Island in Chesapeake Bay and "legally" dispose of him.

This was contrary to Booth's plan to get Lincoln to Richmond. "It won't help our soldiers get released if the old scoundrel is killed," Booth worried. "It's urgent that I complete the kidnapping before the speculators do. Or," he added soberly, "the war ends."

But Booth had no intention of quitting what he saw as his duty. He had not quit when the speculators discharged him; he would not quit now.

Chapter 8

WHO'LL KIDNAP FIRST?

Washington's citizens huddled under the first of March's cold, blustery winds and leaden skies. Heavy rains turned unpaved streets to mire. In spite of the weather, people seemed jubilant. They sensed impending victory.

Inside the nation's governmental centers and in New York, the country's financial heart, many were not happy.

Power plays were going on behind almost every office door; tremendous pressures were building. There was no end to the intrigues, lies, deceits, and double-dealing.

John Wilkes Booth was fuming over his replacement by James Boyd.

Boyd had rushed off to Canada, then had returned to Maryland. He was to go on to Virginia before returning again to Maryland.[1]

Radical Republicans held secret meeting after secret meeting.

The speculators convened to curse the President who would be inaugurated for a second term on March 4.

In the field, Union troops pushed for final victory. And

the Radicals and the Northern speculators' plans were about to blow sky-high. War's end would spell their ruin.

In February, the Confederates had lost Wilmington, N.C., the last major Southern port. Robert E. Lee had placed Gen. Joseph E. Johnston in command of Confederate armies in South Carolina, Georgia, Florida, and Tennessee.[2]

Gen. William T. Sherman advanced steadily through South Carolina following his devastation of Georgia. There was no doubt he would soon be in North Carolina, driving the Confederates before him.[3]

In the Shenandoah, Union Gen. Philip Sheridan's crack 10,000-man cavalry was about to destroy what was left of the weakened Jubal Early command.[4]

Grant was again threatening Richmond and Petersburg with growing numbers of troops and war materiel. The South could muster fewer and fewer men, especially to hold off Sherman's advance in the Carolinas.

On Friday, March 3, the 38th Congress of the United States adjourned in preparation for Lincoln's inauguration the following morning.

Accumulated strain showed in Lincoln's haggard face. Forehead lines were deeper. Melancholy was a frequent companion.

Shortly after noon, March 4, he would take the oath of office for the second time. It was a sharp contrast from his first inauguration. War had followed his first swearing in. Now the war would soon end. He would have succeeded in his greatest single aim—to preserve the Union.

A second major objective had been reached on January 31. Congress had passed the Thirteenth Amendment to abolish slavery.[5] The amendment was still to be ratified, but it seemed certain the required number of states would support it. The amendment freed all slaves everywhere. Slavery as an institution was abolished.[6]

Lincoln stared out the window at the dreary, drizzly day. A heavy rain had fallen all morning. Streets and sidewalks were mud paths. Crowds of people under umbrellas were already making their way along Pennsylvania Avenue toward the Capitol.

The first ceremony would take place at noon in the Senate chambers, where Vice President Andrew Johnson would take the oath of office. The second ceremony would be held outside in the weather, in front of the eastern portico. There the President would be sworn in.

Lincoln turned and padded across the room in his carpet slippers to a chair. Sighing, he pulled on his boots. In December, he had stood on a paper, drawn the outline of both feet, carefully marked the measurements at various points, and mailed the paper to New York. Chiropodists who had visited the White House had given the President's feet some comfort, but only the New York shoemaker had ever made boots that didn't hurt the big Lincoln feet. The President stood, wiggled his toes, and prepared to leave for the Senate Chamber.

Mary Lincoln was also preparing for her husband's big day. A Westerner from "uncivilized" Illinois in snobbish Washington, the First Lady was extremely jealous of her prerogatives. Insecure and sometimes blundering, suffering from migraine headaches, she was short-tempered and self-centered. She had buried two sons, Eddie and Willie. Her eldest, Robert, was grown; her youngest, Taddie, would not live to maturity. Mrs. Lincoln, with family roots in Kentucky, was the subject of malicious rumors of disloyalty to the Union and of being a Southern spy in the Executive Mansion.[7] The head of the family was not the 56 year old President. His wife, 46, ruled by negation, and fear.[8]

When she had arrived at the White House, Mrs. Lincoln had at once changed the established order, fired the White House steward, rearranged the furniture, put famous paintings in storage, hidden heirlooms, ordered new decor, raged over food bills, and accused servants of stealing.[9]

Her funds were always low. At the back door of the White House, she berated butchers and grocers for their charges, and would clamor like the lid on a simmering

91

saucepan until her eyes bugged and her voice failed.[10]

She wanted to be addressed as "Madame President." The best her husband could do was call her "Mother."

The inaugural ball that night would be another trial for the short, plump, dark-eyed woman. She had bought imported fabrics, convinced that the President's wife should be the best dressed woman in the nation, and had gone heavily into debt to achieve the most elegant of gowns.[11] The First Lady, wearing a $2,000 inaugural dress, would be stunning that night. At the ball the President would shake hands with more than 6,000 people. But before the festivity he would slip into his wife's dressing room and ask, "Mother, which women may I speak to tonight?"[12]

The President entered his carriage with Mrs. Lincoln and was driven southwest along Pennsylvania Avenue toward the Capitol. Hacks and pedestrians alike gave way to his vehicle as it lurched through two inches of mud. Pedestrians under umbrellas and bejeweled ladies in barouches were also headed for the Senate chambers. The Senate galleries were already full. Journalist Noah Brookes wrote that the women there "chattered and clattered like a zephyr among the reeds of a waterside."

As the President entered the chambers, spectators and legislators arose to honor him. He prepared to go through the traditional signing of last minute bills passed by Congress the day before.[13]

Booth was present somewhere in that chamber or outside in the crowd of umbrellas. He had obtained a pass through Lucy Hale, his reported fiancee and one of numerous young women admirers. She was the daughter of Senator John P. Hale of New Hampshire.[14] It was doubtful she knew of Booth's divorce in 1864. His wife of five years and mother of his infant daughter were not known even to his closest associates.

Across the hall from the Senate Chambers, Andrew Johnson stopped in the office of Hannibal Hamlin, outgoing Vice President. Johnson was just recovering from typhoid fever and didn't feel or look well.[15]

"You don't happen to have any liquor, do you?"

"Why, no, but I'll have a page bring a little something if you'd like."

"Brandy, please."

The page hurried to the Senate restaurant and returned with the bottle. Hamlin noted with some concern that Johnson downed three glasses.[16]

By the time the noon hour struck, the hour of traditional ceremonies, the incoming Vice President was feeling no pain. He took Hamlin's arm and entered the hall. They took seats on the dais of the presiding officer. Hamlin made the usual courtesy bowing out speech. Johnson was called to take the oath.

Secretary of Navy Gideon Welles, whose flowing white locks and beard made him look like a cross between a biblical patriarch and Father Neptune, whispered to Lincoln, "Johnson is either drunk or crazy."[17]

Ben Pereley Poore, a Washington journalist, was blunt: "The Vice President-elect made a maudlin, drunken speech."

A procession of dignitaries escorted Lincoln toward the eastern portico of the Capitol where the crowds waited.

Lincoln passed into the cold outside air, walked in front of the portico, and stepped upon the platform. He was given the oath of office by Chief Justice Salmon Chase, kissed the Bible, open at the fifth chapter of Isaiah, and prepared to make his second inaugural address. The text was short, four pages on a writing tablet. It was interrupted frequently by applause as he built toward a climax.

A journalist on the platform jotted down his observations. "Every word was clear and audible as the ringing and somewhat shrill tones of the President came to his final paragraph."[18]

"With malice toward none," the President said in a tone which carried across the crowd, echoed off the buildings and reverberated throughout the land, "with charity for all, with firmness in the right, as God gives us to see the right. . . ."[19]

Sunlight suddenly broke through a hole in scowling

skies. A brilliant ray caught the President. There were startled exclamations.

Lincoln's gray eyes took in the crowd's reaction. "Let us strive on to finish the work we are in, to bind up the nation's wounds. . . ."[20]

The words seemed to gain power as they poured forth, ". . . To care for him who shall have borne the battle, and for his widow, and for his orphans. . . ."[21]

A photographer's shutter clicked. The outdoor panorama was frozen on film: the crowded foreground, the raised dignitaries' platform, the spectators on the columned portico behind Lincoln. It was all there in black and white. Later, a darkly mustached man in top hat would be singled out in the picture as Booth. He stood in front of a massive marble statue depicting a pioneer and an Indian scuffling over a tomahawk. Lincoln stood directly beneath him.

The President concluded his remarks, ". . . To do all which may achieve and cherish just and lasting peace, among ourselves, and with all nations."[22] He sat down to roaring applause.

A lasting peace, with malice toward none. It sounded good to a war-weary nation of 36 states, but there were others who bore malice.

"What an elegant chance I had to kill the President on inauguration day if I had wished," Booth boasted to Samuel K. Chester, the actor who had refused to join him in his plot.[23]

And in New York, desperate Northern speculators prepared for the day when their conspiracy would remove the one block to tremendous profits.

In a final attempt to delay defeat, the Confederacy had given Robert E. Lee command of all Southern armies. Until then, the CSA had had no Supreme Commander. Lee had achieved all his remarkable accomplishments with the tiny, ragged, underfed army of northern Virginia, a fighting force that had defeated or held off six of the Union's top generals and all the superior military materiel the Federals could throw at it.

Union Commander Grant's onslaught had been brutal and costly, but Lee had done an incredible job of spreading his thin gray line of hungry, barefoot troops in defending both Richmond and Petersburg. The South's resources were now nearly gone. The life-sustaining pork had never arrived.

Sherman, after slicing a 60 mile wide swath of death and destruction through Georgia to the sea, had turned north. In mid-February, his seasoned troops poured into the South Carolina capital of Columbia. The city was in flames.

On February 22, Union troops poured into Wilmington, North Carolina. The last major Southern port was lost to the Confederacy.[24] On all fronts, victorious Federal bluecoats continued to make steady gains.

The second inauguration behind him, Lincoln pressed for an end to the war, and the implementation of his reconstruction policies.

His enemies made an effort to dislodge the President by appointing a congressional committee to investigate the cotton pass situation. The Washburne Committee, headed by E. B. Washburne, Illinois Congressman, held hearings from January through early February, 1865.[25]

The hearings only served to frustrate the investigators. Lincoln refused to submit lists of persons for whom he had signed cotton passes. The committee finally forced a reluctant Treasury Department official, Hansen Risley, to surrender a list.[26]

Ward Lamon's name wasn't on the list, although the committeemen knew the President's friend had been speculating in cotton.[27] The name of Orville Hickman Browning, another long-time Lincoln associate, did not appear either. Browning later admitted in his book that he had been deeply involved in cotton speculation.[28]

The Washburne Committee adjourned without accomplishing what it had tried to do.

Beaten at this point, the Radical Republicans turned to another method of attack. But this time, those behind the move were more subtle.

Lafayette Baker, NDP Chief in all but name, pushed his bearded face into the tiny cubicle located at the Chaffey Company which Thomas Caldwell called his office. The company manager sat talking with James Barnes.

"Gentlemen," Baker said affably, pretending not to notice the two men's effort to compose themselves, "I hope I'm not interrupting anything."

"Not at all, Mr. Baker; not at all," Caldwell exclaimed, jumping to his feet. "Come in and sit down. Always glad to see a good customer. You know James Barnes, of course?"

The two men nodded to each other as Baker sat down and faced them. "May I speak frankly?"

"Of course, Mr. Baker," Caldwell said.

"Over the years, Thomas, we've done a great deal of business together. I've grown to feel we are friends."

Caldwell smiled, unsure of Baker's errand. The Chaffey Company had many secrets. "I'm proud to count you among my friends as well."

The detective smiled at both men and leaned back in a scarred chair. "That's what makes my visit here all the more unfortunate."

Caldwell's hands shook as he nervously moved some papers. "I don't understand."

Baker speared the shipping agent with an inquisitor's eye, then swung the same hard look to Barnes. "This concerns you, too, I believe," he said flatly. "It seems you have something in the works you haven't told me about."

"Oh?"

"I'm referring to a plan involving the actor, John Wilkes Booth."

Caldwell wet his lips. "Mr. Booth and I have many business transactions."

"How many," Baker leaned forward suddenly across the desk, "involve kidnapping the President?"

Caldwell shifted papers. "I don't think I follow you."

Baker grinned. "Oddly enough, Thomas, I don't think you do, either. And for that matter," Baker continued, jerking his bearded chin at Barnes, "neither do you." He leaned forward again. "I'm not here to arrest you. After all, what kind of a friend would I be to arrest those who helped me sell a little contraband cotton?"

Barnes and Caldwell moved uneasily. Was he trying to entrap them? Trying to infiltrate them as he had done in other parts of the cotton circle? He had boasted about such after the Washburne hearings. He'd expected to receive an advancement to general.

Baker left the men wondering just what his motives truly were. He liked that.

Captain James William Boyd rode through Maryland in the cold, dreary March weather. He had returned from Canada on the first step of his assignment for the War Department and the Northern speculators. Boyd was unsure of the leader behind his orders. He had the impression the mastermind was not one, but a number of highly placed men working together on a daring plan. Boyd was to orchestrate it day by day.

The unhealed wound on his right leg above the ankle was still giving him trouble.[29] After he had been captured in August 1863, it had become worse. Now when he had to walk a great deal, he needed crutches.

Slowly, cursing the pain and the rain, Boyd worked his way down through the southern end of Maryland and to the Potomac, where he crossed into northern Virginia. Wherever he stopped, he asked discreet questions concerning roads through the area. When the road wasn't too bad, he took side trips.

He also discovered partisans. Maryland was more of a problem than Virginia. People lived in every state who did not hold with the official state position in the war.

Boyd was not polished, but he was cool and calculating. He obtained all the information he wanted in both states and rode toward Washington again—in a hurry, for time was running out.

Time was running out for Booth, too. His ego still suffering from being replaced as head of the Northern kidnap attempt, he wanted to beat his replacement in finishing the job. Then the world would never forget John Wilkes Booth.

Chapter 9

IF AT FIRST YOU DON'T SUCCEED . . .

After the first kidnap fiasco on January 18, Booth and his men waited two months to try again.

The actor had assembled his group when news from Richmond indicated the need for speed if any "capture" were to be made before the Confederate capital fell.[1]

Booth fired off a telegram to Michael O'Laughlin on Monday, March 13: "You had better come at once."[2] Messages also went to Atzerodt at Port Tobacco and to the other conspirators. It looked as though Grover's Theatre would offer the best opportunity to attempt the abduction on March 15.

Monday's newspaper carried an item: "Mr. Lincoln is reported quite sick today." On Tuesday, the President was so ill the cabinet met in his bedroom. It did not appear he would be well enough to attend Grover's Wednesday night performance of the German Opera Company's *The Magic Flute*.[3]

Louis Weichmann was curious, but not too upset when on Tuesday the young giant Payne reappeared at the Surratt boarding house. He came up to the third-story bedroom that the clerk shared with John Surratt. Weichmann was asked to leave the room.[4]

On Wednesday afternoon, March 15, Weichmann climbed the stairs to the back attic and opened the door to find Payne and Surratt seated on the bed. They leapt up in alarm. Weichmann saw an array of revolvers, knives, and spurs spread on the bed.

The clerk went downstairs and tattled to Mrs. Surratt. She brushed off her gossipy boarder with the remark that "he mustn't think anything about it. John needs such things for his frequent hunting trips into the country."[5]

That same evening, Payne borrowed Weichmann's military cloak. He and Surratt took Honora Fitzpatrick and Apollonia Dean to Ford's Theatre. Weichmann was told Booth had given the $10 box seat ticket to Surratt to be his guest at the one-night-only performance of *Jane Shore*.

When the party returned home after the performance, Nora and Polly had exciting news. They had sat in the presidential box! At intermission, Booth, who had arranged for the box, had stopped by and visited briefly.

Payne and Surratt had stepped into a side corridor with Booth for a brief chat before the play resumed. The conspirators had arranged to see the play at Ford's in order to study the layout of the theatre and the presidential box. They had set their second kidnap attempt at Grover's until the newspapers had reported Lincoln's illness. They'd given up on Grover's for the night and had gone to check out Ford's.

After the play Payne and Surratt left the boarding house for an all night planning session at Gautier's Restaurant. The meeting lasted until 5 a.m.[6]

While Payne, Surratt, and Booth had been at Ford's Theatre, President Lincoln had surprised patrons at Grover's Theatre by showing up after all. Mrs. Lincoln had been insistent. The President had indulged her. Rising from his sickbed, he had accompanied his wife, Gen. James G. Wilson, and Clara Harris, daughter of New York's Senator Ira Harris, to the performance.[7]

At Gautier's seven men were on hand for Booth: Samuel Arnold, Michael O'Laughlin, John Surratt, George Atzerodt, David Herold, Lewis Payne, and James Wood. They did not know each other well. Arnold had just met Herold and couldn't even remember his name. It was a strange group to coordinate a plan that was sure to draw pursuit and possibly end in death. Yet these strangers worked out their arrangements, entrusting their lives to each other.[8]

The meeting started well. Booth had provided good food and drink, and drank champagne until his deep, rich baritone rose in excitement.

"Gentlemen" Booth said, "We face dark moments. It is rumored that the Confederate Congress has been wrangling so severely with President Davis that it may not reconvene when the session closes next Saturday. Everywhere, the glorious boys in gray are threatened or in retreat. . . .[9]

He paused dramatically. "Ours is a solemn responsibility, yours and mine, to yet snatch victory from defeat, to determine with our own hands whether the South lives or dies." He held his ivory pale hands out to the men.

"Tell us what you want, Cap," Payne said softly, "and we'll do it."

Booth unrolled his papers to reveal the interior of a theatre. "Gentlemen," he boomed, "we shall excite the attention of the whole world by capturing the old tyrant from the midst of hundreds of theatre-goers."[10]

Surratt crowded close to survey the seating arrangements and watch Booth confidently point out the position of each conspirator. Surratt honestly felt that abducting Lincoln would force an exchange of prisoners. He cried out, "Is there a young man in the North with one spark of patriotism in his heart who would not have with enthusiastic ardor joined in any undertaking for the capture of Jefferson Davis and brought him to Washington?"[11]

Arnold was less enthusiastic. He began to argue that the theatre abduction proposal was foolhardy. O'Laughlin sided with him. The others seemed to be moving towards the same point of view.

Booth struggled to retain control. "Sam, you find fault with everything concerned with it."

"No, Wilkes," Arnold protested, "I just want to have a chance, that's all. We might have a chance if we capture him in the streets, where he often walks alone, or when he rides horseback to the Soldiers Home. . . ."

The argument grew hotter. "Do you know, Sam," Booth cried, "you are liable to be shot?"

"If you feel inclined to shoot me," Arnold yelled, "go ahead, but I'll defend my view."

Surratt brought up the rumor that the government suspected a kidnapping plot against the President.[12] "They've commenced to build stockade gates on the Navy Yard Bridge, as though they expected danger from within." Surratt went on. "I'm confident the government has wind of our plan. Perhaps the best thing we could do is to throw up the whole project."

Booth slammed his fist upon the table. "Well, gentlemen, if the worst comes to the worst, I shall know what to do."

Four men rose in anger. "If I understand you to intimate anything more than the capture of Mr. Lincoln," O'Laughlin declared, "I, for one, will bid you goodbye."[13]

The dissenters reached for their hats, and Booth's manner changed. "Gentlemen! Please! Sit down again. I apologize. I've drunk too much champagne."

Tempers cooled. The men resumed their conversation. But Arnold was firm in his conclusion. "If this is not accomplished this week, I forever withdraw from it."[14]

The meeting broke up at dawn on Thursday morning with plans to make another abduction try immediately.

Surratt received word later in the day that the President would visit the Seventh Street Hospital-Soldiers Home where an entertainment for wounded soldiers was planned.[15] Booth's actor friends, John Matthews, Lester Wallack and E. L. Davenport were to appear there in the benefit, *Still Waters Run Deep*.

The report came within an hour of Lincoln's scheduled appearance at 2 p.m., but the band's communications were so perfected by then that the men were spurring their mounts towards the Soldiers Home before two. Booth was followed by Surratt, Herold, Payne, Atzerodt, Wood, Arnold, and O'Laughlin.

The men reined up in a stand of timber well beyond the city's outskirts. Under a threatening sky with a gale whipping their coats, Booth explained the plan. "The road curves sharply there. Surratt and I will ride out of the woods and take our position in front of the carriage as it rounds the bend. We'll be screened from both directions. When the carriage passes this grove, the rest of you spur out behind the carriage. Understood?"

There was a nodding of heads. Freezing cold rain began to fall.

Booth raised his voice to be heard above the wind. "John, you rein in suddenly beside the coachman and grab him. Change into his livery clothes. Payne and I will handle the old scoundrel. Wood, O'Laughlin, Arnold, Atzerodt, and Herold take care of any escort following the carriage. Understood?"[16]

Again, heads nodded. Then the men ducked their faces into their upturned collars to ward off the cold and waited.

The sound of a carriage brought heads up. Booth and Surratt eased their mounts forward, swinging into position ahead of a beautifully matched team pulling a handsome closed vehicle. The other horsemen spurred into position. Booth dropped back toward the coach, then let out an exclamation. "It's not him!"

Surratt thought the startled face inside the carriage might have been Chief Justice Salmon Chase.[17]

The conspirators, warned by Booth's cry, furiously reined in. Horses reared high in the savage effort to turn them. The band fled into the rainy afternoon dark.

Whoever was in the coach made no formal report to the War Department. Months later, the Bureau of Military Justice dredged up the first public or private records of the incident.[18]

Booth's third kidnap attempt had now failed, sending some of the conspirators into panic. They wanted to scatter.

Indeed, Weichmann was reading in his room that night when Surratt burst in, drew a pocket pistol and pointed it at the clerk. "My prospects are gone; my hopes are blasted," Surratt cried.[19]

Payne also came in, flushed but calmer than Surratt. Weichmann saw that the giant carried a large revolver under his vest. Soon an agitated Booth joined them. He strode up and down the room, swinging his riding whip, unaware of Weichmann. When he finally saw the clerk, the actor motioned for Payne and Surratt to follow him.

The three men went upstairs to the back attic for about half an hour. Weichmann's nosy nature was thoroughly piqued.[20] What was going on? Why were they all so upset?

A George Atzerodt came often to the house. A David Herold had come in mid-March to meet with Payne and Surratt. Someone called Wood had showed up. What was the tie-in? What had the guns, knives and spurs meant? What was all the whispering about, the mysterious coming and going?

Weichmann felt he was being left out. Worst of all, they had asked him to leave his own room. And Booth had ignored him. The clerk decided to do more than share his suspicions with Mrs. Surratt, who had pooh-poohed his earlier tattling.[21]

By his own admission, Weichmann was in the habit of repeating "various occurrences" that took place in the Surratt boarding house. As early as February 20, he had talked to D. H. Gleason, a wounded ex-soldier and fellow clerk in the Office of Commissary General of Prisoners. Weichmann had confided that a kidnapping was planned and "the time set was inauguration day."[22]

Gleason had pondered this information for 10 days, then had informed a Lieutenant Sharp, an assistant provost marshal on Gen. Christopher C. Augur's staff. Weichmann also passed the information along to James A. McDavitt, a U.S. enrolling officer. He, in turn, notified his superiors.[23]

Now, in mid-March, Weichmann was so bursting with juicy boarding house gossip that he rushed out to Gleason's quarters. Since Gleason wasn't home, Weichmann had to wait until the next day, then the young man talked about knives and guns, the excited behavior of the three men.

"By God," Gleason exclaimed, "that is strange! There's something wrong going on there, Weichmann."[24]

The snitch made some guesses: "Perhaps they're trying to run the blockade. Maybe they're engaged in cotton speculation."

Gleason thought a moment. "It's probably a good idea to go and tell the Secretary of War, but. . ." He reflected further. "It would be a good thing to keep an eye on them. If anything comes up again, we can report it to the authorities."

Weichmann, suffering from an inferiority complex and jealousy, saw himself now as a stalwart soldier who did not desert his post in time of danger. He would stay to observe the enemy's movements.

The morning after Booth's third try, he had an unsettling experience. The actor answered a knock on his Washington hotel door to find Lafe Baker, NDP Chief, standing there.[25]

"The end has come," Booth thought, his heart skipping.

"Good morning, Mr. Booth. Did I awaken you?"

Booth fought for control. "Oh, no! I was just being lazy this morning. I'm sorry not to be dressed for callers."

"I realize it's a little early, Mr. Booth, but I felt my business was urgent enough that you wouldn't mind my early arrival."

"Oh?"

"May I come in, Mr. Booth?"

"Oh, of course, Forgive me, Colonel Baker. Do come in."

"Soon be General Baker. Just got the word myself."

"General? A promotion!"

"For my undercover work in the cotton pass mess. Nice room, this."

"Won't you sit down, Colonel—uh—General Baker?"

"Oh, no, thanks. I like to move about. You don't mind, do you?"

Booth was sure the detective was prowling, taking in the pictures on the walls, books and plays on the shelves, and the brandy supply on a sideboard. Every fiber was alert. "May I offer you a drink, General Baker?"

"No, thanks. Nice picture of this young lady, Mr. Booth."

"A friend."

"You have many interesting friends, Mr. Booth."

Booth managed to keep his voice calm. "An actor gets to know many people, General Baker."

"Ah, yes, of course." The detective put down the book. "It is a rare gift, however, to have so many friends in high places."

Booth said nothing.

Abruptly, the detective seated himself and reached slowly into an inside pocket. "Mr. Booth—or may I call you John or Wilkes?"

"I'm called both. Whichever you prefer, General."

"Ah, yes; thank you. Well, Wilkes, I have here some personal messages for you." He slowly withdrew three sealed envelopes,[26] looked thoughtfully at them, turned them face down so the writing was not visible, and extended them without haste.

Booth was cautious. "What are they, General?"

"Messages from your friends. Go ahead. Take them."

"If you'll pardon me for saying so, General, it seems a bit unusual for the head of the nation's secret police to be delivering messages to an actor."

Baker smiled. "These are not ordinary messages, Wilkes." The envelopes were thrust into Booth's reluctant hands. Slowly, he turned them over. All three were addressed to him.

"Go ahead," Baker urged. "Open them."

"Thank you, General, but I wouldn't want to interrupt our conversation to read. . . ."

"No, please, Wilkes! Open them! I don't mind!"

"But. . . ."

"I insist." There was a sudden flat, metallic tone to the command.

Booth opened the envelopes.

Baker said, "No need to be concerned, Wilkes. I know they're from Jefferson Davis, Judah Benjamin, and Clement Clay."

Booth's first thought was that the detective had opened and read the messages.

"No need to be alarmed, Wilkes. They're genuine. They

contain instructions. May I suggest you follow those, and let me be on my way?"

Booth was trapped. The messages seemed genuine. He had no time to think of elaborate defenses. Perplexed, but seeing no alternative, Booth obeyed one of the written instructions. He moved to a corner, opened a drawer and rummaged under papers, then approached the detective with the amount of money specified in the letters.[27]

"Thank you, Wilkes." Baker rose. "Thank you very much. Now, if you'll excuse me, I have other business to attend to." He smiled briefly at Booth and walked out.

Booth stood uncertainly in the middle of the room, his mind tumbling. Quickly, he moved to the desk and penned a note to Judah Benjamin in Richmond.[28]

"I don't trust him," he concluded.

Booth sent the letter by courier with instructions to ride hard and return as quickly as possible with an answer.

Agitated and concerned, Booth hurried to John Conness' office.[29]

"Do you know who just came to call on me?" Booth demanded.

"Sit down, Wilkes, and calm yourself. Would you like a drink?"

"Don't tell me to sit down and be calm!" Booth snapped. "Do you know who just left my hotel room?"

"Lower your voice, Wilkes. Here. Take a little brandy."

Booth waved the liquor away. "Baker! Lafe Baker! Do you understand what I'm saying, John? Baker came to me this morning with letters from President Davis, Judah Benjamin, and Clement Clay. Baker's on to us, John!"

"Quit pacing the floor and sit down, Wilkes. Let me tell you some facts."

"The only fact I'm interested in right now is how the head of the secret police knows enough about us to carry personal messages from Confederate leaders to me. To me! Personally!"

"Baker's all right. He can be trusted. I knew Baker in '55 and '56, the rough times in San Francisco.[30] There was no law and order. It was like '51 all over again, so the Second Vigilante Committee was formed. I was one of them, and so was Baker."

"Are you saying that you trust Baker because he served with you on the Vigilante Committee of 1856?"

"There's a little more to it than I care to go into right now, Wilkes."

Booth frowned. Skeletons in the closet? When the vigilantes had cleaned up San Francisco, they had set up a police state of their own. There had been irregularities, including questions about vanished gold.

"Trust Baker, Wilkes. He's with us."

The actor studied the Californian. Conness knew something that made him willing to trust Baker more than Booth would ever have dared.

"Wilkes, a senator has all kinds of privileged information. Some of it cannot be disclosed. Take my word on Baker."

The actor shook his head. "Too many strange things are happening in Washington to suit me. Nobody's what he's said to be; nobody's trustworthy."

"That's politics, Wilkes. But we must play the game, and that requires trust. Now quit fretting and get on with your project. I'll send you word when's the best opportunity for another try."

Booth was more anxious than ever for a reply to his message to the Confederacy. When it came finally, it didn't relieve his anxiety. It read: "Trust him."[31]

Word now came to Booth that the President would pass a certain spot on Saturday, March 18. Booth and an unknown number of conspirators waited seven hours. When the President did approach, he was escorted by a squad of cavalry.[32] Another failure, Booth's fourth.

Baker, accompanied by Lt. Col. Everton J. Conger, called on Booth.[33]

Conger was a veteran secret service officer and had been a lieutenant colonel in the military for two years. In June 1863, Baker had been commissioned a colonel in the First Regiment, District of Columbia Cavalry. At first only a skeletal unit to back up civilian detectives, the recruitment of 1,200 men in Maine raised the unit to full regimental strength. Conger was its active commander, backed by Maj. J. S. Baker of Wisconsin, a relative of Lafe's. A cousin, Detective Luther Baker, later became a lieutenant in this regiment.

"Baker's Mounted Rangers are a set of damned spies and ought to be killed," a major general had angrily told Lafe. The general went on to say that the regiment was really assigned to spy on army officers and report to Lafe Baker what each said and did.

Booth could not be too open about his distrust of Baker. About Conger he could be more explicit. "Make him leave," Booth said.[34]

The second detective was offended, but Booth was adamant. "I don't know him. Talking to too many people is dangerous."

The chief detective tried to defend his operative, but finally indicated with a movement of his bearded chin that Conger was to step outside.

Booth did not record the topic of the second meeting with Baker.

At another party at the home of Eva Grey's parents, Sen. Conness again caught Booth's eye. While the two men were smoking cigars in a corner of the library, Conness said, "I believe the time has come. I expect to have information tomorrow or the next day."[35] Booth nodded and returned to mingle with other guests.

Booth thought Yankee politicians were beyond belief. Their only interest was money. They had no patriotism, no personal honor. They were cowards, hiding behind their office, spouting hypocrisy.[36]

Conness' information about the next kidnap possibility came—Sunday evening, March 19.[37] The conspirators rushed to the location named. And waited in vain into the late night hours. The President did not appear.

On Monday, March 20, the conspirators made a sixth attempt at a kidnap.[38] About the time the President was supposed to pass the ambush site, a warning was given Booth that the kidnapping was expected. Booth ordered his men to scatter, sure he had been betrayed.

Booth's frustration was complete. On that same Monday, Payne and the actor went to the Navy Yard, where Booth bought a leather covered carbine, paying $5 to a "Wakefield" for the weapon.[39]

In the late night of March 20, Booth took Payne and Surratt to a road which ran alongside some gardens. They waited.[40] Eventually the trio heard a horse approaching and tensed, waiting until the horseman was about 30 yards away.

"It's him!" Booth whispered.

He brought the rifle to his shoulder and sighted in the poor light. His finger tightened on the trigger. The gun spewed flame and noise.

The President's hat fell off.

Payne fired twice, a double echo of the actor's shot. Surratt touched spurs to his mount and raced away.

"Come on!" Booth whispered fiercely to Payne. "They'll be after us within minutes!"

The two horsemen spurred furiously away, the President's armed escort thundering after them through the darkness. Within a couple of miles the conspirators had eluded pursuit.[41]

It was another failure! But with a difference. Shots had been fired. The plotters were becoming desperate.

Behind the scenes the reaction was instantaneous. Booth and Payne were in a room at the Herndon House when Col. Conger, in mufti, knocked.[42] "I've been looking for you, Booth," Conger said evenly.

"What is it you want?"

"I've been asked to have a little talk with you."

"By whom? Baker?"

"No matter," Conger countered. "Fact is, you and your friends have been raising quite a lot of dust lately, and not much else. Trying to ambush the President, shooting at people in the dark, behaving like fools at a circus. . . ."

"Fools, Sir!"

"I think that was the word," Conger coolly retorted. "All your reckless attacks and loose talk are creating a very dangerous situation. Anyway, my people think that maybe they hadn't made it sufficiently clear when they told you to stay out of the matter from now on."

Booth was furious. "Sir, I'm a free agent. I cannot be hired and dismissed like a day laborer. I am the servant of my conscience."

"Save your speeches for the stage," Conger snapped.

"By God, Sir, I'll not tolerate your insults! I devised the plan to abduct the President, and I intend to carry it through," Booth stormed.

Conger grabbed the actor by the coat collar and pulled him up tight. "Now listen carefully. If you make another move without orders, you and your friends are going to be found in the Potomac."[43]

Conger released his hold, turned and walked away.

"Say the word, Cap," Payne rumbled, "and I'll kill the tin soldier."[44]

The actor muttered, "We have better things to do!"

Booth left town on Tuesday, March 21. Surratt laid low until Saturday, March 25, when he left for Richmond. Where Payne was is uncertain.

About the same time, President Lincoln, showing signs of ill health, accepted Gen. Grant's invitation to visit his headquarters at City Point, Virginia. Mrs. Lincoln and Tad were to accompany him on the announced trip.

It was rumored that the war was at an end, and Lincoln was going to instruct Grant on surrender terms.

Chapter 10

WAR'S END MAKES DESPERATE MEN

Lincoln's chartered steamer, *River Queen,* with the tug, *USS Bat* for protection, moved down the Potomac en route from Washington to City Point on Thursday, March 23. The President was not well. Poor drinking water was suspected. Mrs. Lincoln viewed her lanky husband with concern. Shortly after his second inauguration, she had bought $1,000 worth of mourning clothes—purple and pearl gray dresses trimmed in black.[1] Only a week had passed since an influenza attack had forced the cabinet to meet in Lincoln's bedroom.[2]

The President was generally understood to be suffering exhaustion when the press said "influenza." But his wife knew his long history of illness: frequent melancholy, headaches, fatigue, mild smallpox in 1863, a 10 day cold in early 1864. Then he had fainted on February 6, following the Attorney General's stormy disapproval of Lincoln's pardoning deserters.

Lincoln had leapt to his feet, shouting. "If you think that I, of my own free will, will shed another drop of blood . . ." and had fallen in a faint.[3] Dr. Robert K. Stone had warned Lincoln of nerves and exhaustion.[4]

A crowd had been on hand to see the President leave Washington with White House guard William Crook assigned to protect him. Crook became seasick that night when the steamer reached Chesapeake Bay near Fort Monroe. The President felt so well he had fish for breakfast the next morning. He became ill later in the day.

After dark on Friday, March 24, the steamer reached City Point where the Appomattox empties into the James River. Grant's headquarters were on a high bluff.

When the general boarded the steamer, the President apologized, "I'm not feeling very well. I got pretty well shaken up on the bay coming down and am not altogether over it.[5] Over the next several days, however, the President's health seemed to improve. He conferred with Gen. Grant, Gen. Sherman and Adm. David Porter.

On Sunday, April 2, besieged Petersburg at long last surrendered. Richmond fell the next day, and the Confederate cabinet fled the ruined city. Lincoln rode over the Petersburg battlefields where dead and dying still lay upon the ground, his face a mask of sadness.[6]

The President was somewhat cheered after the 15 mile ride to Petersburg where Capt. Robert Lincoln, on Grant's staff, greeted his father. But after returning to City Point, to the sight of Confederate prisoners in deplorable condition, Lincoln's face once again settled into lines of sadness.[7]

On April 4, Adm. Porter asked Lincoln to visit Richmond with him. Porter insisted it would be a way to gather again the reins of government in the fallen Confederate capital. It was a strange, silent visit. Only the blacks, who had somehow heard the President was coming, lined the shore as Lincoln was rowed to a landing. "Dar comes Massa Linkum, de Saviah ob de lan'—we is so glad to see him," Crook recorded the freed slaves as crying out.[8]

The President shook every outstretched black hand as he moved along the street with six sailors in advance, six in the rear, and the President's small party in the middle. Crook, armed only with a Colt revolver, held Tad by the hand and considered the sailors' short carbines as they moved up the silent, brooding streets of the fire-blackened capital.

Everywhere, sullen white spectators thronged. Windows were crowded. Men clung to telegraph poles and trees to glimpse the President and his son—yet nobody made a sound. In the oppressive silence nobody called out either in welcome or insult.

The party reached the war-ravaged Jefferson Davis home. A black house servant produced fine old whiskey for the Yankees, and everyone took a "pull" except Lincoln. The President asked Crook to accompany him alone through the city where some homes still burned among blackened shells. The silent crowd was now so thick that it was difficult to move. Eventually the two men reached the capitol.[9]

They were shown the room Davis and his cabinet had occupied, its furniture wrecked and stripped. "This must have been President Davis' chair," Lincoln remarked, lowering his long body into the hacked relic.[10]

An ambulance took the President back to Adm. Porter's flagship, *Malvern,* lying to in the James River. With a sigh, Crook saw his charge safely aboard. Throughout the night, before the ship sailed, the guard heard rumors of efforts to get aboard to kill the President. The *Malvern* cast off all lines the following morning for the run back to Washington.[11]

For Booth, time had about run out. On Saturday, April 1, he left Washington for New York where he insisted on a meeting with the speculators[12] the next day. Petersburg had fallen; Richmond's fall was hours away. Victorious Federals were pouring across Virginia in a widening sweep that threatened to engulf what little was left of Lee's valiant troops.

Booth's original purpose in abducting Lincoln seemed lost. "We've been betrayed!" he cried in his deep throated, dramatic way. "I think the scoundrel responsible is Baker. He knows of my activities. He's been to my very doorstep to let me know. I warn you, he may be planning arrests!"[13]

The speculators listened with growing concern. The fall of Richmond meant the end of their dreams.

"As soon as he has everything he wants, he'll betray every one of you, along with me. We'll all end up in Old Capitol Prison, or in the Potomac. That's what they threatened me with." Booth began to stamp about the floor as he told of Conger's threat. "We're all dead men if we don't do something soon!"

Booth was instructed to return to Washington to wait for orders.[14]

The President had now touched off a major political-military situation. On Thursday, April 6, at City Point, he had authorized Gen. Godfrey Weitzel to give permission to the "gentlemen who had acted as the Legislature of Virginia in support of the Rebellion" to meet and take measures to withdraw that state's troops from fighting the Federals.[15] Secretary of War Stanton saw the action as allowing Virginia lawmakers to proceed as though nothing had happened, setting a precedent for all future insurgent legislatures to reconvene and be recognized.[16] The authorization had Washington in an uproar.

On Palm Sunday, April 9, General Lee met with Grant at Appomattox Courthouse and signed surrender papers.

Although only the Army of Northern Virginia was officially included in the terms, Lee's action, as supreme Confederate Commander meant the war was over.[17]

Washington went wild. Impromptu parades, bonfires in the streets, loud celebrations were everywhere.

Booth moaned at the news. "If it is true," he wrote, "it means the end."[18] He expected the politicians and their cronies to strip the South bare. It seemed that all "we have planned and striven for has come to naught."[19] Booth also wrote, "I believe that Eckert, Baker, and the Secretary are in control of our activities."[20]

Booth could think of three reasons why War Secretary Stanton could be behind the situation in which the actor found himself. First, removing Lincoln would assure the War Secretary's continuance in office. When the war was over, Stanton might not be needed by Lincoln. Secondly, under the Radical Republicans' plan for reconstruction, which Lincoln opposed and Stanton supported, the War Department and the Secretary of War would be vital in a military occupation of conquered states. Military governors and districts, all under Stanton, would make him the most powerful man in the land. Finally, Stanton could forward his own plans for becoming President through the power and publicity he would receive as the nation's most influential man.[21]

Booth's suspicions of Major Eckert were less firm. Still, if the War Secretary advanced, so would Eckert, especially if the two were involved in a conspiracy to remove the President.[22]

Baker, Booth knew, could expect similar advancements. His unchecked power would grow even greater since secret service agents would be needed all over the South. The trouble with Baker was that his true position was hard to pin down.[23] He knew about Booth's kidnapping efforts and had carried messages from the top Confederate officers to him. But whose side was he on? Booth did not know.

Baker had a lot of business to attend to that dramatic week. The day following Lee's surrender, the chief of the secret service went to Stanton.[24] "Mr. Secretary, I have some disturbing news."

Stanton brushed a hand over his perfumed beard. "Be quick about it. I'm busy."

"I have most of the information, but the most important thing I don't yet . . ."

"What are you talking about, Baker?" The secretary continued to study papers on his desk.

"I'm talking about the fact that there's going to be an attack on Lincoln."

"For more than a year, the town's been full of such rumors. Now why do you come in here and waste my time?"

"Sir, I know this plan is in action."

"You *know*, Baker?"

The detective nodded. "Yes, Sir. For some time, as you know. I've been in possession of facts regarding the treason of several high ranking army officers who're planning to help kidnap the President. I've been waiting for the right moment to catch them in the act."[25]

"So?" Stanton glanced up briefly.

"We know there's going to be an attempt to kidnap Lincoln, but we don't know just where it is to occur, or how."[26]

Stanton's notoriously short temper exploded. "That's all you've got? You have come in here with nothing more specific than what you've just told me?"

Baker protested, "No, Sir, we know more than that, Mr. Secretary. We've learned an assassination attempt may be made instead of kidnapping."[27]

"Assassination!" Stanton spun towards Baker. "That's one of the most common rumors in this city."[28]

"Mr. Secretary, we've learned everything except the name of the assassin. I have some ideas on that———."

"Out with them then! What do you think you know, Baker?"

Baker lowered his voice. "Eckert has made all the contacts."[29]

"My secretary? Maj. Thomas Eckert, in charge of my military telegraph?"

115

"Yes, sir. And the deed is to be done on the 14th."

"In four days? Baker, you've taken leave of your senses."

"I assure you, Mr. Secretary, these are the facts."

"I do not believe them!" Stanton jumped up. "Baker, you are a grievance of mind to me. I want you out of my office and out of my sight. I don't want to hear another word out of you. In fact, I think I'll send you to New York on a special mission."

"But Mr. Secretary——"

"No buts, Baker!" Stanton interrupted, his voice rising. "You're a party to it, Baker. Let's wait and see what becomes of it."[30] The secretary turned abruptly to his work. "I'm busy, Baker. Come back tomorrow."

The next day, Baker was called into Stanton's office. The secretary was blunt, "I've been checking into what you said yesterday."

"You're satisfied I'm not a party to it?"

"On the contrary, Baker. Look at this." Stanton handed the detective a document. Baker studied it. Vice President Andrew Johnson, who would succeed Lincoln, was the "perpetrator of the crime," with Baker carrying out the assignment.[31]

"That's a forgery!"[32]

"Is it Baker? It shows that you have been in charge of a plot to kidnap the President. It makes you a party to the deed."

Faced with strong opposition from Stanton and other cabinet members, the President sent a second telegram to Gen. Weitzel denying he had called the Virginia lawmakers together: "I have done no such thing. I spoke of them, not as a legislature, but as 'the gentlemen who acted as the legislature of Virginia in support of the Rebellion,' " he wired.[33] It appeared Lincoln was backing down from what Stanton considered a colossal blunder—or was it another clash between the President and ambitious, powerful men?

Baker had inside information on the subject to share

116

with Earl Potter. He said he had been present when Stanton learned of Lincoln's independent action and that the War Secretary had reacted strongly.

"Stanton erupted in an insane tirade. That's the first time I realized his mental condition, his insane and fanatical hatred for the President."[34]

"What'd Stanton do?"

"There are few in the War Department who respect the President or his strategy, but there aren't many who would countermand an order he has given. Stanton even sent a telegram to Gen. Weitzel countermanding the President's order of the 6th."[35]

Potter listened in silence as Baker recalled the scene in the War Secretary's office. "He laughed in a most chilling manner," Baker continued, "and said, 'If he (Lincoln) would know who rescinded his order—we will let Lucifer tell him. Be off, Tom, and see to the arrangements.' "[36]

"Do you realize what you're saying, Lafe? Tom Eckert and Stanton?"

The chief nodded. "That's the first time I knew Stanton was one of those responsible for the assassination plot."[37] Baker was fighting a rising excitement. "Always before, I thought that either he didn't trust me—for he really trusts no one—or he was protecting someone—until it was to his benefit to expose him. But now I know the truth and it frightens me."[38]

"Frightens you?"

"I'm afraid I may become the sacrificial goat."

Booth, too, was concerned over personal danger, now compounded by Lee's surrender.

"But by the Almighty God," he wrote in his diary, "I swear that I shall lay the body of this tyrant dead upon the altar of Mars."[39] [Lincoln frequently referred to Stanton as Mars.[40]]

Booth wrote on, "If by this act, I am slain, they too shall be cast into hell, for I have given information to a friend who will have the nation know who the traitors are."[41]

News came from the New York speculators. Booth

117

wrote of "a new plan, other arrangements to be made. I am to have charge."[42]

Two days after Lee surrendered, Booth made his way through celebrating crowds in Washington and near the War Department was caught up in the press of surging humanity. Men yelled, shouted, screamed, cheered, laughed, and wept. An impromptu band had sprung up.

Secretary of War Stanton appeared and made a short speech. The crowd roared for Vice President Johnson whose words were bitter: "And what shall be done with the leaders of the rebel host? I know what I would do if I were President! I would arrest them as traitors; try them as traitors, and hang them as traitors!"[43]

Many in the crowd cheered his words. Someone began the cry, "To the White House." Booth let himself be carried to the Executive Mansion where the crowd's chant brought Lincoln to an upper window west of the portico. The sight of the haggard face seemed to drive the crowd wild. Endless cheers poured from aching throats until President Lincoln raised his hands for silence.

"My friends," the President said, "you want a speech, but I cannot make one at this time. Undue importance might be given to what I should say. I must take time to think. If you will come tomorrow evening, I will have something to say to you."[44]

The cheering rose briefly, then fell as Lincoln again asked for silence. "You have a band with you. There is one piece of music I have always liked. Heretofore, it has not seemed the proper thing to use in the North. But now, by virtue of my prerogative as President and Commander in Chief of the Army and Navy, I declare it contraband of war and our lawful prize. I ask the band to play, 'Dixie.' "[45]

The crowd went wild as the Confederate national tune was struck up.

The next night, the crowd was back to hear Lincoln's promised speech. Booth and David Herold stood among the flickering shadows made by the candles which alone were allowed to illuminate the grounds.[46]

Speaking of the thousands of black soldiers who had been pressed into gray uniforms, Lincoln said: "If universal amnesty is granted to the insurgents, I cannot see how I can avoid exacting in return universal suffrage, or at least suffrage on the basis of intelligence and military service."[47]

Booth protested to Herold, "That means nigger citizenship. Now, by God, I'll put him through."[48]

U.S. Marshal Lamon that same day approached the President with a request. "Lincoln, I've got to go to Richmond on a reconstruction convention matter, and I'll need a pass for myself and a friend."[49]

The President reached for a blank card and wrote, "Allow the bearer, W.H. Lamon and friend, with ordinary baggage, to pass from Washington to Richmond and return. April 11, 1865. A. Lincoln."[50]

On the night before the marshal left Washington, he called on John P. Usher, Secretary of the Interior.[51] "I'd like you to do me a favor. Persuade the President to exercise extreme caution, and urge him to go out as little as possible while I'm absent."

"Why don't we go together and ask him?"

Usher and Lamon visited Lincoln and Lamon asked "Will you make me a promise?"[52]

The President replied, "I venture to say I would, Ward, but I'd like to know what it is you want me to promise?"

"Promise me you won't go out after nightfall while I'm gone, particularly to the theatre."[53]

The President turned to the Secretary of the Interior. "Usher, this boy is a monomaniac on the subject of my safety. I can hear him—or hear of his being around—at all times of the night, to prevent somebody from murdering me. He thinks I shall be killed; and we think he is going crazy."[54] Lincoln stood up. "Well, I promise to do the best I can towards it." He shook his friend's hand. "Good-bye, God bless you, Ward."

Did Lamon know something special? Certainly he didn't

tell his friend Lincoln all he knew, for the marshal was going to use the presidential pass for himself and Beverly Tucker, the Confederate agent. They were going to discuss cotton and in particular make arrangements for the Northern speculators to put their deals through to completion.[55]

Capt. James William Boyd had run into a little trouble in early April. Taking his orders from the War Department, thieves under his direction, had been rounding up good mounts in Prince Georges County, Maryland.[56]

Boyd had learned that a retired provost marshal, Captain Thomas H. Watkins, a resident of Upper Marlboro, had attempted to assault sexually the wife of one of Boyd's colleagues. On a night in late March, Boyd had shot Watkins in the back of the head. Confederate guerrilla John H. Boyle was suspected, but Boyd admitted his guilt in a letter to his friend Moe Stevens in Tennessee. In addition, Boyd wrote that the government knew what he had done and had looked the other way.[57]

His freedom was more important to someone than having him tried for murder.

On Thursday afternoon, April 13, Booth ran into E.A. Emerson, a stock company actor at Ford's. He was to play the part of Lord Dundreary in the next night's production of *Our American Cousin,* starring Laura Keene.[58] When the men greeted each other, Booth reached out and took a cane from Emerson's hands, gripped both ends of the cane, and threw it over his shoulders. Emerson had often seen Booth do this.[59]

Booth held the cane behind his shoulders as he loudly asked, "Ned, did you hear what that old scoundrel did the other day?"

"Who're you talking about, Wilkes?"

"Why, that old scoundrel, Lincoln."

Emerson was surprised, even a little dumbfounded. "For God's sake man, speak low! The first thing you know, you're going to get yourself in trouble!"[60]

Booth took no notice. "He went into Jeff Davis' home

in Richmond, sat down and threw his legs over the arm of his chair and squirted tobacco juice all over the place."

He added somberly, "Somebody ought to kill the old scoundrel."[61]

"For God's sake, John, stop where you are! I'm going to leave you!"[62]

Booth's dark eyes flashed. He pulled the cane down over his shoulders, broke it in two, dropped the pieces, and strode off.

Emerson slowly picked up the two halves and stared after his friend.

Chapter 11

TARGET DAY FOR ASSASSINATION

On Good Friday, April 14, 1865, morning sun burned off a light fog early. A beautiful spring day was assured.

Booth, usually a late sleeper, arose at 7:30 a.m.

Lewis Payne was sleeping late at the Herndon House. David Herold was sitting on the edge of a bed at the Navy yards and wondering what time it was. Mary Surratt was already cleaning her house after breakfast. Her son, John, was believed to be in Elmira, New York.[1]

Sam Arnold was clerking in the commissary store at Fort Monroe. In his pocket was a letter from Booth urging him to come to Washington at once. Arnold knew that meant the kidnap plan had been revived. George Atzerodt, whose usual bed was an old carriage at Port Tobacco, was given room 126 at 8 that morning when he registered at the first class Kirkwood House, 12th Street and Pennsylvania Avenue. Directly below was Vice President Andrew Johnson's suite.[2]

Michael O'Laughlin was deep in dreams. He had been out late the night before, visiting women whose nickname had been taken from their profitable association with Hooker's Army Division.

Ned Spangler, scene shifter at Ford's Theatre, who rarely slept in a regular bed, that Friday morning arose from his makeshift quarters backstage at the theatre and prepared for a day's carpentry.

Dr. Samuel A. Mudd was already looking over his farming operation down in Maryland.

Booth breakfasted in Washington's National Hotel dining room with Miss Carrie Bean, a merchant's daughter. The actor spoke briefly with another young woman, Lucy Hale, as he left the hotel and went to the barbershop for his morning shave.[3] There he met Henry Johnson, his former valet.[4]

As the actor left the barbershop, he met Michael O'Laughlin. The two men went to the National Hotel for a private talk.[5] Three days before, O'Laughlin said, he had made contact in Baltimore with a sea captain who used the code name, T.B. Road. O'Laughlin used the name of John Stevenson. He had completed certain arrangements and returned to Washington. O'Laughlin was feeling uncertain.[6] "I keep hearing all these different names," O'Laughlin began. "who's really in on this project?"

"A number of people are going to help. A major is to come to Ford's Theatre during intermission at the end of the second act. He'll tell the President he's needed at the War Department."

"When will this be, Wilkes?"

"Just as soon as the old tyrant attends his next theatre performance."

"What about the guards?"

"The regular guards are to be enticed into the saloon and drugged into unconsciousness. Other guards will take their place."

"I still don't see how you're going to. . . ."

Booth interrupted. "A troop of cavalry will come to the theatre and escort him away. The President's carriage will pick up the Secretary of State at his home. Then the Vice President will also be captured."

122

"All three in one carriage?"

"Yes. Nobody's going to stop the President's carriage, especially if it seems to have a cavalry escort."

O'Laughlin shook his head dubiously. "You've still got to get them out of the city. How're you going to do that?"

Booth explained that the carriage with Lincoln, Johnson and Seward, escorted by cavalry, would leave Washington for Maryland by way of the Navy Yard Bridge. "The password has been arranged; the coach will proceed to Surrattsville, to Bryantown, then on directly to Benedict's Landing, where a ship is waiting."[7]

O'Laughlin asked, "Then what?"

"The three captives will be taken aboard. The coach and team will be disposed of. Nobody will find them. The ship will take the captives away."

O'Laughlin was still doubtful. "Assuming everything works all right to that point, what're you going to do with the prisoners?"

"They'll be secreted someplace. You don't need to concern yourself."

The plan was so fantastic, so grandiose; it sounded just like something the dramatic, publicity-seeking Booth would do. It had dash and daring, risk and originality. In short, it was all highly improbable.

Possible failure had not been mentioned. All was entrusted to a handful of followers, many unknown to each other. Yet Booth went grandly ahead with reckless daring.

"What about Secretary Seward? He's still reported confined to his home with a broken collarbone and fractured jaw from that April 5 carriage accident.[8]

Booth said, "We may have to make other arrangements for Seward."

O'Laughlin asked, "How about you and me and the others?"

"I'm going to Europe. I've arranged for extensive bank credits in England and France. I've got a ship waiting for me at Nanjemoy Creek near Port Tobacco." The actor smiled. "Let me reassure you, Mike, everything's been worked out. The first ship at Benedict's Landing will take the prisoners away. A second ship will pick me up at Port

123

Tobacco. We'll head for the Bahamas. . . ."⁹

O'Laughlin interrupted, "What about me?"

The actor laid a friendly hand on O'Laughlin's shoulder. "I've made arrangements for you to follow in about six weeks. You'll leave Baltimore for England. In about three months, we'll all meet in Liverpool."

O'Laughlin protested, "Wilkes, you know I don't have that kind of money for travel."

There was an edge to Booth's tone. "Someone will bring it to you. They'll get in touch with you through an ad in the Baltimore newspaper."¹⁰

O'Laughlin was very unhappy. In the smuggling business with Booth he usually obeyed without knowing the reasons, but this was different. O'Laughlin realized he didn't know much of anything, not even the name of the ship's captain he had contacted by code name on the dark Baltimore pier.

"I'll see you later." Booth ushered his friend out. A few minutes later, he went downstairs, walked up Sixth Street to H, and stopped briefly at the Surratt boarding house where he spoke with Mrs. Surratt.¹¹

Many Washingtonians were preparing to attend traditional Good Friday services which began at noon. Mrs. Surratt was going to St. Patrick's Church with one of her boarders, Nora Fitzpatrick.¹² Boarder Louis Weichmann had been allowed off work and planned to attend rites at St. Matthews Church.

Booth had no interest in such observances. He continued on to Ford's Theatre where he received his mail when in Washington.

Ford's Theatre was a three-story brick edifice which fronted directly on the narrow sidewalk and unpaved Tenth Street. In 1833 the First Baptist Church of Washington had been erected on the site.¹³ Years later, it had been abandoned. When John T. Ford, a Baltimore theatre entrepreneur, came to Washington in 1861, he saw the building's raised platform at its east end as a stage, the former pews as seating for theatre-goers.

The Board of Trustees of the church leased the building

to Ford for five years in December, 1861, with an option to buy. The building burned down on December 30, 1862. Ford rebuilt the gutted brick structure into a popular theatre, first known as Ford's Atheneum.[41]

His main competition was Leonard Grover, who had rebuilt the old National Theatre on E Street, Northwest, and Pennsylvania Avenue and called it Grover's Theatre.

President Lincoln often slipped into Grover's or Ford's for a few minutes, sometimes accompanied by small son, Tad. Occasionally they watched awhile from the back row, then left, unobserved by most theatre patrons. Lincoln went back to his work apparently refreshed by a good laugh.[15]

Diagonally across the unpaved street from Ford's was a three-story red brick building owned by William Petersen. A tailor, Petersen rented out some of his rooms to transient soldiers, or to actors who played at Ford's.[16] Just past Ford's on the south, was Peter Taltavul's bar where Booth often drank a great deal of brandy.

Behind the theatre was the 30 foot wide "Baptist's Alley," with stables some 200 yards straight back. Shanties of black women were in rows along the theatre's drab rear wall.[17]

Booth entered the theatre lobby and stood until his eyes adjusted to the dim light. He glanced at the clock hung above the center lobby door. "Any mail for me?" he asked Thomas Raybold, ticket seller at Ford's.

Raybold handed him several pieces and a small bundle.

Out in the bright light of day, the actor sat down in the entryway. One letter was in feminine handwriting. Two other letters in the same hand were hidden in his saddle blankets.[18] Booth glanced briefly at the simple signature, "Lola."

Lola Alexander was the attractive, and promiscuous, wife of the Federal Cavalry's Col. Julius Alexander. She was known to prefer handsome and famous men like Booth—and men who could provide her with information of various kinds. Both Vice President Andrew Johnson and his personal secretary, Col. Browning, had received seductive letters from Lola.

"Oh, dear Colonel," she had written Browning, "please do come to New York. It is so beautiful. I have a parlor and a bedroom at your disposal."[19]

In her first letter to Booth, on Feb. 20, addressed to the National Hotel in Washington, she had written, "It was nice to see you tonight and I hope you return soon. You are always welcome. I hope that you do not think me silly for enclosing the valentine."[20]

Lola's second letter, dated March 19, had been simple and to the point: "Mr. Booth, if you come to town as supposed, I will be crushed if you do not stop and see me. Please do. Lola."[21]

Lola's third letter provoked him mightily. Dated April 12,[22] it had none of the wiles and seductiveness of the first two messages. It read, "Mr. Booth, I am now doing what I declared to myself I would not do, but I do value our friendship.

"You, sir, were rude to me. I am not used to gentlemen friends being rude to me, and I do not like it; nor will I condone it."[23]

The letter carried suggestions of more than a lover's quarrel. "You do not own me, not even a little. I saw in you a side I did not dream existed. How can you be so jealous of the dead?"[24]

Mrs. Alexander was chiding Booth over Col. Ulric Dahlgren. The Dahlgren Raid was rising up to plague the actor again. Mrs. Alexander drove her knife deeper: "And do you not know that a good soldier follows orders without question? And he was a good soldier. Besides, I have it from the best of authority that he was following the orders of the Commander in Chief. So how could he do otherwise."[25]

Considering her amorous letters to Vice President Johnson, his secretary Colonel Browning, and other escapades with top echelon brass, there is no doubt that somebody had told Mrs. Alexander more than how lovely she was.

"You seem to forget that he paid with his life for what he believed good and necessary."[26] Booth read on with

126

mounting emotion. "When you have served your cause with half the dedication and loyalty he showed, then perhaps you may have earned the right to criticize, but I doubt that this will happen. If you want to see me again, I will expect you to be civil; otherwise, I will not see you. Lola."[27]

"Oh, that damn woman!" Booth exclaimed, startling passersby. Twice Dahlgren had risen from the grave to cause Booth anguish.

Booth went to James W. Pumphrey's stable to hire a saddle horse. The actor said he would engage her then and return for her about 4 p.m. The mount Booth preferred to ride was not available, so the actor chose instead a small bay mare with a white spot on her forehead.[28] Pumphrey warned that she was spirited and known to break her bridle when tied.

"I'm going to Grover's to write a letter," Booth answered. "There's a stable behind the theatre." The actor mounted the little horse. When he let her have the rein, she proved quick and fast. Exactly what he wanted.

At Ford's Theatre, a White House courier approached the box office and spoke to Harry Ford, theatre treasurer. The President wishes to know if he may have a private box for himself and party tonight?"[29]

"Certainly! Certainly!" Harry Ford exclaimed. "I'll take care of that request myself."

"Mr. and Mrs. Grant have been invited," the messenger added.

This news intrigued Ford. The city would want to see the military hero. Besides, Good Friday evening usually had one of the lowest attendances of the year. Handbills and newspaper advertisements in the afternoon papers might pick up the attendance.

Ford called a theatre employee. "As soon as rehearsal is over, prepare the presidential box. Remove the partitions between seven and eight so there'll be room for the President and Gen. Grant. Bring up chairs and a sofa."[30]

Ford took a pencil and scrawled in large letters across

127

the poster on the side of the box office: "The President and his party will be at the theatre tonight."

Newspaper ads and handbills were quickly prepared. The Washington *Evening Star*'s emphasis was on the importance of Grant being in attendance: "Lieut. Gen'l. Grant, President and Mrs. Lincoln have secured the State Box at Ford's Theatre TONIGHT, to witness Laura Keene's *American Cousin*."[31]

George Atzerodt was finishing a morning drinking bout at the Kirkwood House bar. He made several references about "Vice President Johnson," whose hotel suite was just below his. He met David Herold later and went to Naylor's stable where Herold hired a horse.

E.A. Emerson was standing in the lobby with Harry Ford when Booth came in about 1 p.m. and saw the announcement about the President's party.[32] "Why," Booth exclaimed, "that old scoundrel is going to be here tonight."

Ford replied, "Yes, John, but I wouldn't speak of him that way if I were you."

Emerson watched as his fellow actor turned and walked rapidly away.

Booth went to Grover's Theatre and upstairs to Deery's Saloon, where he wrote a long letter to the *National Intelligencer*, put the letter in an inside pocket, and walked out.

Back at the National Hotel he bathed, then called at the Kirkwood House to see Atzerodt, who wasn't in. Booth left a note under his door and, after a drink at the Kirkwood bar, approached the desk clerk, "Is the Vice President in?"

"No, Mr. Booth, he isn't."

"Is his secretary, Col. Browning?"

"Sorry, Mr. Booth."

"It's all right. May I have a blank card, please?"

The clerk handed it to Booth. He scribbled, "Don't wish to disturb you. Are you at home? J. Wilkes Booth."[33]

Booth had just gone when Browning came in. In his room, Browning found Booth's card. Was it for Johnson or him? There was no indication. The secretary decided it was meant for him.[34]

Booth returned to the desk. "May I see Mr. Browning?" The clerk replied, "I'll see if he's in."

Booth handed his card to a bellhop who went upstairs while Booth roamed aimlessly around the lobby. The boy reappeared and whispered to the clerk. "Sorry, Mr. Booth. Col. Browning is not at home."[35]

Booth's black eyes flashed. "He's not?" The actor glanced up the stairs where he had seen Browning disappear a few minutes before.[36] "I see. Very well. Thank you." Booth walked out rapidly, a hand striking his thigh in agitation.

Sometime that afternoon, Booth went into Peter Taltavul's saloon and saw Ed Henson, who closely resembled David Herold.[37] Henson, Herold, and Booth were friends and fellow smugglers. He waved to Booth. "Have a drink, Wilkes?"

Booth accepted, ordering brandy. He lifted the glass in salute.

"You know, Wilkes, it's not going to be the same anymore."

"What isn't, Ed?"

"You know." Henson's eyes darted around the room. Booth knew Henson meant the smuggling. "The end of the war sure put an end to some things, eh?"

"Indeed, Ed, indeed."

"To tell you the truth, Wilkes, I'll miss the excitement. I wish I had me some more good times like we used to have."

Booth's dark eyes narrowed. "You really want some excitement, Eddie?"

"Sure do, Wilkes. Sure do."

The actor thumped his glass on the bar. "I'll keep you in mind, Ed, if I hear of anything."

At the Herndon House, at Ninth and F Streets, in an upstairs corner room, Booth found Payne lying on the bed, hands clasped behind his head. "I've got the plan for tonight. Meet me back here tonight. A horse will be in

129

the little stable behind Ford's Theatre."

"Right, Cap."

Booth rushed out.

Decorating of the presidential box had been delayed until rehearsal was finished about 2 of that afternoon. Ned Spangler and carpenter Jake Ritterspaugh were helping. John Burrough, nicknamed Peanuts, volunteered, too.

While the partition between boxes seven and eight was being removed, Spangler suddenly exploded: "Damn the President and Gen. Grant."[38]

"What're you damning those men for?" Burroughs demanded. "They never did you no harm."

"They ought to be cursed for getting so many men killed."

Three straight backed chairs and a sofa were placed inside the box to the right of the audience. A black walnut rocker, upholstered in red damask, was put in box seven next to the red flower papered wall screening the box from the balcony audience.[39] The rocker would seat the President closest to the audience, directly over the stage apron 12 feet above. Red lace curtains would hide the lean, haggard face. The rocker would place Lincoln about four feet in front of the door to box seven. In back of the sofa and closest to the door to box eight, the President's personal attendant could be seated.

The boxes were only accessible from the right, or south, side of the theatre's second floor, behind a semi-circular arrangement of cane bottom chairs in the dress circle. Entry to the two upper tier boxes was through a single white door which led into a single small antechamber. Beside this door, in the blind corridor, a cane bottom chair was placed for the White House guard. Anyone reaching the President would first have to pass the officer.[40]

The only other way into the President's box was over the front railing some 12 feet above the stage apron. Young Ford, on a ladder on the apron, finished adjusting a blue and gold U.S. Treasury flag across the front of the box.

"How does it look?" Harry called down to an actor.

"Looks good, Harry, except there's a bare spot right in the middle, under the center post just above the blue flag."

"Get me that picture of George Washington." The Washington portrait was hung above the Treasury flag.

Harry spotted the scene shifter inside the box. "What do you think, Spangler?"

"Looks fine to me, Mr. Ford."

Ford backed down the ladder and stood looking up at the decorated box. "Well," he said, "I guess Ford's Theatre is ready."

About 2:30 that Good Friday afternoon, Booth climbed the stairs to the Surratt boarding house.[41] Weichmann opened the door before the bell rang.

"Ah, Mr. Weichmann. On your way out?"

"Mrs. Surratt has asked me to drive her into Maryland to collect some money owed her. She just gave me $10 and asked me to rent a horse and buggy. I'm to drive."[42]

"Splendid, Mr. Weichmann! Splendid! I'm sure you'll enjoy the ride. Well, don't let me keep you. I've come to see Mrs. Surratt."

Weichmann moved down the stairs as Booth entered the second-story parlor. The big youth paid six dollars for a rig and returned to the boarding house. On the way, he had seen Atzerodt trying to rent a horse at a livery stable on G Street.[43]

As Weichmann came in he saw his landlady and Booth in earnest conversation by the hearth. He climbed to his third-story bedroom, got some clothing, and returned to the curb, where he waited by the horse until Booth left, and Mrs. Surratt descended the stairs. Before she entered the buggy, Mrs. Surratt exclaimed, "Oh, wait! Let me get something of Mr. Booth's."

She returned with two packages, both wrapped in brown paper and tied with twine. "It's glass," she explained, setting one package carefully on the bottom of the buggy.[44]

Weichmann slapped the reins on the horse's rump and headed for Maryland.

Booth wrote several letters that afternoon. The one he had written earlier to the *National Intelligencer* was delivered to Editor James C. Welling. It was a long letter which opened with the ominous words, "By the time you read this, I will either have accomplished my purpose or be myself beyond the reach of any man's hand."[45]

Reference was made to his loving peace more than life, of having loved the Union beyond expression. For four years, he had waited for the dark clouds to part and restore the former sunshine.

"My prayers have proved as idle as my hope. God's will be done. I go to see and to share that end."

The letter rambled on, disjointed, the product of an aggravated and anguished mind. "This country was formed for the white, not the black man." Lincoln's policy was preparing the way for "total annihilation."

His government "is the most corrupt in the nation's history." Lincoln's friends had become wealthy. Lincoln had sold out to the "scavengers of Wall Street."

The *Intelligencer* would do a great service to the nation if it would print the names "of his friends and speculators who have been and wish to exploit the now bloody, defeated Southern states."[46]

Thirty-five names followed.*

James Speed; Ward H. Lamon; Leonard Swett; Judge David Davis; Orville H. Browning; Judge James B. Hughes; Gen. John [James] W. Singleton; Sen. Edwin D. Morgan of New York; Sen. William Sprague of Rhode Island; Rep. Oakes Ames of Massachusetts; Schuyler Colfax, Speaker of the House; Hugh McCullough, Sec. of the Treasury; Hansen A. Risley; Judge Ebenezer Peck; Judge Joseph Casey; Gen. Adelbert Ames; Gen. John A. Dix; William P. Dole; Thurlow Weed; Jeremiah S. Black; Thomas C. Durant; Leonaidas Haskell; Jay Cooke; Henry Cooke; James Fiske, Jr.; Simeon Draper; William T. Mellen; Eben Jordan; George Frances Train; H. M. Hoxie; Benjamin E. Bates; William O. Bartlett; Alexander T. Stewart; John A. Stewart; and Abel Rathbone Corwin.

Booth concluded, "Each of these men named have only their pecuniary enrichment in mind and care for very little else."

The letter was never published.[47]

Booth's second letter was addressed to Col. William A. Browning, and began with a dramatic lament: "My Dear Colonel, 'Tis true; the last cup from the bottle bears the bitter dregs. How bitter it is to be deceived by such a trusted compatriot, one whose cause was mine in summer's heat and barren cold of winter."[48]

Booth had accused Browning of lying, but "you assured me that the act was that of a heinous madman, too soon sent to command too much, and unworthy of the task assigned. But you swore the act was his, and his alone, done without the sanction of the principal."[49]

The pen continued to scratch. Was Browning really Booth's friend? Was Browning trying to deceive Booth? Or had Browning himself been deceived?

Why, Booth continued, had Browning avoided seeing him? He had seen Browning arrive at the Kirkwood House. But when Booth sent up his card, "the word came back that you were not at home. What was meant was that you were not at home to me. Ah—how bitter the dregs, when the first cup was so sweet!"[50]

The lure had been held high while the dagger had been fondled under the coat. But "we will have judgment . . . and some behavior is only expiated by bloodletting. . . ."[51]

A time would come when the colonel would be asked, "Why did he do it? Was he mad?" Browning could answer, "Yes, 'twas madness born of tyranny and dying with the tyrant."[52]

Booth signed the letter, folded it, slid it into an envelope, and walked out into Washington's waning afternoon.

Witnesses saw the actor in various places throughout the remainder of the day. He picked up the little bay mare and demonstrated her speed to James Maddox, property man at Ford's.

"She can run like a cat," Booth boasted and touched

spurs to the mare. James P. Ferguson, a nearby restaurant keeper, watched her go.[53]

Charley Warwick saw Booth trotting the lively bay up the avenue, but his eyes were on Booth. "He was faultlessly dressed," Warwick said, "in elegant riding boots with slender steel spurs on his feet."[54]

Booth tethered the mare in front of Grover's, went into Deery's, and had a brandy. He walked to the desk and addressed another of several letters he'd written that day.

Booth was talking to actor John Matthews, when Matthews saw Gen. Grant drive by in an open carriage. "Why, Johnny, there goes Grant. I thought he was going to the theatre this evening with the President."[55]

Booth looked after the carriage, suddenly shook Matthews' hand, mounted his horse, and galloped down Pennsylvania Avenue after the carriage.

Gen. Grant saw a horseman ride by, wheel his mount and ride back to peer into the carriage.

Mrs. Grant remarked, "That's the very same man who sat near us at lunch with some others, and tried to hear our conversation."[56] Grant thought it was merely some rider's idle curiosity.

Grant and his wife obviously were leaving town. Their luggage was with them. That meant the general's customary military escort would not be present at the theatre.

As Booth popped in and out of various Washington spots, one of his fellow conspirators rode out of town on horseback with a companion.

David Herold, after picking up a horse at Naylor's, had ridden into Maryland with a 16 year old neighbor, Johnny Booth, to sell a horse to Judge Joseph Parker. The younger boy was the son of a blacksmith named James Booth, who was no relation to the actor. They lived two houses down the street from the Herold home.[57]

Shortly before 5 o'clock, Booth was seen drinking in Peter Taltavul's bar. His companions were Ned Spangler and James Maddox. Moments later, Booth met a drunken Atzerodt on the street and spoke briefly before riding his mare into the alley behind the theatre. He called to Spangler to get "Peanuts" Burroughs to hold the mare.

In about half an hour, Booth again entered the theatre, then left to have dinner at the National Hotel.

At approximately 7:45 p.m., as the curtain was to rise on the first act of *Our American Cousin,* Booth met Michael O'Laughlin in front of Ford's.[58] Booth was very excited. O'Laughlin could see that he had been drinking. "Everything's gone wrong! The major sent word that he would not be here."

"Which major is that?"

Booth did not reply but rushed on, "The major with the President has refused to go through with it."

O'Laughlin wasn't sure who Booth was talking about. He thought maybe it was Maj. Thomas Eckert who would not be here, and Maj. Henry R. Rathbone who would not cooperate.[59]

Booth ran on, his face flushed, his eyes bright with drink. "Everyone wants to call it off again. I refuse. It must be done tonight! Tonight, do you hear?"

O'Laughlin understood what Booth was saying. It was no longer a risky public kidnapping from the theatre and a wild dash to Maryland and waiting ships. The night's new task was assassination.[60] "You'd better forget it," O'Laughlin suggested in a low voice. "Call it off."

Booth's baritone voice rose. "I won't, Mike! I won't! It's got to be tonight!"

The heated reply attracted the attention of an artillery sergeant. O'Laughlin, already nervous, persuaded Booth to go inside the theatre. The angry actor and his concerned friend, began making new plans.[61] Time was short, the situation critical. It was decided to wait until the "major" could be consulted. With that, O'Laughlin returned to the street. Booth stood alone downstairs in the lobby and glanced at the clock. It was a little after 8. The presidential box was still empty.

Booth entered Payne's room at the Herndon House shortly after 8. A few minutes later, Atzerodt also entered.[62] "Where are the others?"

"They haven't come."

Atzerodt controlled a small sigh of relief. "Then we can do nothing."

Payne pulled out a long, heavy knife. He began to whet it on a small stone.

Booth's dark eyes glittered. "The plan has been changed. The capture plan won't work. We are too few. Things have gone wrong. Too many people have backed out. Seward's confined to his home. He can't be moved."[63]

Payne continued to sharpen his long blade without evidence of emotion.

"What . . . what can we do?" the carriage maker asked.

Booth stared hard into Atzerodt's eyes. "Kill them," he said fervently.[64]

The German's body jerked involuntarily. "Kill . . .?"

"Much safer, George. Quickly done and over. No captives to worry about." The actor spun to face him. "I'll take the President. Payne will handle Seward. You'll kill the Vice President at the Kirkwood House."

"But . . . I did not think to kill . . . I was only to capture. . . ."

Booth snapped, "It doesn't matter what you thought! The only alternative now is to kill all three!"

Atzerodt wrapped his arms around himself. "No," he said, "No! I will not kill Vice President Johnson!"[65]

Booth's temper flared. "You'll be hanged anyway! It's death to every man who backs out!"

Atzerodt's drinking made him bold. "No."

Booth shrugged. "Then Payne and I will do it. We strike just after 10."

Payne put up his whetstone and carefully sheathed the long blade. "Yes, Cap," he said. He stood, calm and ready.

Atzerodt walked numbly into the night. He saw Booth mount the bay mare and spur her toward Ford's Theatre.

It was 9 o'clock.

Chapter 12

LINCOLN'S FINAL DAY OF LIFE

The Lincoln family breakfasted together on Good Friday, April 14. Capt. Robert Lincoln had arrived the day before with Gen. Grant.[1]

Mrs. Lincoln had brought up the subject of the theatre. She wanted to see Laura Keene in *Our American Cousin*. Reluctantly, Lincoln had agreed to go. He suggested inviting Gen. and Mrs. Grant, along with Secretary of War Stanton and his wife. Grant had conditionally accepted, but no word had been received from the Stantons.[2]

The President thought the people would enjoy seeing the general. As for the Stantons, well, it would be surprising if they accepted. The War Secretary did not approve of the theatre.

Mrs. Lincoln put down her napkin and turned to 21 year old Robert. "How about you, son? Would you like to join your father and me at Ford's tonight?"

The President's gray eyes twinkled. "Mother," the President said, "a young man in uniform, home from the front, with a pretty young senator's daughter waiting for him, isn't too likely to prefer his parents' company to hers."[3]

"I'll let you know," Robert said. "But I don't think so."

His mother was a little unhappy—she wanted to know how many to count on—but she let it pass. The box would be big enough for Robert and his girlfriend if they decided to come at the last minute.

The President left for his upstairs office. Several callers were waiting to see him. He had invited Gen. Grant to be a special guest at the 11 a.m. cabinet meeting. The President was anxious to learn of the possible surrender of Joe Johnston's troops.

At the War Department, Gen. Grant, preparing a budget for cutting military personnel now that peace had returned, spoke to Secretary Stanton.[4] "The President has asked me to come to his office and attend today's cabinet meeting. I'll have to leave early. I've also been invited to attend the theatre tonight with the President and his party."[5]

"My wife and I are always invited to those things, but we never go. Surely you're not going, General?"[6]

Grant studied his cigar.

The War Secretary was instantly agitated. "I heartily disapprove, General Grant! It is too dangerous. Your life would be in danger! Numerous assassination threats have come to me through the secret service, and other sources."

Grant was used to a military escort. Besides what could happen in Washington?

"Lincoln makes light of these things," Stanton continued. "But I realize the seriousness of them. I'm afraid for you to attend the theatre, General. I urge you not to go."

Grant chewed on his cigar, staring at the War Secretary, who rushed on, "If possible, persuade the President not to attend."

"I'd like an excuse not to go. But. . . ."

"Have no hesitancy over breaking the engagement," the Secretary interrupted.

Grant's aide, Col. Horace Porter, lit the cigar which the general puffed into life. "I could send the President word that I haven't seen my daughter in a long time."

"Capital!" the War Secretary exclaimed. "Withdraw your acceptance. You and Mrs. Grant could take the evening train to New Jersey. Isn't that where your daughter's in school?"

The general stood, thinking how his reneging would look to the Commander in Chief. But it would look good to Mrs. Grant. Twice within two days, the emotionally unstable Mrs. Lincoln had made the general's wife acutely uncomfortable. The two women would not be happy in close quarters.[7]

In March, when the Lincolns were at City Point, a grand review of the Army of the James, under the command of Maj. Gen. Edward O. C. Ord, had been planned. President and Mrs. Lincoln were invited to see the review.

Mary Lincoln and Julia Dent Grant had been riding in an army ambulance over a corduroy road toward the reviewing area. Gen. Adam Badeau and a driver were escorting the two women. As usual, Mrs. Lincoln was overdressed. She was in a good mood, which Gen. Badeau instantly ruined by commenting that all wives had earlier been ordered to the rear, except Mrs. Charles Griffin, wife of Gen. Griffin.[8] She had a special permit from the President.[9]

Mrs. Lincoln's famous instantaneous rage jerked her up from her seat to stand unsteadily in the jostling ambulance. "What do you mean by that, Sir? Do you mean to say that she saw the President alone?"[10]

As the surprised general turned to peer over his shoulder, the plump little First Lady continued, "Do you know that I never allow the President to see any woman alone?"

Smiling, Badeau tried to calm Mrs. Lincoln.

"That is a very equivocal smile, Sir! Let me out of this vehicle at once!" She started to jump out. "I will ask the President if he saw that woman alone!"

The following day, Mary Lincoln again exploded. She arrived by ambulance at a scheduled review already in progress. Maj. Gen. Ord's wife, a beautiful woman, was "riding with extreme grace a spirited bay horse," as a newspaper article phrased it. Mrs. Lincoln learned that Mrs. Ord had ridden side by side with the President in a procession preceding the review. The First Lady was instantly so insanely angry that she tried to leap once more from a moving vehicle. Mrs. Grant, sitting beside her tried to restrain her and was soundly berated for her pains.

Stanton interrupted Grant's thoughts. "I was saying my wife and I never have any hesitancy in turning down the President's theatre invitations. Including this one."

Grant smiled faintly. "It isn't easy to tell the President of the United States and my Commander in Chief that I don't want to attend the theatre with him."

"Don't fret about it, General. If you decline, the Lincolns will find someone else. Over the years, cabinet members have declined such invitations, and the Lincolns don't seem to be offended. Lincoln wanted you so he could show off his victorious general to the public, I'd guess."[11]

"I have already accepted conditionally. I'd have to break the engagement."

"Do so," Stanton urged. "I assure you, to go would be dangerous."

"But the President is going out in such circumstances."

"I have repeatedly asked Lincoln not to expose himself," the secretary responded. "Yet he has ignored my warnings not to go to theatres and other public gatherings."

Grant turned to Samuel Beckwith, his cipher operator. "Summon a messenger. I'll send a note to my wife."

At the cabinet meeting Secretary of the Navy Gideon Welles took his seat at the large table as John P. Usher, Secretary of the Interior; Postmaster General William Dennison; and Hugh McCulloch, Secretary of the Treasury, came in. Attorney General James Speed took his seat, nodding to the President.

Lincoln acknowledged the presence of Frederick Seward, a son of the Secretary of State. The young man had come to report his father was still confined to his bed. The man who had tried to wrest the 1860 Republican nomination from Lincoln was in a steel harness about neck and throat. His broken arm and fractured jaw were still very painful.

Grant's arrival brought applause. Lincoln stood and shook hands. Grant presented his aide, Col. Porter.[12]

"Is there any news of General Sherman?" Lincoln asked.

"None when I left the War Department telegraph a few minutes ago."

So Johnston had not yet surrendered. Lincoln tried to

sound cheerful. "There could be news before the day's out." He hesitated, then mentioned a recurring dream that had come to him again in the night. "This is the eighth time I have dreamed this same dream," he murmured.[13] He seemed to lapse into reverie.

Lincoln was noted for his strange dreams. He always spoke of them with caution, as though doubtful that he should share such profoundly personal matters. Even his longtime friend, Ward Lamon, was not immune to the melancholy that the retelling of a Lincoln dream could bring upon a listener.[14]

Earlier that week, Lamon had asked why Lincoln seemed so depressed. The President replied he'd had a strange dream. Pressed to tell Lamon and Mrs. Lincoln about it, the President had said, "It seems strange how much there is in the Bible about dreams. There are, I think, some 16 chapters in the Old Testament and four in the New in which dreams are mentioned, and there are many other passages scattered throughout the Book which refer to visions.

"If we believe in the Bible, we must accept the fact that in the old days, God and His angels came to men in their sleep and made themselves known in dreams.

"I had a dream the other night which has haunted me ever since. After it occurred, I opened the Bible, strange as it may seem—to the 28th chapter of Genesis, which relates to the wonderful dream Jacob had."

The President said he had turned to other passages, "and seemed to encounter a dream or a vision wherever I looked."

He kept on turning the pages and everywhere "my eyes fell upon passages recording matters strangely in keeping with my own thoughts—supernatural visitations, dreams, visions, and so forth." Lincoln had paused, his manner sad and weary.

Mrs. Lincoln had exclaimed, "You frighten me! What's the matter?"

Her husband replied that he thought he had done wrong to mention the subject. "But," he'd added sadly, his long face sorrowful, "somehow the thing has got possession of me, and like Banquo's ghost, it will not let go.[15]

"About 10 days ago," Lincoln began, "I retired very late. I had been up waiting for some important dispatches from the front. I could not have been long in bed when I fell into a slumber, for I was weary.

"I soon began to dream. There seemed to be a death-like stillness about me. Then I heard subdued sobs, as if a number of people were weeping. I thought I left my bed and wandered downstairs. There the silence was broken by the same pitiful sobbing, but the mourners were invisible.

"I went from room to room; no living person was in sight, but the same mournful sounds of distress met me as I passed along. It was light in all the rooms. Every object was familiar to me. But where were all the people who were grieving as if their hearts would break? I was puzzled and alarmed. What could be the meaning of this?"

In his dream, Lincoln had walked on through the White House until he came to the East Room. "There I met with a sickening surprise. Before me was a catafalque, on which rested a corpse wrapped in funeral vestments."

Soldiers were on guard duty around the body, with a crowd of people weeping pitifully or gazing upon the corpse, "whose face was covered." In his dream, Lincoln asked one of the soldiers, "Who's dead in the White House?"

"The President. He was killed by an assassin!"

A loud cry of grief from the crowd awakened Lincoln from his dream. "I slept no more that night," he concluded to his wife and Lamon. "And although it was only a dream, I have been strangely annoyed by it ever since."[16]

Mrs. Lincoln had exclaimed, "That is horrid! I wish you had not told it! I am glad I don't believe in dreams, or I would be in a terror from this time forth."[17]

Gideon Welles cleared his throat, "You were mentioning a recurring dream you had again last night, Mr. President," Welles prompted.

"It relates to your element, the water," Lincoln said to the Secretary of the Navy.[18]

142

As Lincoln began, Stanton bounced through the door, apologized for being late, and spread a roll of papers before him. "I waited by the telegraph as long as possible, but there was no word from Sherman."

The subject of reconstruction was introduced, the President declaring, "I think it providential that this great rebellion is crushed just as Congress has adjourned and there are none of the disturbing elements of that body to hinder and embarrass us."[19]

Secretary of War Stanton nervously shuffled his papers. He was there to represent the hard line of the Radicals. Congress versus Lincoln was an old story, but the final, telling struggle was about to begin.

Lincoln went on, "If we are wise and discreet, we shall reanimate the states and get their governments in successful operation, with order prevailing and the Union established, before Congress comes together in December."[20]

Radical Republican congressmen would not be pleased. This cabinet session would send tempers even higher. Lincoln hoped there would be no persecution and no bloodshed. "No one need expect me to take part in hanging or killing these men, even the worst of them."

Grant asked for an opinion about capturing Jefferson Davis or letting him escape out of the country.[21]

"Hang him" was the general opinion. What did the President think?

Lincoln began telling a story.[22] "When I was a boy in Indiana, I went to a neighbor's house one morning and found a boy my own size holding a coon by a string. I asked what he had.

"He says, 'It's a coon. Dad cotched six last night, and killed all but this poor little cuss. Dad told me to hold him until he came back, and I'm afraid he's going to kill this one, too, and oh, Abe, I do wish he would get away.'

"Well, why don't you let him loose?" I asked.

" 'That wouldn't be right, and if I let him go, Dad would give me heck. But if he would get away himself, it would be all right.' "

The President looked around the table. "Now, if Jeff Davis and those other fellows will only get away, it will

143

be all right. But if we should catch them, and I should let them go, 'Dad would give me heck.' "

The cabinet got the point. A demand to punish Confederate leaders would get no support from Lincoln.

The War Secretary peered over his small glasses and brought up the other subject on which the President was sure to disagree. Gideon Welles wouldn't like his first proposal, either. But it was a way into the subject of military control of the South under Stanton. "I suggest the Treasury Department be empowered to issue permits to all who wish to trade, and that the War Department order Confederate ports to receive all trading vessels."[23]

Welles was instantly alert to the War Secretary's power grab. "It would be better," the Navy Secretary said carefully, "if the President issued a proclamation stating the course to be pursued by each of the several departments."[24]

Stanton got the warning to stay out of the Navy's jurisdiction. But he had only used the ports as an opening gambit. He was after a greater prize. "After a great deal of reflection," he began, "I have arrived at a plan regarding reconstruction of the South."[25] Someone had to plead the Radical Republicans' hard line policies. What more logical person than the most power hungry man in the nation?

Stanton began reading. In a few words, he was suggesting that the South be treated as a conquered nation and ruled by military occupation. Stanton proposed Virginia be under Federal authority.

Welles pointed out that Virginia already had a skeletal government and a governor.[26]

Stanton read on. State governments would be re-established along lines that caused some members to see vengeance as the driving force.

Welles became the opposition spokesman.[27] "I believe that is in conflict with the principles of self-government which I deem essential," he declared.

"I realize the matter needs more work. However, the President had asked me to draw this up in time for today's meeting, and I have endeavored to do my best."[28]

The President suggested that the matter should be carefully deliberated.

Stanton retreated and turned to another proposal: that the states of North Carolina and Virginia be united under one military governor and the state lines obliterated.[29]

This brought instant discord. Wasn't that the exact opposite of why the war had been fought? The object was to keep the states united, not altered.

In a sudden lull, Welles asked once more to hear about Lincoln's recurring dream.

The President picked up the story Stanton's arrival had interrupted. "I seemed to be in some indescribable vessel, and I was moving with great rapidity toward an indefinite shore," Lincoln began, then paused.

"I have had this dream preceding Sumter and Bull Run, Antietam, Gettysburg, Stone River, Vicksburg and Wilmington."[30]

Gen. Grant reminded Lincoln that Stone River was no victory. The general added, "Nor can I think of any great results following it."

The President nodded. However, he said, the dream usually had come before good news and great victories. He expected that's what it meant this time. "I had the dream last night, and we shall, judging from the past, have great news very soon. I think it must be from Sherman."

In the dream, Lincoln saw a ship sailing rapidly away, badly damaged, with Union vessels in close pursuit. The dream also showed land battles with the enemy routed and Federals in possession of a "vantage ground of incalculable importance."[31]

The President was his usual soft-spoken self, yet there was a hint of iron in him that day. He was back in the saddle after last summer's near disastrous events. He had made compromises, had played politics, and had won the election. He had kept his pledge to keep the Union intact. He had freed the slaves. To date, he had won everything for which he had fought. Now the vast issue of reconstruction must be dealt with. It would be a time of power politics. The winner would determine whether the South

145

rose again, or whether it was raped and pillaged.

The cabinet postponed any decision until Tuesday.[32]

The meeting, a surprisingly friendly session, ran long. No major decisions were made. About 2 o'clock, the President glanced around the table for last minute comments. There were none.[33]

As the meeting adjourned Gen. Grant, trailed by his aide, approached and thanked the President for being allowed to attend.

"It was especially amicable," Lincoln responded. "I'm glad you could be present."

"I appreciate your invitation to the theatre tonight, Mr. President. However, Mrs. Grant has planned a visit to the children in Burlington, New Jersey. She will be sorely disappointed if the visit is delayed."[34]

"There'll be plenty of time to see the children," Lincoln chided, looking down from his great height. "The people are expecting to see the man who won the war."

Grant was saved further embarrassment by the arrival of a messenger. A note from Mrs. Grant said she hoped they could take the 6 o'clock train. Grant handed the note to Lincoln. "I must decide not to remain in Washington," Grant said.[35]

The President's face grew sober. "I understand, Gen. Grant," he said. "Go to your children. And have a safe journey."

Shortly before 2:30, the President lunched with his wife. He returned to his office, nibbling on an apple, and summoned Andrew Johnson, who had repeatedly, but unsuccessfully, tried to see the President since Johnson's drunken behavior on inauguration day.[36] Lincoln greeted him warmly and called him, "Andy." The two talked for less than half an hour, but Johnson's step was much lighter when he left than it had been.

The best clue to what had been discussed was the President's remark to his secretary, John Nicolay, "Reconstruction is a brand new problem. The Vice President should be acquainted with it. He should also understand the President's wishes in the matter."[37]

Shortly after Johnson left, Lincoln was alone at his desk when he heard a commotion outside his door. He opened the door to see a former slave barred by a uniformed guard with a rifle.

"There is time for all who need me," Lincoln said. "Let the good woman come in."

Mrs. Nancy Bushrod took a while to compose herself in front of the President's desk.[38] She had been jokingly admitted to this point by outside armed guards. They knew the distraught woman would be stopped further on. The soldier at Lincoln's door would not let her pass, but she had cried out, "For God's sake! Please let me pass!" and Lincoln had heard her.

Mrs. Bushrod told Lincoln she and her husband had been so relieved when they were freed as slaves on a plantation near Richmond that Tom had enlisted after they both ran away to Washington. But his pay from the Army of the Potomac wasn't coming through, and the Bushrods had many children. Could the President help her?"

"Come this time tomorrow," Lincoln said, "and the papers will be signed and ready for you."[39]

Mrs. Stanton stopped at the War Department after a shopping trip to speak to her husband. "How should I decline the Lincoln's invitation?"

Stanton peered at her in surprise. "Why, just send regrets."

Mrs. Stanton sighed. Since curtain time was only about four hours away, she would send a messenger: "Mr. and Mrs. Stanton regret they will be unable to attend the theatre tonight."[40]

The President pulled out his pocket watch and checked the time. He had promised his wife a carriage ride. He arose and was washing his hands in the corner closet of his office when Assistant Secretary of War Dana came in.

"Jacob Thompson, the chief of the Confederate secret service in Montreal, is expected in Portland, Maine, tonight. He's believed headed for England. The provost marshal wants to know what instructions you have."

The President began drying his hands. "What would Stanton say on the matter?"

"Arrest him," Dana replied.

The President hung up the towel. "No, I think not. When you have an elephant by the hind leg and he's trying to run away, it's best to let him run."[41]

The President went downstairs and escorted his wife to the driveway. Coachman Francis Burns smartly swung his spirited team to the steps.

"Should someone go with us?" Mrs. Lincoln asked.

Her husband helped her into the carriage. Burns heard him reply, "I prefer to ride by ourselves."

The President settled beside her and nodded to Burns. The driver clucked to the horses.[42] Burns heard the President and his wife laughing over something and smiled to himself. The President was in good spirits.

Mrs. Lincoln remarked on her husband's attitude. "You almost startle me by your great cheerfulness."[43]

He became serious. "Mother, I consider that this day the war has come to a close. We must both be cheerful in the future. Between the war, and the loss of our darling Willie, he have both been very miserable."[44]

The mention of Willie sobered Mrs. Lincoln. The laughter stopped. The President had touched a very sensitive spot.

On February 20, 1862, 12 year old William Wallace Lincoln had died of pneumonia. He had been born the year after Eddie, the first Lincoln son, had died. The Thursday after he died, Lincoln began observing a part of every Thursday to remember Willie and all boys lost in the war.[45]

Mrs. Lincoln now asked her husband, "Do you remember what you said to a member of the Christian Commission when our little boy died?"

Her husband remembered. He had said, "I think I can say with sincerity that I hope I am a Christian. I had lived until my boy Willie died without realizing fully these things. The blow overwhelmed me."[46] He had added, "It has been my intention for some time, at a suitable opportunity, to make a public religious profession."

As the carriage whirled along that Good Friday afternoon, the President spoke of personal matters, something he rarely did. "Mother, when reconstruction of the South is completed, I'd like us to take a trip to Europe. Also I especially would like to go to the Holy Land. I should like very much to visit those sacred places."

Mrs. Lincoln asked what they would do when his term was over.

"Maybe we'll return to Springfield. Perhaps we can buy a farm along a river."[47]

Burns couldn't hear the President's words, but something Lincoln said apparently made Mrs. Lincoln laugh loudly.

"I never felt so happy in my life," Lincoln told his wife.

The carriage turned back to the White House.

Mrs. Lincoln said she was concerned about who would accompany them to the theatre. Their oldest son didn't plan to go. The Grants had backed out. So had the Stantons. The First Lady had invited the daughter of Senator Ira Harris of New York, and the senator's stepson. Clara Harris was a nice looking young woman who wore her dark hair in spitcurls over her forehead and in many ringlets down her neck.[48] Major Henry R. Rathbone, a tall, slender Union officer, was engaged to Clara.

The President returned to his office before leaving for the theatre. Some people waited to see him, but he decided to make a hurried trip to the War Department telegraph.[49] William Crook, who had the 8 a.m. to 4 p.m. shift, fell into step with him.[50]

The President had insisted that the guards, in plainclothes, walk beside him. They were to appear as friends, not policemen. The two came to the turnstile dividing the White House grounds from the enlosure to the War Department.[51]

The President always took the same route and usually talked to Crook. Today he seemed more depressed than Crook ever remembered. The President's walk was unusually slow. Yet a short time before, Lincoln had made his wife laugh aloud.

Some drunken men, celebrating too early or still celebrating from days before, blocked the path. Crook stepped ahead and cleared the way. After they passed, Lincoln looked sadly at the guard.[52] "Crook, do you know, I believe there are men who want to take my life? And I have no doubt they will do it." His calm, sure voice dismayed the guard, who asked, "Why do you think so, Mr. President?"

"Other men have been assassinated." The President said it matter of factly.

"I hope you're mistaken, Mr. President."

In his usual tone, Lincoln then said, "I have perfect confidence in those who are around me, in every one of you men. I know no one could do it and escape alive. But if it is to be done, it is impossible to prevent it."[53]

Lincoln asked Stanton for any late news, and said, "Grant has cancelled his engagement to attend the theatre this evening, and you are unable to come."

Stanton apologized for the late cancellation, but the President waved the remark aside.

Stanton asked, "Then you're not going tonight, either?"

"Oh, yes," Lincoln replied. "We're still going."

"You must have a competent guard."

The President seemed to change the subject. "Stanton, did you know that Eckert can break a poker over his arm?"[54]

The question surprised Stanton. "No. Why do you ask such a question?"

"Well, Stanton, I have seen Eckert break five pokers, one after another, and I am thinking he would be the kind of a man to go with me this evening. May I take him?"

The War Secretary shook his head. "I have some important work for Eckert this evening. I couldn't spare him."[55]

In a rare display of anger, Lincoln replied, "I will ask the major myself, and he can do your work tomorrow."

The President went into the adjoining cipher room and

told Eckert of the evening's plans. Lincoln concluded, "I want you to be one of the party, Maj. Eckert, but Stanton says he can't spare you. Now, Major, come along. You can do Stanton's work tomorrow. Mrs. Lincoln and I want you with us."[56]

The muscular major listened politely. He was in a doubly tight spot. The Commander in Chief was asking a lowly major to attend a social function and act as bodyguard. There could be no higher honor, and protocol decreed instant acceptance. Eckert also owed his job to Lincoln.

In February, 1862, a month after Stanton entered the cabinet, Eckert, then a captain, had learned that the new War Secretary didn't like his work. Eckert had sent in his resignation. The War Secretary was angry that word had leaked to Eckert in time to allow him to resign. On a Sunday afternoon, Eckert and a friend were ushered in to see Stanton. In a loud voice, Stanton had berated Eckert, "Well, Eckert, why have you neglected your duties by absenting yourself from your office so frequently?"[57]

Quietly, Eckert defended himself. He had been at his post for three months without taking off his clothes, except to change his linen. He had remained all night at the telegraph and seldom slept in his hotel bed. But if his services were not acceptable, he wanted his resignation accepted.[58] Eckert felt an arm on his shoulder. It was Lincoln's.

"Mr. Secretary," the President had said, "I think you must be mistaken about this young man neglecting his duties." Lincoln declared he had seen Eckert at his post for three months, before breakfast, late at night, and before daylight. He had never seen any reporters or outsiders in the office.[59]

Stanton had picked up Eckert's resignation as well as the document dismissing Eckert and had torn them to pieces.

"You are no longer Capt. Eckert," Stanton had said. "I shall appoint you major as soon as the commission can be made out."

Maj. Eckert now looked at Lincoln and said, "I thank

you, Mr. President, for inviting me to accompany you to the theatre tonight. But I'm sorry, Mr. President, I cannot accept. The work to which the Secretary referred must be done this evening. It could not be put off."[60]

Crook fell in beside the President as they turned back toward the White House. Every trace of Lincoln's depression was now gone. He spoke as usual, telling Crook about Mrs. Lincoln and his plans to attend the theatre. "It has been advertised that we will be there, and I cannot disappoint the people. Otherwise, I would not go, I do not want to go."[61]

At the White House, it was time for John Parker, the night guard, to replace Crook, but Parker was two hours late in arriving.

As the President climbed the White House stairs, he paused and looked down at Crook. "Good-bye, Crook," he said, startling the guard. As far as he could remember, Lincoln had never before said anything except, "Good night, Crook."[62]

About that time news was circulating through the streets and homes of St. Joseph, Minnesota, that the President had been murdered in Washington. St. Joseph was 40 miles from the nearest railroad and 80 miles from any telegraph communication.[63]

Also, at 10 o'clock that morning, residents of Booth's hometown, Manchester, New Hampshire, were speaking in the past tense of Lincoln's assassination, discussing the event as if it had already happened.[64]

By noon that day, a well-known surgeon of high standing in an unnamed New England town had been informed of the President's death.[65]

At 2:30 that Good Friday afternoon, a writer on the Middletown, New York *Whig Press* asserted that he had been informed that the President had been shot and "it was currently so reported in the village of Pine Bush and in the town of Crawford before 12 o'clock of that day."[66]

The *Newburgh Journal* confirmed the reports in the

Whig Press, but was more conservative in its editorial opinion.[67]

From 12 to 4 hours before the President was to sit in his box, his death had been reported in half a dozen scattered parts of the country.

It was late; Lincoln should have been dressing for the theatre, but people still waited at the office to see him. One was Speaker Schuyler Colfax, who had seen him in the morning. Colfax commented on Lincoln's exposing himself to danger when he had walked through the fallen Confederate capital of Richmond.

The President replied he would have been alarmed if someone else had done it. "But," he added, "I was not scared about myself a bit."[68]

Lincoln thought of the theatre party. Would the Speaker like to come?

"No, thanks." Colfax said, adding his excuses.

It was time for Lincoln to join his wife. As he and Colfax left his second floor office, an usher brought word that George Ashmun was waiting to see the President. "He doesn't have an appointment," the usher said, "but the Congressman says it will only take a minute."

Lincoln owed a lot to ex-Congressman Ashmun of Massachusetts. He had been in charge of the 1860 convention that had nominated Lincoln.[69]

It was already 10 minutes to 8; the curtain at Ford's had gone up five minutes before, but in politics an ex-congressman is worth a few minutes' time. "Show him in." Lincoln turned to Colfax, "Would you mind waiting outside for me?"

Ashmun's first words were annoying. He had a friend who was in a spot because of a large cotton claim against the government. Could the President appoint a commission to look into the situation?

"I'm done with commissions!" Lincoln's rare anger was surprising. "I believe they are contrivances to cheat the government out of every pound of cotton they can lay their hands on!"[70]

Ashmun sputtered, "I hope that the President means no personal imputation?"

Lincoln apologized.[71]

Fifteen minutes had passed when Mrs. Lincoln, dressed for the theatre, stepped into the office. She was polite, considering, that her husband had already made them nearly a half-hour late, and they still had to pick up Maj. Rathbone and his fiancee.

The President asked Ashmun if he'd come in the next day and they would finish their talk. Lincoln picked up a card and wrote: "Allow Mr. Ashmun and friend to come in at 9 a.m. tomorrow. A. Lincoln. April 14, 1865."[72]

The two men and the waiting Colfax walked downstairs. Mrs. Lincoln and the newspaperman, Noah Brooks, were now waiting on the front porch.

Lincoln told Senator William Stewart, who had come with Mr. Ashmun, "I am engaged to go to the theatre with Mrs. Lincoln. It is the kind of engagement I never break."

The President and Mrs. Lincoln finally settled themselves in the coach. Burns released the brake and slapped the reins. The team pulled away.[73]

Some minutes before, night guard John Parker had talked briefly with White House doorman Tom Pendel, one of the original four policemen detailed to White House duty.[74]

Pendel asked the guard who had relieved Crook, "John, are you prepared?"

Before Parker could answer, guard Alphonso Dunn exclaimed, "Oh, Tommy, there's no danger."

"Dunn, you don't know what might happen," Pendel had replied. The doorman urged Parker, "Now you start down to the theatre and be ready when he reaches there. And see him safe inside."[75]

Chapter 13

NIGHT OF THE ASSASSINATION

The presidential carriage picked up Maj. R. Rathbone and his fiancee, Miss Clara Harris, at the Harris residence, Fifteenth and H Streets.[1]

The party moved through Washington's streets as the temperature dropped. The weather had been clear at 6 o'clock on that Good Friday. A light wind blew from the southwest with temperatures in the mid-50's.[2]

Driver Burns turned the last corner onto Tenth Street towards Ford's Theatre about 8:30 p.m. and brought the team into a smart trot as they neared the brick structure, passing barrels holding black tar torches which burned irregularly in the brisk air. Beside the barrels shills called out, "This way to Ford's Theatre."[3]

The President carried his overcoat as security against the night chill. Personal aide Charles Forbes carried the ever present heavy plaid shawl Lincoln favored, winter or summer.

The last to alight was Maj. Rathbone, unarmed and in mufti. Rathbone offered his arm to Miss Harris. Mrs. Lincoln took her husband's and all entered the lobby.

Doorman John Buckingham bowed deeply.

White House Guard John Parker had arrived in time to check out the lobby, the stairs to the dress circle and the presidential box. Everything had seemed satisfactory, and he had returned to the lobby to wait for the President's party.

On stage, Miss Kay Hart and E.A. Emerson were

speaking their lines when they caught sight of the President.[4] The actors began applauding. The audience turned to see the late arrivals, and the orchestra began "Hail to the Chief." The presidential party followed Parker around the second story dress circle and down a sloping aisle, bringing them to the upper tier box nearly even with the stage. The guard pushed open the white door to the tiny antechamber.

In response to the prolonged applause, whistles and cheers, the President did something he had never done before. He stepped forward to the box rail, in front of the lace curtains, where the audience could clearly see him, and bowed. The crescendo of sound rose even higher. The music and the cheers continued even when the President's lips moved. "Thank you. Thank you." and his hands motioned for them to sit down.[5]

The man who had held the Union together stood near the post which separated the arches of boxes seven and eight, a picture of Washington almost at his right hand. The blue Treasury flag stretched across both boxes.

Finally, applause slowed. Lincoln backed into the shadows and sat down in the rocker next to the balcony wall. The music stopped. Partially rising from the rocker, the President said in a low voice to the actors, "Now, Mr. Emerson, please go on."[6] Then he vanished behind the curtains.

The audience could no longer see those inside the box. Backstage, however, 16 year old W.J. Ferguson, the callboy, could see Mrs. Lincoln, in a cane chair, on the President's right. Five cane chairs and one armchair were unoccupied.[7] Closest to the door of box eight, Forbes was seated on a straight chair.

The President was sitting about four feet in front of the door to box seven. The locks on both doors were inoperative.

Outside those doors, in the antechamber and between the one outside white door through which anyone reaching the President would have to come, guard John Parker looked at the plain chair provided for him.

156

It was the custom of White House guards to remain in the little passageway, but Parker couldn't see the play from there. He got up, carried the chair through the white door, and put it outside the antechamber. He still couldn't see the stage.[8]

After awhile, he peered around and saw an empty seat at the front of the gallery. He left his post and moved quietly down to the empty seat. Now he could see.[9]

Lincoln's back was totally unguarded.

Booth popped in and out of the theatre no less than five times before 10 o'clock. The doorman noticed that the actor was excited, his cheeks aflame as though he had been drinking. Booth was a familiar figure around the theatre and was allowed to come and go as he wished.[10]

Parker soon tired of the play. He arose, walked away from the gallery, and back to the dress circle. The white door was closed. The guard walked behind the dress circle, down the stairs to the lobby, and stuck his head out into the night air. He approached the presidential carriage at the curb and roused Burns dozing inside.[11] "How about a little ale?"

Burns yawned, hunched his shoulders against the chill, and said that sounded like a good idea. As the two men passed through the theatre doors on their way to Taltavul's Star Saloon, they saw Forbes who had left the Presidential party alone in the box. Forbes joined Parker and Burns at the bar.

In the box, the President was reminiscing about the drive that afternoon. He whispered with his wife about their plans, the return to Springfield, and future travels.[12]

"There is no city I desire to see so much as Jerusalem," the President repeated.[13]

Mrs. Lincoln leaned closer to her husband.

Booth left the lobby and went out into the night. He rode up the alley behind the theatre and dismounted from his frisky mare about 9:30 p.m.

"Spangler!" Inside her shanty, on the alley back of Ford's, Mary Jane Anderson, a black woman, saw Booth dismount and heard him repeat his call.[14]

On the third call, the scene shifter stepped out into the alley. The moon had not yet risen. It was cold. "Hold my horse, Ned." Booth shoved the reins into the scene shifter's hands.[15]

"I can't, Mr. Booth. I've got a scene change coming up."

"Then get Peanut John." Booth disappeared into the theatre.

Inside her home, Mrs. Anderson heard the horse stamping her hooves and moving restlessly on the cobblestones as John Burroughs held her reins.

Booth approached the set from behind, drew off his gauntlet gloves, and greeted actors and stagehands waiting their cues.

He shaded his eyes against the lights, peering toward the presidential box. The curtains and smoky lamps prevented him from seeing anything. The actor turned to utility man, J.L. Debonay. "Is it all right to cross behind the set?"

"Sorry, Mr. Booth. The dairy scene is on. You'll have to go under the stage."[16]

Booth knew the play, knew the lines, and when each person would be on stage. In about half an hour, only actor Harry Hawk would occupy the stage. Booth nodded and entered the subterranean passage which took him underneath the President's box and out into a narrow outside passageway between the theatre's south wall and Taltavul's saloon.

In the box, Lincoln whispered to his wife. "I just felt a cold chill."

Mary turned toward the back chair where Forbes had been sitting. He was gone, but the shawl was there.[17] Mrs. Lincoln indicated its location.

"No," he whispered, "I'll just slip on my overcoat."

The President stood up to put on the coat.

Maj. Rathbone noticed the President's action. He had not seen Lincoln move since he had sat down more than an hour before.[18]

Behind them, door seven was still open. Door eight was closed. The President, in his overcoat, sat down again. Rathbone's eyes returned to the play.

Booth came out the far end of the tunnel, turned west, emerged on Tenth Street and went into the saloon.

Forbes, Burns, and Parker were drinking at the far end of the bar.[19]

"What'll it be, Mr. Booth," Taltavul asked, "the usual?"

"No, thanks, Peter. Think I'll have some whiskey."

The barkeeper raised one eyebrow. Whiskey for the famous brandy drinker? He shrugged. [20]

"A little water, too, please." Booth laid money on the bar as Ed Henson got up from a nearby table. He walked a little unsteadily to the bar to greet Booth. "Buy you a drink, Mr. Booth?"

"Thanks, Eddie. I've already ordered."

Taltavul set whiskey and a glass of water on the bar before Booth.

"Then join me at my table."

Booth carried his whiskey and glass of water to Henson's table.

"Did you see the President's carriage outside, Mr. Booth?"

"Yes, Eddie."

"He didn't get here until about the middle of the first act, but he made it, and I guess that's what counts, huh, Mr. Booth?"

Booth lifted his glass. "That's what counts, Eddie."

The two men sipped their drinks. Booth seemed to be studying his one time smuggling companion. The dark eyes made Henson uncomfortable. "What'cha looking at me like that for, Mr. Booth?"

"Eddie, how serious were you this morning? I mean about wanting some excitement?"

"I've never said anything to you I didn't mean, Mr. Booth."

Booth glanced around the room and saw an older man watching him at a nearby table. He decided the man was

159

drunk. At the far end of the bar, the President's men were still drinking and talking.[21]

"Eddie, I've got a bit of business to do. Meet me on the road to upper Marlboro near Good Hope Hill about midnight."

"You mean across the Potomac in Maryland? How about the guards?"

"Shh! Keep your voice down! You can get across the bridge. Now that the war's over, the guards aren't so strict. Will you do it?"

"Sure, Mr. Booth." Henson raised his glass. "Just like the old days."

Booth's eyes glittered as one of the President's three men summoned the bartender and ordered another round. "Not a word to anybody, you understand, Eddie." The actor finished his drink and stood. He was aware the older man at the nearby table was still eyeing him with distaste. Booth turned his dark eyes on the man, who raised his nearly empty glass and called, "Hey, Booth."

The actor stared at the drunk, who shoved himself unsteadily to his feet. "Booth, you'll never be the actor your father was."[22]

Booth smiled. "When I leave the stage," he said, "I will be the most famous man in America. You can bet on that!"[23]

Booth pushed his way through the front door, nodded to the doorman and asked what time it was.

"Step into the lobby," the doorman replied, "and you can see for yourself."

Booth entered and glanced at the clock.

It was time.

Deliberately, he turned toward the stairs that led to the dress circle and the unguarded President's box.

George Atzerodt was to go to Johnson's room at the Kirkwood Hotel about 10:15 p.m., knock on the door, and shoot Johnson pointblank when he opened it. However, the carriage maker from Port Tobacco, Maryland, went to the "Oyster Bay" restaurant until about 10 p.m. From there he went to Naylor's Stables, picked up his

160

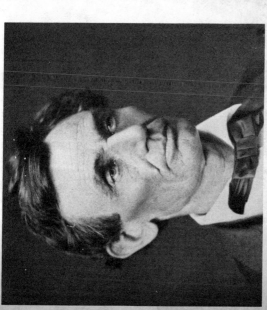

Abraham Lincoln was the sixteenth President of the United States and the first President to be assassinated. Sunn Classic Pictures' film, "The Lincoln Conspiracy," re-examines the April 14, 1865 assassination. On the left is believed to be the best photo of Lincoln without his beard, taken about 1859. On the right, Lincoln is pictured as he appeared in 1864.

In Sunn Classic Pictures' film, "The Lincoln Conspiracy," Abraham Lincoln is portrayed by John Anderson (left) who has played Lincoln more than 600 times in his career. John Wilkes Booth is played by Bradford Dillman, a veteran of many feature films and television productions.

To inspect conditions and bolster troop morale, President Lincoln visits the troops on the front line during the Civil War. Wearing his legendary stovepipe hat, Lincoln confers with General George McClellan and 15 members of his staff on the battlefield at Antietam, Maryland, on October 3, 1862.

Sunn Classic Pictures' film, "The Lincoln Conspiracy," was filmed in historic Savannah, Georgia. Elaborate planning goes into the shooting of every scene in a motion picture. Here, "stand-ins" pose for cameramen while they adjust their equipment and shooting angles. "The Lincoln Conspiracy" required a cast of more than a thousand.

Carey Street, the main business district of the Confederate capitol of Richmond, Virginia, lies in ruins after undergoing extensive shelling and burning in the final days of the Civil War as Northern troops overran the city, destroying everything in their path. The photo is dated Spring of 1865.

Colonel Lafayette C. Baker, Chief of the National Detective Police (federal secret service), confronts John Wilkes Booth in his Washington City hotel room in a scene from Sunn Classic Pictures' film, "The Lincoln Conspiracy." Colonel Baker is played by John Dehner and Bradford Dillman stars as Booth.

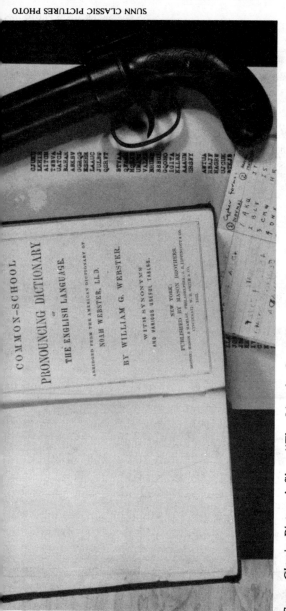

Sunn Classic Pictures' film, "The Lincoln Conspiracy," is based on heretofore unpublished secret service documents, congressmen's diaries, cipher-coded manuscripts, and other documents from more than 20 private collections. Pictured are some of the 1865 documents used in the film. The pistol and cipher-coded manuscript page were the property of Colonel Lafayette C. Baker, Chief of the National Detective Police (NDP). The cipher decoding dictionary and cipher notebook were owned by NDP detective Luther Potter.

John Wilkes Booth, played by Bradford Dillman (left), and Edwin Henson, portrayed by Ed Lupinski (center), escape across the Rappahannock River after Lincoln's assassination in a scene from Sunn Classic Pictures' film, "The Lincoln Conspiracy."

JOHN WILKES BOOTH

IZOLA DARCY BOOTH

OGARITA BOOTH

IZOLA FORRESTER

Historians have long contended that John Wilkes Booth was an unmarried madman actor. Booth was married in 1859 to Izola Darcy, an actress who used the stage name Martha Mills. Booth kept his wife and daughter, Ogarita, on a farm near Harpers Ferry, Virginia. Also pictured is Izola Forrester, Ogarita's daughter and Booth's granddaughter.

NATIONAL PARK SERVICE PHOTO

This John Wilkes Booth diary, now on display at Ford's Theatre in Washington, D.C., is missing 18 pages. Secretary of War, Edwin M. Stanton, testified before Congressional investigating committees that the pages were missing when the diary was given to him in April of 1865. The missing pages contain the names of some 70 high government officials and prominent businessmen who were involved in a conspiracy to eliminate Lincoln. The purported 18 missing pages were recently discovered in the attic of Stanton descendents.

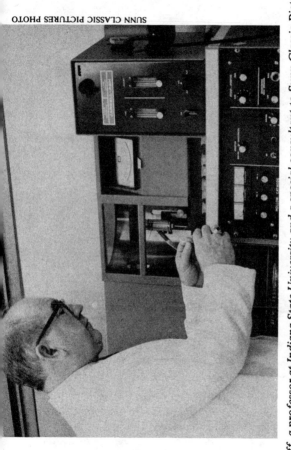

Dr. Ray A. Neff, a professor at Indiana State University and a special consultant to Sunn Classic Pictures on "The Lincoln Conspiracy," performs an atomic absorption spectrophotometer analysis on strands of Colonel Lafayette C. Baker's hair to determine the cause of his death on July 3, 1868. Results showed that Colonel Baker, Chief of the National Detective Police, died of arsenic poisoning. Colonel Baker's beer was laced with arsenic by a War Department employee.

JEFFERSON DAVIS

JUDAH BENJAMIN

JACOB THOMPSON

BEVERLY TUCKER

Late in 1864, several Confederate leaders conspired to have Lincoln kidnapped and brought to the Confederate capitol of Richmond, Virginia. Their purpose for kidnapping Lincoln was to hold him for ransom and to force release of Southern troops being held in Northern prisons. The key leaders behind this plot included Jefferson Davis, Confederate States President; Judah P. Benjamin, Confederate Secretary of State; Jacob Thompson, Confederate Secret Service Chief, and Beverly Tucker, Confederate diplomatic agent. John Wilkes Booth was the man chosen to kidnap Lincoln.

SEC. EDWIN STANTON

SEN. ZACHARIAH CHANDLER

SEN. BENJAMIN WADE

SEN. JOHN CONNESS

"Radical" Republicans in Lincoln's own party conspired to have him removed from office prior to the assassination in 1865. Their motive was to prevent the President from instituting "soft" peace terms with the South which called for bringing southern states back into the Union. The Radicals favored dividing the South into military districts and ruling them as conquered territories. John Wilkes Booth was directly involved in the Radicals' plot. Secretary of War Edwin M. Stanton, who was not an elected official, sided with the Radical Republican conspirators who included Senators Zachariah Chandler (Michigan), Benjamin Wade (Ohio), and John Conness (California).

Northern commodities speculators and financiers of the Union war effort conspired to have Lincoln forcefully removed from office because they felt he was personally preventing them from making a financial killing in cotton speculation. Leaders among this group were Jay Cooke, Philadelphia financier; Henry Cooke, Washington banker; Thurlow Weed, politician-journalist; Robert D. Watson, cotton speculator; and Ward Hill Lamon, U.S. Marshal of Washington, D.C. Lamon, Lincoln's closest friend, was usually able to manipulate the President on behalf of the northern speculators. John Wilkes Booth also played a role in the northern speculators plot against Lincoln.

JAY COOKE

PENNSYLVANIA HISTORICAL SOCIETY PHOTO

HENRY COOKE

LIBRARY OF CONGRESS PHOTO

THURLOW WEED

LIBRARY OF CONGRESS PHOTO

ROBERT WATSON

RAY A. NEFF PHOTO

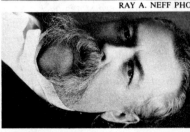

WARD H. LAMON

The assassination of President Lincoln occurred April 14, 1865 at Ford's Theatre on Tenth Street in Washington, D.C. Once a Baptist church, the three-story building was converted into a theatre that remains in use to this day. President Lincoln frequently visited the theatre for relaxation.

When Lincoln was assassinated by John Wilkes Booth, he was attending a performance of ''Our American Cousin'' at Ford's Theatre in Washington. Pictured is Lincoln's original theatre program, blemished by his fatal bloodstains. This dramatic historical event is re-examined in Sunn Classic Pictures' film, ''The Lincoln Conspiracy.''

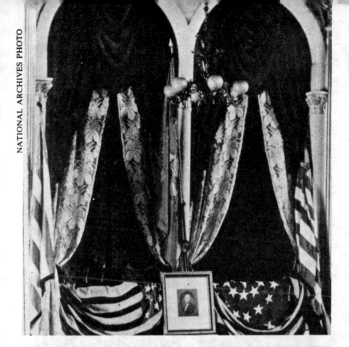

President Lincoln and Mrs. Lincoln were viewing the play, "Our American Cousin," from the Presidential Box at Ford's Theatre when Lincoln was fatally shot. The bottom photo shows a reconstruction of the seating arrangement on the tragic assassination night. Lincoln was seated in the rocking chair on the left.

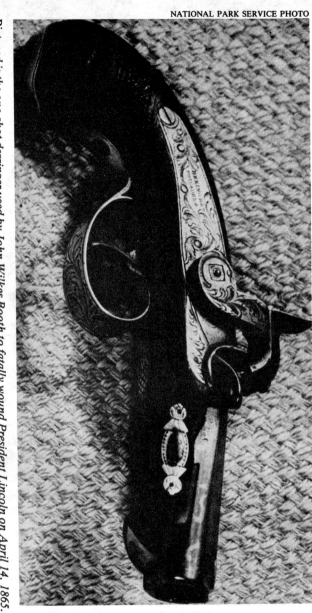

Pictured is the one-shot derringer used by John Wilkes Booth to fatally wound President Lincoln on April 14, 1865. The pistol is now on display at Ford's Theatre National Historic Site in Washington, D.C.

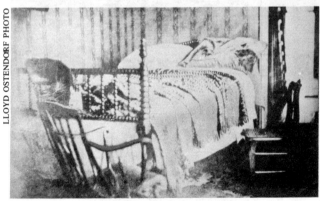

Following the shooting of President Lincoln, his near lifeless body was removed from Ford's Theatre's Presidential Box to the William Petersen home across the street at 453 Tenth Street, Washington, D.C. The lower photo of the bed with the bloodstained pillow was taken immediately after Lincoln died during the early hours of April 15, 1865.

Shortly after the assassination of President Lincoln, assassin John Wilkes Booth escaped from Washington, D.C. over this bridge known as the Navy Yard Bridge in 1865. It was the only escape route not closed by government authorities.

EDWIN M. STANTON

COL. LAFAYETTE BAKER

CHARLES A. DANA

MAJ. THOMAS ECKERT

Four high government War Department officials, charged with the protection of Lincoln, knew of a conspiracy plot to eliminate the President and failed to take preventive measures. These same people directed the conspiracy cover-up after the assassination. Lincoln's Secretary of War, Edwin M. Stanton, orchestrated the cover-up, assisted by Colonel Lafayette C. Baker, Chief of the National Detective Police (federal secret service); Major Thomas Eckert, Chief of the War Department Telegraph Office and Charles A. Dana, Assistant Secretary of War.

Following Lincoln's assassination, massive rewards totaling more than $300,000 were offered for the capture of John Wilkes Booth and other suspects in the assassination plot. The rewards prompted frequent shootings of Booth look-alikes, including the killing of Captain James William Boyd at Garrett's farm in Virginia. After announcing this "Booth" shooting to the press, the government passed off the corpse as that of John Wilkes Booth.

THEODORE ROSCOE PHOTO   NATIONAL PARK SERVICE PHOTO

On April 26, 1865, U.S. government troops shot Booth look-alike Captain James William Boyd at Richard Garrett's farm near Bowling Green, Virginia. The left photo shows the house as it existed around 1865. It was on this front porch that Captain Boyd died from bullet wounds. The right photo shows the run down Garrett farm many years later.

LLOYD OSTENDORF PHOTO

JOHN WILKES BOOTH

JAMES WILLIAM BOYD

RAY A. NEFF PHOTO

The government claimed John Wilkes Booth, Lincoln's assassin, was killed by federal troops at Garrett's barn in Virginia 12 days after he assassinated Lincoln. The truth is, Booth was never in the barn. The man killed was Captain James William Boyd, a former rebel agent who worked for the War Department and who bore a striking resemblance to Booth. The government passed off the Boyd corpse as that of Booth at an official inquest in Washington. Meanwhile, Booth and contraband smuggler Edwin Henson escaped to freedom and were never apprehended by authorities.

HENRY JOHNSON

DAVID HEROLD

EDWIN HENSON

The government claimed John Wilkes Booth escaped from Washington City with co-conspirator David Herold. However, newly discovered evidence reveals Herold was miles away from Washington that evening and that Booth actually escaped town with fellow contraband smuggler Edwin Henson who also resembled Herold. Along their escape route, they met Henry Johnson, Booth's valet, who supplied them with fresh horses and supplies as the three galloped to freedom.

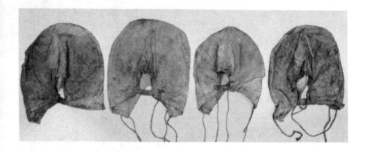

The eight people arrested as Booth's co-conspirators in the Lincoln assassination were subjected to excessive physical torture while confined to prison awaiting their trial. Day and night, the prisoners wore leg chains, stiff wrist shackles and cotton-padded hoods an inch thick, with openings only for the nose and mouth.

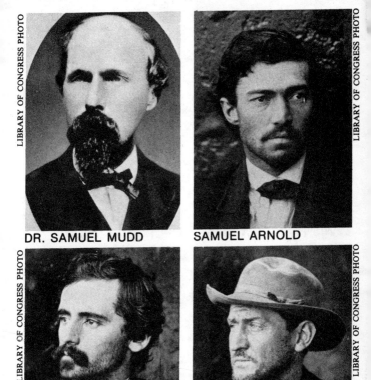

DR. SAMUEL MUDD

SAMUEL ARNOLD

MICHAEL O'LAUGHLIN

EDWARD SPANGLER

Following Lincoln's assassination, the government imprisoned more than 2,000 suspects in the assassination plot. Eight of the suspects were tried as having conspired with Booth to assassinate the President. Four of these suspects were sentenced to life in prison. Imprisoned were Dr. Samuel Mudd, medical doctor; Samuel Arnold, commissary clerk; Michael O'Laughlin, feedstore clerk; and Edward Spangler, Ford's Theatre stagehand.

LEWIS PAYNE (PAINE)

GEORGE ATZERODT

DAVID E. HEROLD

MARY E. SURRATT

Four of Booth's alleged assassination co-conspirators were sentenced to be hanged even though much of the evidence against all eight of the co-conspirators was manufactured by the War Department. Witnesses were paid large sums of money—from $250 to $6,000—by the government to testify against the individuals. Those hanged on July 7, 1865 were Lewis Payne (Paine), unemployed; George Atzerodt, carriage maker; David E. Herold, drugstore clerk; and Mary E. Surratt, boarding house owner.

The four John Wilkes Booth co-conspirators sentenced to be hanged on July 7, 1865 within 24 hours of their sentences being announced, were forced to walk by their own coffins and graves enroute to the gallows. This scene is re-enacted in Sunn Classic Pictures' film, "The Lincoln Conspiracy."

After what became known as the famous Conspiracy Trial of 1865, four people were sentenced to life in prison and four others were sentenced to be hanged within 24 hours for their presumed roles with Booth in the Lincoln assassination. Mary E. Surratt became the first woman in American history to be hanged. The historical hanging took place at the Arsenal Prison in Washington, D.C. on July 7. None of the conspirators were allowed to testify in court and later evidence showed that most were framed by paid government witnesses.

MAJ. HENRY RATHBONE **CLARA HARRIS**

MARY LINCOLN **SGT. BOSTON CORBETT**

Strange twists of fate plagued many of the people connected with the Lincoln assassination. Major Henry Rathbone and Clara Harris, the Lincoln's Theatre guests, were soon married. A few years later, Major Rathbone fatally shot his wife and spent the rest of his life in a German insane asylum. Mrs. Mary Lincoln, distraught over the assassination events, was declared insane and committed to an insane asylum by her son, Robert Lincoln. Boston Corbett, who the government credited with shooting John Wilkes Booth (Captain James William Boyd) became a clerk with the Kansas State Legislature. He went beserk one day and shot up the gallery. He, too, was sent to an insane asylum and later escaped into obscurity.

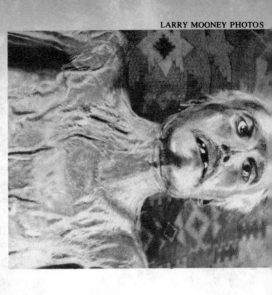

The death of John Wilkes Booth remains a mystery. Following Lincoln's assassination, some historians traced him to England and India. Others speculate that he faked his death in India and returned to the United States under the assumed name of David E. George or John St. Helen. On his deathbed, this individual claimed he was John Wilkes Booth and since there was a reward for the body of Booth, the mortician did not bury the corpse but had it carefully preserved. The above photos are purported by some people to be the John Wilkes Booth mummy, now in a private collection.

rented mare, and after having a drink with the hostler, galloped about town. His assignment was to kill Johnson, but he was not going to do it.[24]

By Lafayette Square, just beyond the White House, a tall muscular man in a dark coat approached the four-story home of Secretary of State William Seward. The giant held a bottle of medicine in his hand. Under his coat was a large Navy revolver and a Bowie knife. He reached a hand toward the bell.

Booth moved behind the dress circle patrons and paused, glancing toward the President's box. The guard's chair was empty. He knew Parker was still downing drinks next door.

Capt. Theodore McGowan, sitting in the aisle leading to the President's antechamber, felt someone push behind him. McGowan pulled his chair forward to let the man pass. The captain knew Booth but did not glance up at the man's face, only saw that the figure stopped a few feet away.[25]

Leisurely, the fellow surveyed the theatre, then produced a small pack of visiting cards from his pocket and selected one. He stood a second with the single card in his hand. McGowan saw him approach what he called "the President's messenger."[26] The captain didn't notice whether the messenger took the card or merely looked at it, then allowed the man to approach the white door.

James P. Ferguson, who operated a restaurant adjoining Ford's Theatre, saw Booth as he passed near the President's anteroom. Ferguson saw Booth stand a moment beside the white door, then put both hands and one knee against it and push.[27] The door opened. Booth vanished inside. Ferguson's eyes flickered back to the stage.

In the box, Mrs. Lincoln, snuggled beside her husband, glancing up and murmured, "What will Miss Harris think of my hanging onto you so?"[28]

The President smiled down at his wife. "She won't think anything about it."

In the anteroom, Booth saw no guard. He sheathed

Bowie knife. He would not need to use it. He reached into his pocket for a small brass pistol. The name, Deringer, was engraved on the side. The 44 caliber, six-inch, single shot weapon had been capped earlier for instant firing. A heavy, lead slug about the size of a marble was in position ahead of the charge.[29]

Silently, the actor stood outside the open box door holding his breath against the excitement, the liquor, the tension. He listened for the cue from the stage when only one man would be between himself and the back alley.

On stage, the matronly and scheming mother had just discovered that the American backwoodsman was not rich enough for her daughter. "Go to your room," she cried to her daughter. "You may go to your room at once."[30]

As mother and daughter exited, Harry Hawk stood alone on the stage, gazing after the haughty woman. "Society, eh?" Hawk spoke the lines of Asa Trenchard. "Well, I guess I know enough to turn you inside out, old woman, you sockdologizing old man trap!"[31]

Laughter rippled through the house.

Booth took a quick step from the antechamber, crossed the three or four feet to the President's back, and quickly extended the pistol. Lincoln started to turn his head to the left. The derringer's explosion ripped through the laughter.

The call boy, Ferguson, was standing across the stage from the President's box, talking to Miss Keene. Her back was to the box. At the sound of the shot, Ferguson saw Lincoln lean back in his rocking chair. The left side of the sad, haggard face came to rest against the red wallpaper.[32]

Maj. Rathbone had been watching the stage. The pistol shot jerked his head around. Through the smoke some seven or eight feet to the major's left, Rathbone saw a man standing between the door and President Lincoln.

The assailant dropped his pistol and sprang toward the box railing.

Rathbone thought he heard someone cry, "Freedom!"

Booth cried, "Sic semper tyrannis!"[33] Thus always to tyrants.

The unarmed major sprang. The actor wrestled free

and made a violent stroke with the knife toward the major's chest. Rathbone instinctively threw up his left arm. The knife struck him between the elbow and shoulder. Blood flowed from a wound an inch and a half long.

Booth again headed for the front of the box. One hand gripped the railing near the picture of Washington.

Again, Rathbone sprang forward clutching at Booth's clothing. Booth vaulted over the railing to the stage apron a dozen feet below. He landed off balance on his left knee, a piece of the blue flag trailing from his spur. The fall had snapped Booth's left tibia about two inches above the ankle, but the actor immediately sprang to his feet, fled across the stage into the darkness backstage.[34] Harry Hawk stood on stage in stunned surprise.

From the President's box, a dense cloud of gun smoke was drifting into the auditorium. Rathbone, his arm covered with fresh blood, pointed and yelled, "Stop that man!"

Orchestra leader William Withers, returning from backstage to the pit, saw a man come running toward him. He hit Withers so hard he was spun around. Two quick cuts were made with the knife, nicking Wither's clothing at his neck and side. Withers went down. As he fell, the orchestra leader recognized Booth.[35]

Ferguson saw Booth rushing toward him and Miss Keene as they stood backstage.

Booth ran between the star and the call boy, not pausing as he covered the 30 feet to the little door opening into the alley. Although many people had recognized Booth, the actor reached the door with no one laying a hand on him.

Theatre carpenter, Jacob Ritterspaugh, heard someone cry, "The President has been shot!" He lunged for the running man who struck out with a knife.[36] The carpenter jumped back and rushed up to Spangler. "That was Booth!"[37]

The scene shifter slapped Ritterspaugh with the back of his hand. "Shut up! Don't say which way he went!"[38]

"What do you mean, slapping me in the mouth?"

Spangler cried, "For God's sake, shut up!"

Utility man Debonay had recognized Booth in the center of the stage, a long knife in his hand.[39]

No one pursued as Booth vanished backstage until Joseph B. Stewart moved. The six-foot, six-inch tall Washington lawyer and former Union Army officer had been seated in the right front orchestra seat when the pistol had gone off. Stewart glanced up in time to see a man sail over the box railing and fall to one knee on the stage, his back to the audience.[40] As he rose, the man turned full face to the audience and Stewart was quite sure he recognized Booth. As Rathbone called, "Stop that man!" Stewart had given chase.

About 20 feet away from the stage door, Stewart saw it open and slam shut. He reached the door but couldn't find the way to open it.[41]

Burroughs had risen from the carpenter's bench in the alley when he heard a pistol shot from inside the theatre. No shot was called for in the play. He turned uncertainly toward the door, still holding the horse's reins. The little rear door banged open and Booth sprang through. "Give me that horse!"

Booth lifted one foot into the stirrup, struck Burroughs with the butt of the heavy knife, and kicked the fallen man in the chest.[42]

Mary Jane Anderson had seen the theatre door swing open and Booth rush into the alley. She saw something glittering in his hand. He seemed to move so quickly that he didn't have proper control of the mare.[43]

Stewart, still the only one in pursuit, finally managed to open the stage door and step into the alley. The moon was just beginning to rise. He saw a horse moving at a quick, agitated run. He was within 10 feet of the horse's left flank when the rider swung the horse away, and the big man missed a grab at the reins. The rider crouched forward on the saddle, and the horse swept rapidly away to the left toward F Street.

Less than a minute had passed since the shot had been fired.

Maj. Rathbone rushed across the box into the antechamber where John Parker should have been standing guard. He threw himself at the closed white door and tried to pull it open. A piece of wood about three feet long and four inches wide was solidly wedged between wall and door. Rathbone yanked, but the brace would not move.[44]

Miss Harris stood beside the railing and called to the audience below, "Water! Water!"

Mary Lincoln stared at her husband. Except for a slight movement of his head at the moment the explosion occurred, he had not moved. Suddenly, the horrifying truth hit her, and she began to scream, the anguished sounds raising gooseflesh on a suddenly silent audience. "They've killed him!" As the terrible screams continued, patrons finally sprang to life.[45]

Men in uniform and civilians tried to open the white door to the antechamber, shouting and pointing. Finally, with a tremendous surge of strength from his uninjured right arm and with blood pouring from his left, Rathbone yanked the plank free and the door swung open. Anxious men yelled questions as Rathbone blocked their way. "Please," he cried, "doctors only!"

Dr. Charles Leale, only 23, pushed his way in and identified himself. He was assistant surgeon of U.S. Volunteers.[46]

Rathbone recognized a Col. Crawford in the antechamber. "Keep people out unless they're doctors," the major ordered and turned back into the box.

Miss Harris was crying hysterically. "Please," she begged, "Oh, please! Won't someone help him?"[47]

Dr. Leale turned to Mrs. Lincoln, pressed against her husband's unresponsive breast. "Oh, Doctor," Mrs. Lincoln cried, "Is he dead? Can he recover?"[48]

Dr. Leale assured her he would do what he could, motioning for men crowding into the box to remove her. She was led to the sofa where Miss Harris began patting Mrs. Lincoln's plump hand.

The doctor was young, but he was all doctor as he took charge. "Get a lamp," he ordered. "Lock that door. Admit no one except physicians." He turned to the crowding, curious men. "Hold matches until the lamp gets here."[49]

As matches flared, burned brightly, and then faded away to be replaced by new bursts of light, Dr. Leale examined the President. He ran his fingers along the President's beard, up the jawbone, and toward the back of the head. Suddenly, he stopped. He felt blood behind Lincoln's left ear.[50]

Rathbone was calling for medical attention. "I'm bleeding to death." Leale checked Rathbone's wound, saw that it was not serious although blood was flowing brightly, and turned back to the President.

Dr. Charles Taft was hoisted into the box by men shoving and lifting him from stage to railing. The second physician placed himself under the younger man's direction. They began opening the President's clothes.[51]

The President's eyes showed evidence of brain damage. The bullet had gone in the left side of the head, behind the ear near the top of the spine. There was no exit wound.

Lincoln was placed on the floor. The two physicians began doing what they could as Dr. Albert F.A. King joined them in the box.[52]

"His wound is mortal," Leale announced.

The other doctors nodded.

Mrs. Lincoln screamed, "They've killed him! They've killed him!"

Someone suggested the President be removed to the White House. Dr. Leale shook his head. "No. It is impossible for him to recover."[53]

Four soldiers lifted the long, limp body and eased it down the aisles past the frightened, bewildered audience. The President was carried downstairs to the lobby toward a rising crescendo of sound from the crowd gathering on Tenth Street.

An infantry captain, seeing the situation, swept his sword from its scabbard and snapped to attention. "Surgeon," he said, "give me your commands, and I will see that they are obeyed."[54] Leale pointed across the street.

The sword sliced through the air. A mighty roar of command, coupled with explicit blasphemy, cleared the way for the President's carriers.

The party reached the first house across the street. No one was home. A man with a candle motioned to Dr. Leale from 453 Tenth Street. The captain's sword flashed again. Dr. Leale led the way up the steps of the William Peterson home and down the hall to a tiny bedroom.[55] The bed was pulled from the wall and the long body placed on it diagonally.

Fingers, thrust into the wound, could not touch the bullet. From the patient's slightly protruding right eye, the doctors correctly concluded the 44 caliber ball had entered behind the left ear and lodged in the brain just behind the right eye.

Theatre patrons rushed into the street, shouting the fearful news: "They have shot the President!"[56]

As the news spread in ever widening circles, Booth's little bay mare pounded through the quiet streets of Washington toward the Potomac River.

Across the street from Ford's Theatre, beyond the screaming and shouting of shocked and furious crowds, the doctors looked down on the stripped, long, underweight body.

There was only one wound, but it was mortal.

The death watch began.

Chapter 14

MORE BLOOD AS DEATHWATCH BEGINS

"Secretary Stanton! There's bloody work at Seward's house! He has been murdered or nearly so! Several of his household are dying!"[1]

The Secretary of War peered out his front door at a babbling young man. "I'll come at once."

Five hours before, at his usual quitting time, Stanton

had stopped by his telegraph office and had said to Eckert, "I've changed my mind about tonight, Eckert. I will not return."

Maj. Eckert had stood politely. "Yes, Mr. Stanton." The two men had said goodnight, and the secretary had gone home.[2] A short time later, Maj. Eckert had also left the War Department. Whatever the "important work" was that the War Secretary wanted done, it obviously was not going to be done that night.[3]

Now Stanton's carriage sped toward the Secretary of State's home, half a dozen blocks or so from Ford's Theatre.[4]

An excited pedestrian, recognizing the Secretary of War, rushed up to the carriage. "President Lincoln has been shot! The President's still in the theatre!"

Stanton arrived at the Seward home at the same time as Secretary of the Navy Welles. Strangely, the War Secretary did not immediately tell him about the shooting of Lincoln.

The two men entered the Seward mansion where five people had been attacked, and three were thought to be dying. They climbed stairs bright with fresh blood and entered the third floor bedroom of the Secretary of State. Gas jets had been turned up. Signs of struggle were everywhere.[5]

The two secretaries were told of a rampaging man who had struck the household like a tornado.

A few minutes past 10 o'clock, William Bell, the black servant, had heard the front doorbell ringing incessantly. The servant had adjusted his white coat and opened the door to a tall, powerfully built man wearing a broad brimmed hat and carrying a bottle. The stranger had immediately pushed his way into the house.[6] "I want to see Mr. Seward. I was sent here by Dr. T. S. Verdi with this medicine." The giant thrust the bottle forward.

"You can't see him," Bell replied. He held out his hand. "You'd better send it up by me."

The stranger had started up the stairs with the servant protesting. Seward's son Frederick, Assistant Secretary of State, appeared at the top of the stairs in dressing gown and slippers. "You can't come up. My father is sleeping and must not be disturbed."⁷

The young giant began pushing up the stairs. When Frederick argued with him, the big youth seemed about to yield. "Very well, Sir, I shall go," he said. He had turned away only to swing back, a Navy colt revolver in his hand. Pointing the weapon at Frederick, he'd pulled the trigger. The gun misfired. The intruder then pistol-whipped young Seward who fell across the banister. The attacker continued to smash the pistol down until the weapon broke. Unconscious, Frederick slid to the hall floor.

Screaming, "Murder!" Bell fled down the stairs and rushed toward Gen. Christopher Augur's next door office.

Dropping the revolver, the attacker whipped out a Bowie knife and lunged into the invalid's dimly lit room.

George Robinson, a male attendant, had just started to the door. The assailant rushed forward, slashing Robinson's forehead, then sprang upon the defenseless secretary in the bed. The knife rose and fell in powerful, savage thrusts, ripping Seward's right cheek, the right side of his throat, and slashing deeply under the left ear. So much blood spurted, it seemed his throat must have been cut.⁸

Maj. Augustus Seward, another son, burst into the room and grappled with the still furiously hacking aggressor. Robinson staggered to his feet and tried to help Augustus wrestle the attacker off the bed and toward the door. The injured Secretary of State fell off the bed.

Fanny Seward, the secretary's daughter, rushed into the room, was struck and knocked down. Mrs. Seward, an invalid, tottered onto the scene and saw a sight which shortened her life. In the subdued glow of the gas light the attacker was driving his long blade wherever he could into chests and arms.⁹

Suddenly the man had muttered, "I'm mad" and broke off the attack to clump noisily down the stairs and into the night. He left behind two hysterical women and five men thought to be dying.

Frederick's skull was split. Sergeant Robinson had suffered apparently fatal knife wounds in the chest and shoulder. Maj. Seward had sustained severe wounds. He appeared to be half scalped. The Secretary of State was so covered with blood about the face and throat, he was presumed dying.[10]

Bud Hansell, a state department messenger whom the stranger had met in the hall as he stumbled from the bedchamber had not uttered a word before the intruder plunged the blade deep into his chest.[11]

Stanton and Welles left Seward's room aghast. The Navy Secretary said, "I heard that Seward was attacked, but I couldn't believe it until I saw it with my own eyes. Now I am half afraid to relate another rumor I heard on the way here. It was reported the President had been shot. I didn't believe that, either."

"It's true," Stanton replied, "I talked to a man who had just left Ford's Theatre."[12]

"Then I will go at once to the White House."

Stanton shook his head. "The President is still at the theatre."

"Then let us go there immediately."

The two cabinet members reached the bottom of the stairs and pushed their way through a throng of dignitaries. News of the Seward attack had spread rapidly.

The War Secretary ordered Montgomery C. Meigs, builder of the Capitol dome and now quartermaster general, to take charge at the Seward mansion.[13]

Meigs asked where the two secretaries could be reached. When they told him, he cried, "Don't go! There's murder in the streets!"

Welles said to Stanton, "I'm going at once. I think it is your duty to go."

Stanton nodded. "Yes. I shall go."

As the two men entered their carriage, Maj. Thomas Eckert rode up on horseback. The chief telegrapher had been shaving in his dressing room shortly after 10:30 when Thomas A. Laird had rushed in to blurt out the news about Lincoln.[14]

Laird was one of two War Department telegraphers present at Ford's Theatre that night. The other, George C. Maynard, had reported directly to the cipher room.

"Don't go," Eckert pled with Stanton, who seemed to hesitate. Welles became insistent.

"I've just come from there," Eckert declared, holding his mount steady as the shouting, pushing crowd surged around him. "It's unsafe for you to expose yourself."[15]

John Wilkes Booth galloped toward the Navy Yard Bridge which crossed the Eastern Branch of the Potomac. The further shore was Maryland. Chesapeake Bay and the Atlantic were to the east. Richmond was 100 miles south.

Before his carriage left, Stanton sent word to Seward's neighbor, Gen. Auger, to alert his command. As Stanton settled into the carriage, Meigs, yelling for a cavalry escort, flung himself into the vehicle. Two mounted troopers swung in behind. The carriage whirled southeast toward Ford's Theatre[16] through huge crowds hurrying toward Tenth Street.

A terrible rumor was gripping the city: the South was rising in one final desperate act of vengeance. All Union officers were in danger of assassination. A bloodbath was just beginning; Lincoln and Seward were only the first on the list of men to be slain.

Silas T. Cobb, sergeant of the guard, heard hoofbeats and stepped out of the little frame house that served as sentry station at the bridge's north end. Nobody was supposed to cross the bridge after 9 at night without a pass.[17]

The horseman reined in.

"Who are you, sir?"

"My name is Booth."

"Where are you from?"

"The city."

"Where are you going?"

"I'm going home."

"Where would that be?"

"Charles."

"Don't you know that travelers aren't allowed to pass after 9?" The sergeant figured the rider was some rich man's son who had been having a good time in Washington. "All right," Cobb said. "You can pass."

Booth gave the mare her head. Her hooves clattered

over the wooden span as her rider urged her eastward into Maryland.

L. A. Gobright, Associated Press representative in Washington, hurried to the commercial telegraph office with a short bulletin: "The President was shot in a theatre tonight and perhaps mortally wounded."[18] At Ford's, the reporter talked with Superintendent of Police, Maj. A. C. Richards who had seen Booth leap from the box. Many witnesses had identified Booth as the attacker. Within a few minutes, Gobright had enough facts for a follow-up story. He even had the luck to have the murder weapon handed to him by the hysterical man who had found it.

The AP man filed a second telegram, a curious message for a reporter. The morning edition of the *New York Tribune* read, "Our Washington agent orders the dispatch about the President 'stopped.' Nothing is said about the truth or falsity of that dispatch."[19]

Had somebody forced or persuaded the AP correspondent to miss the scoop of the century?

Before details of the night of terror could be flashed from Washington to morning newspapers, the commercial telegraph went dead.

George Alfred Townsend of the *New York World* later wrote: "Within 15 minutes after the murder, the wires were severed entirely around the city, excepting only a secret wire for government use, which leads to Old Point."[20]

The commercial telegraph wires were still dead at midnight. When Maj. Eckert was approached about the problem, he said he was "too busy."

Someone who knew a lot about telegraphy had destroyed the capital's outgoing commercial telegraph and prevented the public from knowing the facts about the assassination for several hours. Only someone familiar with telegraphy, working inside the main terminal area, could have so effectively sabotaged the news wire.

Leonard J. Farwell, a former Wisconsin governor, apparently was the first man to realize Andrew Johnson, the next President of the United States, might also be in danger.

A patron at Ford's Theatre, Farwell had heard the pistol shot and had seen the assassin leap from the box. Farwell had run down Tenth Street and up two blocks to the Kirkwood House. He shouted, "Guard the doors! The President is murdered!"[21] then rushed up the stairs to the Vice President's room and pounded on the door. "Governor," Farwell cried as Johnson opened the door, "Someone has shot and murdered the President!"[22]

Johnson lit a lamp and turned around in disbelief. The two men gripped each other's arms.[23] Johnson rang for servants and ordered, "Get some guards up here." Another servant was told to stand outside the door to keep everyone out.

"The President's dying," Farwell reported. "Seward is already dead. The rumors are that you're slated for assassination, too. In fact, all the Cabinet members are marked for death."[24]

Stanton and Welles stopped at the Petersen house where a squad of soldiers secured the door. Others patrolled the general area of E and F Streets, as far as Eleventh on the west and Ninth on the east.[25]

The secretaries climbed the front steps and hurried down the narrow hall.

Mrs. Lincoln sat in the front parlor, staring into the coal grate. Miss Harris and Laura Keene sat beside her. Maj. Rathbone and Capt. Robert Lincoln stood nearby.[26]

Stanton briefly paid his respects in the little room where the President lay.

Located under the stairs, the room's tenant was Pvt. William T. Clark of the Thirteenth Massachusetts Infantry. A short time before, actor John Matthews had rented the room where one day, he had found John Wilkes Booth smoking a pipe on his bed—the bed where Lincoln now lay dying.

The President was quiet. Soon there would be spasmodic contractions of the forearms. The chest muscles would become fixed and the President would hold his breath.

The spasm would end in an explosive expulsion of air from the lungs.[27]

The doctors had covered him with mustard plasters from ankles to shoulders. Hot water and heated blankets had been requisitioned.

Soldiers had been sent to bring Lincoln's family physician, Dr. Robert K. Stone. Troopers had also summoned Joseph K. Barnes, Surgeon General of the U.S. Army, and the Rev. Dr. Phineas D. Gurley, pastor of the Presbyterian Church the President sometimes attended.

Stanton stood looking down at the President whose face now twitched on the left side. The upper left eyelid was swollen and dark. The inner angle of the right eye was black and puffy. The left side of Lincoln's mouth was pulled slightly to one side. The doctors frequently removed blood clots from the wound to relieve intracranial pressure.[28]

Stanton was told, "His pulse is faint, 44 the last check The right pupil is dilated. The left is contracted. Neither are sensitive to light."

"What are his chances?"

"It is hopeless, Mr. Secretary."

Stanton took over the Petersen back parlor as the temporary seat of government. He sat at a small table where he could see down the long, narrow hallway and observe any approach from the front entrance. Here, virtually a dictator, Stanton took control of the situation and the nation.

Outside on Tenth Street, White House guard William Crook was allowed through a ring of soldiers, but was not permitted to enter the front door.[29]

The man to whom the President had said, "Good-bye, Crook" instead of his customary, "Good night," glimpsed Capt. Robert Lincoln leaning on the shoulder of Senator Charles Sumner, Radical Republican from Boston.

Five to 10 minutes after Booth had passed the guard station at the Navy Yard Bridge, a second horseman rode up.[30]

"What's your name?" Cobb asked.

174

"Ah, Smith. My name is Smith."

"Where're you heading?"

"Home to White Plains."

"How come you're out so late?"

The rider used what the sergeant thought was "a rather indelicate expression," explaining he had been in bad company.

"Bring your mount up here to the guardhouse door," Cobb ordered.

The horseman eased the roan into the light so it shone full on his face and his mount.

"You may pass," the sergeant said.

The echo of hooves had only just died away over the north end of the Navy Yard Bridge when a third horseman rode up. Cobb walked over.[31]

"Did a man on a roan horse just cross here?"

"Yes. Why?"

"I'm John Fletcher, foreman of the Naylor's livery stable in the city, and I'm chasing a stolen horse."[32]

Sergeant Cobb looked over the third rider and made a decision. "You can cross, but you can't come back."

Fletcher turned back toward Washington.

To the stableman, the roan's rider had looked like David Herold, but the rider was Herold's look alike, former smuggler Ed Henson. Henson caught up with Booth near the top of Good Hope Hill[33] where he heard his name called out. "Henson!"

"Mr. Booth, I was afraid I had missed you. You been traveling fast."

"You saw no others on the road?"

"None."

"We killed the President, Eddie. And some of his cursed cabinet, too. Are you with me, Eddie?"

"You know I am, Mr. Booth. All the way."

"When we get across the Potomac, it'll be all free and clear. Friends, all the money we need! We'll be heroes, my lad!" Booth patted the mare's neck. "Now if the horses hold out and my leg!"

"What happened?"

"I jumped to the stage, must have sprained my left ankle. It's starting to hurt like the very devil." Booth turned his mount toward Upper Marlboro east of Washington. Marlboro was the last major stop before the Patuxent. Down that river at Benedict's Landing, a ship of British registry, flying Canadian colors,[34] waited for two crewmen.

Booth and Henson rode on through the night toward the river.

Assistant Secretary of War Charles Dana was aroused from a sound sleep and hurried to the Petersen house where he saw cabinet members and the Chief Justice of the U.S. Supreme Court gathered in a room off the President's.

Stanton was bustling with activity. "Sit down here," he told Dana. "I want you."[35]

The War Secretary began dictating telegrams, orders closing escape routes out of the city. All the Washington exits were closed before midnight except the Navy Yard Bridge which Booth and Henson had crossed shortly after the assassination.[36]

Before midnight, Col. Thompson was covering roads northwest of and paralleling the Potomac toward Tendleytown, Barnesville, Darnestown and Frederick in Virginia.[37] This was a direction Booth was not likely to take because it was predominantly Union territory. But it had been the first to be closed.

Also before midnight, Com. Parker was ordered to stop all vessels on the Potomac River from Washington to Point Lookout on the very tip of the Maryland peninsula where the Potomac flows into Chesapeake Bay.[38] This area was southeast of the capital and another route that Booth was unlikely to take.

At midnight, Gen. Slough, Gen. Gamble and Maj. John M. Waite sealed off Virginia, northwest of Washington as far as Fairfax, Leesburg, Charlestown, Cumberland

and Harpers Ferry.[39] This too was an unlikely route.

At 3 a.m., Gen. Morris sealed off the area to the northeast of the capital, including Baltimore, Maryland. No trains or boats were permitted to leave.[40]

At about the same time, Stanton had blocked all southwest roads going directly into Virginia. This would have been effective had Booth remained in Washington. By the time Stanton closed the route, Booth had ridden 50 miles.

In the morning hours of Saturday, Provost Marshal McPhail closed off the area east of Washington known as southeast Maryland, plus the cities of Annapolis and Upper Marlboro.[41]

By Easter Sunday, the mouth of the Patuxent River was closed, and the entire western shore of the Chesapeake Bay east of Washington was under military and naval patrol.[42]

Booth's act had caused a virtual blockade of the whole Atlantic coast from Baltimore to Hampton Roads, Virginia, yet the assassin slipped through because the closings had been piecemeal, beginning in the least likely direction and moving slowly toward the route Booth was most likely to have taken. The only road not closed by Stanton pointed south from Washington to Port Tobacco, the route Booth would most probably use because it led toward the Confederacy.

In all wires issued from the War Department during the night of April 14, this route was not once mentioned. No precautions were taken to guard it. It was the one obvious route that should have been instantly and tightly closed. Stanton had been advised by the eavesdropping Louis Weichmann through Capt. Gleason that this was the route the kidnappers planned to use in spiriting Lincoln from Washington to Richmond 100 miles south.

Earl and Andrew Potter hurried to their secret cipher room on Tenth. Soon telegrapher Guy Wittick's coded message was flashing to Col. Lafayette Baker in New York.[43] Their "conference" lasted more than an hour.

Earl Potter called in detectives for instruction. "We know the kidnap plot centered around a crew of smugglers.

Since we feel sure that Booth is directly involved, he'll attempt to get out of the country by ship."

By 11 o'clock that night, many witnesses had reported to the Metropolitan Police Station that they had identified Booth as the President's assailant. Police Superintendent Richards also began to pick up bits of information about Booth's friends. He had come up with the address of the Surratt boarding house. Detectives planned a post-midnight raid at 541 H Street. [44]

Provost Marshal O'Beirne, on his own initiative, sent someone to search Booth's room at the National Hotel and found the actor's trunk.[45]

Against the wishes of his friends, Vice President Johnson finally went to Lincoln's bedside. O'Beirne had wanted a squad of soldiers to accompany Johnson, but Johnson had refused guards. With Farwell and O'Beirne on either side, Johnson walked through the almost deserted streets, past the picketed cavalry horses and the two soldiers patrolling in front of the Petersen house.[46]

The Vice President was silent as he was led into the bedroom, where, hat in hand, he gazed soberly at the dying Lincoln.

Johnson whispered a few words to Robert Lincoln and clasped his hand before going to the back parlor to speak briefly with Stanton. The Vice President held Mrs. Lincoln's hand a moment, then walked out into the night.

His brief stay, violating protocol, immediately caused tongues to wag.

James Tanner was a one-legged corporal who'd attended Grover's Theatre the evening of April 14 and didn't at first believe reports about Lincoln being shot.[47] He returned to his own small room next door to the Petersen house to find the street filled with people. Waiting with them for news from next door, he saw Gen. Auger emerge from the Petersen house and call, "Is there someone who knows shorthand?"[48]

Tanner struggled through the crowd to the front entrance of the Petersen house. Gen. Auger told Stanton that the young man took shorthand. The War Secretary explained that the next room and hallway were filled with witnesses. Tanner was to take their statements. It was midnight as he began work.

"Within fifteen minutes," Tanner declared, "I had testimony enough to hang Wilkes Booth."[49]

But Stanton still had not sent word to the newspapers or to the military leaders identifying Booth as the Presidential assassin.

As mysteriously as it had ceased, the commercial telegraph finally began working again, and AP correspondent Gobright was able to file his next story. He now added a paragraph incomprehensible to a newsman. For about two hours, Gobright had known Booth was the suspect. The nation's readers were anxious to know this, too, but at the end of a long dispatch filed about 1:30 a.m., Saturday, Gobright added this cautious note: "Some evidence of the guilt of the party who attacked the President is in possession of the police."[50]

Throughout the night, a procession of the high and mighty of Washington political circles continued to arrive at the Petersen house to look down at the unconscious Lincoln.

Mary Lincoln coming in on one of her visits saw Senator Charles Sumner holding the President's cold hand.

"Live," Mary whispered, bending to kiss the President's cheek, "Live but one moment to speak to me once—to speak to our children."[51]

Robert alternated between spending time with his distraught mother and staring in silence at his father whose life signs were waning.

"Why didn't he shoot me instead of my husband?" Mrs. Lincoln demanded wildly when she had been led back to the front parlor. "I must go to him!"

Robert tried to calm her. "Mother, please put your trust in God and all will be well."[52]

Stanton, in his temporary seat of government down the

179

hall, was becoming impatient with the First Lady's outbursts.

With Miss Harris and Miss Keene supporting her, Mrs. Lincoln had again left the parlor to enter the small room and stand beside her husband's deathbed. Mrs. Lincoln bent low and brushed her cheek against her husband's bearded jaw. When a labored breath suddenly burst between the parted lips, she jumped back, screamed, and collapsed in a faint.

Her shriek and the reaction of the other two women brought the bearded War Secretary hurrying in. He jabbed an impatient finger at Mrs. Lincoln's senseless form. "Take that woman out and don't let her in again!

"Get everyone out of here and keep them out, except for the physicians. Doctor Barnes, can't you turn his face toward the wall?"[53]

Police Superintendent A. C. Richards gave the first pull on the net set to capture Booth and his accomplices.

About 2 a.m., Detective John A. W. Clarvoe and a squad of officers went to the Surratt boarding house to bring in John Surratt and John Wilkes Booth.[54]

With nearly a dozen men stationed outside, Clarvoe yanked at the bell.

Louis Weichman answered the door. He said Surratt wasn't home. He hadn't seen Booth, and he wouldn't admit the detectives until he had checked with the landlady.

When Weichmann knocked on her door, she cried, "For God's sake, let them come in! I expected the house to be searched!"[55]

Weichmann admitted the officers who found only terrified women boarders in front of whom the clerk decided to show off. "Gentlemen, what do you mean by searching this house so early in the morning?"[56]

Clarvoe demanded, "Do you mean to tell us you don't know what happened last night? John Wilkes Booth has murdered the President!"

When Mrs. Surratt came out of her room, her boarder blurted, "Wilkes has murdered the President!"

"My God!" Mrs. Surratt threw up both hands. "Mr. Weichmann, you don't tell me so!"

About 1:30 in the morning, the formal notification of Lincoln's death was copied in final form by Attorney General James Speed.[57] All cabinet members present signed it. In the tiny room under the stairs, the President still breathed.

Nearly four hours after the shooting, Stanton sent newspapers the first official news.[58] A War Department news dispatch was sent to Gen. John Dix in New York who distributed the material to the media.

The first telegram, sent at 2:15 a.m., was the merest summary: "Last evening, about 10:30 p.m., at Ford's Theatre, the President . . . was shot by an assassin."[59]

The telegram answered most essential questions except the one people were certain to ask, "Who fired the shot?"

The second release sent at 3:20 a.m., gave a clue, but too late for many morning paper deadlines. "The President still breathes, but is quite insensible." Seward had rallied and might live. Frederick Seward's condition was critical. The attendant stabbed through the lungs was not expected to live. Maj. Seward's wounds were not serious. At last it was stated, "Investigation strongly indicates J. Wilkes Booth as the assassin."

Stanton's release added that there was doubt whether Booth was the man who had gone on a stabbing rampage at the Seward home.

The third press telegram at 4:44 a.m. reported, "The President continues insensible and is sinking." There was an additional bit of news: "It is now ascertained with reasonable certainty that two assassins were engaged in the horrible crime; John Wilkes Booth, the one who shot the President, the other a companion . . . whose name is not known. . . ."[60] One of the suspects (Stanton didn't say which) was thought to be heading for Baltimore. The other had not been traced.

It was around 3 a.m. Saturday morning when Atzerodt decided to turn in at the Pennsylvania House, where he had to share a room with a stranger. Atzerodt didn't sleep well. Within two hours, he was up and fleeing north, stopping to pawn his revolvers in Georgetown.[61]

Captain James William Boyd heard the rumors of the attempt on Lincoln's life with disbelief.

Booth's shot wrecked his plan to kidnap Lincoln on behalf of the Northern speculators. If his name became involved in the Booth plot, Boyd was in great danger. Booth's pursuers would not be reasonable. Nobody would believe a Rebel secret service captain had been hired by Union industrialists with the blessing of the War Secretary. And his murder of Captain Thomas Watkins over a woman, hushed up earlier, could be unearthed again to help convict him in an assassination conspiracy.

Boyd reached into his pocket and looked at his old La Roix watch, given to him years before by a Judge Reed. He snapped the cover open. One minute to midnight.

All he could do was run, Boyd decided. He soon had his gear packed and was headed for Maryland.

A few hours later, Charles Dana's brother, Lt. David D. Dana sent a wire to the War Department: "I have reliable information that the person who murdered Secretary Seward is Boyce or Boyd, the man who killed Captain Watkins in Maryland. I think it is without doubt true."[62]

Booth's broken leg forced him to halt. He had to have medical help. The nearest doctor he knew was Samuel Mudd, near Bryantown.

There was another possibility of escape in that direction after Booth's leg was cared for. A second ship of British registry, also flying the Canadian flag, was waiting at Port Tobacco.[63] After the leg was treated, if troops didn't cut them off, Booth and Henson could ride on to the second ship, take it down the Potomac to Chesapeake Bay, thence on to the Atlantic and England.

About 4 a.m., after a ride of 60 miles but still only 30 miles from Washington, Booth and Henson reined in at the farm home of Dr. Mudd, about five miles north of

Bryantown in Charles County.[64] Dr. Mudd looked out of his bedroom window at a man holding the reins of two horses. A second man was in the saddle.

"My friend fell off his horse and broke his leg," the man called. "He's hurting and needs medical attention."[65]

Dr. Mudd went downstairs. The uninjured rider gave his name as Tyson, his injured friend was Tyler.

The rider wore a long, heavy beard. Dr. Mudd wasn't sure if it was artificial or real. A shawl was kept about his neck and the lower part of his face.

The doctor put the injured man on a bed in the front room, cut off the long leather boot, and examined the leg.[66]

"How bad is it?"

"The front bone is broken. It's nearly at right angles, about two inches above the instep." Dr. Mudd said it was a painful break but medically not serious.

The patient murmured, "My back's hurting me something terrible, Doctor."

Dr. Mudd examined the victim's back but found no apparent cause for pain. He had only limited supplies at home, he said, but would do what he could.

In the bedroom he said, "Frank," (his name for the former Sarah Frances Dyer, whom he had known since childhood and had married in 1856) "there's a man downstairs with a broken leg. Will you tear some strips for bandages?"[67]

Her husband splinted the leg as best he could. "Tyson" and the doctor assisted "Tyler" upstairs to bed.

About 6 a.m. Saturday morning, White House guard John Parker, who had vacated his post and allowed the President to be shot, showed up at the Washington police station with Lizzie Williams, a drunken streetwalker, in custody. She was released by the precinct captain.[68]

Back at the Petersen house, Dr. Abbott checked the President's condition and wrote: "Pulse failing. Respiration twenty-eight."

An hour later, as a heavy rain sluiced down, Dr. Abbott

made his final entry: "Symptoms of immediate dissolution."

Surgeon General Barnes touched Lincoln's skin, then turned to an officer. "Have Mrs. Lincoln brought in."

Cpl. Tanner, standing near the head of the bed, made his shorthand notes as the quarter hour came and went. "His forced breathing subsided a couple of minutes after 7 o'clock." There was a gentle rising and falling of the thin chest after that.

The Rev. Gurley stood by the bed. Stanton sat in a chair. At the head of the bed, Robert Lincoln sobbed.

At 7:21 a.m., the President took his last breath.

Mrs. Lincoln gasped.

Still, the heart beat on—slower, weaker.

Dr. Barnes felt for the fading pulse. Dr. Leale's finger was on the President's right wrist. Dr. Taft's hand was on the chest, directly over the faltering heart.

The pulse continued after the breathing stopped. Five seconds. Ten. Sixteen. Then nothing.

It was twenty-two minutes and ten seconds past seven o'clock. Abraham Lincoln, the 16th President of the United States, was dead!

Stanton stared intently at the President's face as Dr. Barnes gently crossed the lifeless hands over the still breast.

Dr. Gurley stepped forward and lifted his hands. "Our Father and our God," he began.[69]

Tanner frantically snatched at his pocket where he'd put his pencil and notebook. The notebook slid out, but the point on his only pencil was broken. "The world lost the prayer," Tanner lamented, "a prayer that was only interrupted by the sobs . . ."[70]

The Secretary of War did not raise his head until Dr. Gurley intoned, "Thy will be done. Amen."

Tanner thought he had never seen a more agonized expression on a human countenance than on Stanton's. Tears streamed down the War Secretary's face. Stanton whispered, "Now he belongs to the ages."[71]

The silence began again, a stillness so absolute that for about five minutes, the pastor could clearly hear the watches ticking in various pockets.

184

A few minutes later, those who had watched Lincoln die were startled to see that the sad, melancholy face had changed. About his mouth was a faintly happy expression. The man who had loved to tell a joke but had carried such a burden seemed to be almost smiling.[72]

"It resembles the expression of someone who has found peace," a watcher whispered.

The others nodded.

It had taken 56 years, a Civil War, and a bullet to end Lincoln's life. Now he was at peace!

Chapter 15

ESCAPE TO THE SWAMPS

An hour before Lincoln's death, Louis Weichmann hurried out of the Surratt boarding house into heavy rain and bought *The Chronicle*.

Booth obviously had shot the President, but who had attacked Seward? The assailant's description reassured Weichman at once.[1] "Thank God, that isn't John Surratt!"

After breakfast, Weichmann and another Surratt boarder, John Holohan, walked toward police headquarters.[2] Newsboys were unable to keep up with the demand for papers. The rejoicing over the week's war victories was silenced, and Washington turned to mourning. Small clusters of people discussed the night's tragic events. Black people on the streets wept.

Weichmann turned into Tenth Street as six soldiers emerged from the Petersen house. On their shoulders they bore Lincoln's coffin. For the next few hours the President's body would belong to the pathologists and the embalmers.

As the bells tolled the sad news through the continuing downpour, Secretary of War Stanton indicated he personally would supervise the dressing of Lincoln's body late that afternoon.[3] In the meantime, the chase went on, and Stanton worked on reward posters.

Lt. David Dana set up headquarters in a hotel at Bryantown in Maryland. He was a scant half dozen miles south of his quarry, John Wilkes Booth.[4]

About 7 a.m., Dr. Mudd sent a servant upstairs to invite "Tyson" to breakfast. He came down looking rested and talking freely.

Mrs. Mudd sent a tray upstairs to "Tyler".[5] At the table, she inquired, "Mr. Tyson, do you live in the country?"

"No," he replied, chewing heartily. "I've been frolicking around for five or six months."

In Washington, Sen. William M. Stewart of Nevada rushed to the Kirkwood House to report Lincoln's death and found Andrew Johnson in a drunken stupor. His clothing was disarrayed. Mud matted his hair.

The senator summoned a doctor and a barber, saying, "He's going to be sworn in as the next President of the United States in an hour or so. Get him ready."[6]

In New York, Lafayette Baker examined a telegram from Stanton with real satisfaction. The War Secretary needed him. The wire read, "Come here immediately and see if you can find the murderer of the President."[7]

On Monday, April 10, Stanton had refused to listen when Baker had told him he knew of a kidnap-assassination plot. Later, he had made it appear that Baker was in charge of the plot.[8]

Baker took the Saturday train to Washington, already having heard by clandestine cipher more about the Friday night assassination than his boss could have guessed.

Mrs. Mudd looked out the kitchen window at her husband showing the talkative young guest around. She heard Tyson ask Dr. Mudd how far it was to the river.[9]

"Oh," the physician replied, "about 18 or 20 miles." She saw her husband pointing toward Zekiah Swamp—a narrow belt of dense undergrowth, treacherous quicksand,

and desolation, alive with mosquitoes, snakes, and wild animals. The swamp ran southward from Bryantown to Allen's Fresh, a tiny settlement where the Wicomico River broadened into a wide backwater of the Potomac.

The chatty young man asked to borrow a razor, so his friend could shave, and inquired about the possibilities of obtaining a carriage.[10] Dr. Mudd provided a razor and said he would see if he could arrange for a carriage.

The search for Booth and the yet unnamed Seward attacker went on. Hard riding cavalrymen splashed through the rain and the mud. Detectives asked questions and pored over the contents of Booth's trunk found in the National Hotel. It held many clues. It was only a matter of time before the NDP would corral Booth's known friends and uncover a lead on the assassin's whereabouts.

The orderly succession of government continued. Less than 25 hours after Lincoln was shot and less than four hours after he died, the nation had a new President. Andrew Johnson, sobered by a physician and made presentable by a barber, was sworn in at the Kirkwood House as the Lincoln cabinet and some congressmen watched.

Johnson immediately asked the cabinet to stay on. The 17th President spoke a few temperate words to the spectators and the nation. "The course which I have taken in the past in connection with this rebellion," he said, "must be regarded as a guarantee for the future."[11]

Radical Republicans were delighted. Everything Lincoln had fought for could be presumed dead along with the late President. A few hours after the swearing in, some Radical Republicans called on President Johnson and declared, "Lincoln's death is like a blessing from heaven."[12]

Blacksmith James Booth was furious. He lived at 642 8th Street, the second house from the J.J. Herold family, who lived at 636 8th. His teenage son, Johnny, had failed to return from a Good Friday afternoon ride into Maryland with David Herold. The blacksmith started looking Friday evening.[13] He took the same road that Lt. Dana had—the way to Dr. Mudd's and Bryantown. The road was crawling with soldiers, but the angry father wasn't concerned about them or John Wilkes Booth. All the blacksmith wanted was his errant son. He didn't pick up his trail until early Saturday morning.

On the second floor of the White House, the body of Abraham Lincoln lay in a guest room preparatory to the Saturday autopsy. Two pathologists from the Army Medical Museum began their grim task.[14] The lanky body was stretched upon a board framework. Towels and sheets covered the remains of "what, but a few hours before, was the soul of a great nation," as Edward Curtis, an assistant surgeon, put it.[15]

As the undertakers took over, newly sworn in President Johnson stopped by for a moment. Later, Stanton supervised the clothing of Lincoln's body.

Six honorary pallbearers were named, including Lincoln enemies and kidnap plotters, Senators Ben Wade of Ohio and John Conness of California.[16] Honorary pallbearers from the House of Representatives included Elihu B. Washburne of Illinois whose House committee had tried to implicate Lincoln in the cotton pass scandal. Schuyler Colfax, of Indiana, who had declined to attend the theatre with Lincoln, was also among the honorary pallbearers.[17]

At the Mudd home, Henson, alias Tyson, received some distressing news. No carriage was available because the next day was Easter, and most of the nearby farmers planned to use their rigs. The injured man would have to ride off on horseback, just as he had come.[18]

John Best, the Mudd gardener, made a crude crutch for the man with the broken leg. Soon Mrs. Mudd heard him hobble downstairs, aided by "Tyson." It was Mrs. Mudd's first glimpse of the visitor's face. His heavy whiskers became partly detached before he reached the bottom of the stairs, Mrs. Mudd noticed, and also saw he had no mustache. Seeing, too, that the man was in great pain, she suggested that he wasn't able to travel. But in the late afternoon the visitors mounted their horses and rode off.

About an hour later, Dr. Mudd returned from Bryantown to announce that President Lincoln had been murdered. Soldiers were in the area looking for the assassin or assassins.

The Mudds talked of the two visitors who had come and gone. Mrs. Mudd mentioned that the injured man had been wearing false whiskers. Dr. Mudd had not seen the man's face.

"Frank," the physician said to his wife, "those men were suspicious characters. I'll go to Bryantown and tell the officers."[19]

On Easter Sunday at church, Dr. Mudd had seen his relative, Dr. George Mudd, and had asked him also to report to authorities about the visit of two men early Saturday morning.[20] On Tuesday afternoon, April 18, George Mudd arrived at the Samuel Mudd home in company with two soldiers. One was Lt. Alexander Lovett, who thought the injured man was Booth.

In the presence of his wife, Samuel Mudd explained why he had sent for the army officers. The two men had come to his home about 4 a.m. the morning of April 15.[21] After helping the injured man into the house, he put him on a parlor sofa until a light could be had.

Dr. Mudd told Lovett, "He seemed to be very much injured in the back, and complained very much of it. I did not see his face at all. He seemed to be tremulous and not inclined to talk, and had his cloak thrown around his head and seemed inclined to sleep, as I thought, in order to ease himself, and every now and then he would groan pretty heavily."[22]

Lovett asked what the doctor had done.

"I had no proper pasteboard for making splints, and went and got an old bandbox and made one of it. As he wanted it done hastily, I hurried more than I otherwise would. He wanted me to fix it up anyway, as he said he wanted to get back home and have it done by a regular physician."[23]

How long had it taken?

"I do not suppose I was more than three-quarters of an hour making the examination of the wound and applying the splint."

The back pain, Dr. Mudd thought, was from horse-back riding. The leg injury "was a straight fracture of the tibia about two inches above the ankle."[24]

Dr. Mudd said the talkative young man had given his name as Tyson and that of the wounded man as Tyler. He didn't hear either of the men address the other by a first name.[25]

"Did anything excite your suspicions, Dr. Mudd?"

"Upon reflection upon these circumstances," he answered, "after breakfast, when I was leaving for my farm work, this young man asked me if I had a razor about the house, that his friend desired to take a shave, as perhaps he would feel better."

After dinner, when Dr. Mudd checked on the patient, "I noticed that he had lost his mustache, but still retained his whiskers."

The questioning went on. Dr. Mudd told about the crutch made for the injured man, the conversations with the younger talkative man. Dr. Mudd and he had ridden over to the physician's father's place to see about borrow-ing a carriage. But the next day was Easter, and no car-riages were available. The young man decided he would go to Bryantown to seek a conveyance for his injured friend.[26]

"When I returned home leisurely, I found the two men were just in the act of leaving." Dr. Mudd told Lt. Lovett that the men had left about 4 or 5 o'clock Saturday after-noon.

Dr. Mudd also told Lovett of Booth's visit to the coun-try the previous winter, and that Booth had bought a horse at that time. Dr. Mudd insisted he had not known that the injured man was Booth. He had not seen the patient's face clearly at any time.[27]

Only after the soldiers had gone did Dr. Mudd remem-ber the boot which he had cut from the injured man's leg.

Booth and Henson disappeared into Zekiah Swamp and were soon lost in dense growths of dogwood, gum, and beech, planted in sluices of water and bog. Frequent deep ponds dotted the wilderness place. No human in-habitants were thought to live in the swamp.[28]

Unknown to the military, a few black men had cabins in the swamp. Trappers trailed raccoon and opossum in the bogs, and sometimes even hunted men ventured into the area.

Oscar Swann, a black man, was moving through the swamp near his isolated home about 9 o'clock Saturday night, when two men hailed him from the darkness. "Which way to the Cox farm?"

Swann could not see their faces, but the voices were those of whites. In Southern Maryland, it didn't pay a black man to concern himself with more than that single fact. Swann called back, giving directions.[29]

"Get your horse and show us the way."

As Swann obeyed, he saw a small man and a lame one with a crutch.

"He broke his leg," the small man said.

"Yessuh."

About midnight, after three hours of plodding through the swamp, their guide approached the Cox farm, called Rich Hill. Col. Samuel Cox walked out into the night holding a candle. "How do you do?"

Before the Negro left, he saw the two men mount their horses and ride away from the Cox farm.[30]

Samuel Cox, Jr., saw his father ride out that morning. The fugitives were secreted in a gully a half mile southeast of Rich Hill. Booth's suffering was intense, but Cox moved the men two miles further to a pine tree thicket where he thought them safer.

The colonel told his adopted namesake, "I want you to bring my brother here."

Shortly after breakfast, young Cox approached Huckleberry, as the Thomas A. Jones residence was called. Jones was a foster brother to the senior Cox. He considered Lincoln "the enemy of my country."[31] A native of Port Tobacco, farmer Jones had nightly rowed the two mile crossing of the Potomac to, or from, Virginia with persons who wanted to cross the river unnoticed.[32] But the war was over now.

Young Cox said his father wanted Jones to come see him about getting some seed-corn.

Cox met Jones at the gate.[33] "Tom, I had visitors about 4 o'clock this morning."

"Who were they? What did they want?"

"They want to get across the river," Cox replied, answering the last question first. "Have you heard that Lincoln was killed Friday night?"

"Yes, I've heard," Jones answered.

"Tom," Cox said, "we must get those men across the river."

He said of Booth, "He showed me in India ink upon his wrist the initials of J.W.B. He told me that he knew I was a Southern sympathizer who had worked for the Confederacy, and he threw himself upon my mercy."

Jones was disturbed. He had often risked his own life for the Confederacy, but the Confederacy was dead. "Sam," Jones replied, "I'll see what I can do, but the odds are against me. I must see these men. Where are they?"

Cox said he had sent them to a "thick piece of pine." His overseeer, Franklin Robey, had guided them there. They had agreed upon a certain whistle signal, then Robey had left them with food for one day and a pair of blankets.

Jones rode alone to the spot where he saw a bay mare, saddled and bridled, standing in a small clearing made for a tobacco bed. He advanced cautiously and gave the low whistle signal Cox had taught him.[34]

A young man appeared out of the underbrush with cocked carbine. Jones thought the rifleman looked scarcely more than a boy.

"I come from Cox. He told me I would find you here. I'm a friend. You have nothing to fear from me."

After a moment's study, the young man lowered the gun. "Follow me."

After about 30 yards' walk into thick undergrowth, Jones saw John Wilkes Booth for the first time. He was reclining on the ground, his head supported on one hand. His carbine, pistols, and knife were nearby.[35] A blanket was partly drawn over him.

Henson said, "This friend comes from Col. Cox."

Jones noticed how pale the injured man's face was and that he showed signs of great suffering. He had never seen a more strikingly handsome man. Jones forgot his reluctance to help the President's murderer. Somehow he would get Booth across the river to safety. "I'll bring you food every day and get you across the river as soon as possible; just as soon as it won't be suicidal to make the attempt."[36]

Cox, standing on the hill near his home, later saw Henson lead two horses deeper into Zekiah Swamp.[37] He heard two pistol shots. Sometime later Cox rode down to the spot and searched for the horses, but never found a sign. They must have been led into one of the large quicksand areas and shot.

Lafayette Baker arrived in Washington but couldn't immediately see the War Secretary, so he went to see Gen. Augur for information.[38]

The general was blunt. "Neither your services nor the services of your forces are required."

The jealousy among the military, civilian, and secret service was apparent. The tremendous rewards that Stanton was preparing to announce would work as much for Booth as against him.

Lafe Baker angrily called a meeting with the Potter brothers. "When I was down from New York on Monday, the 10th, Secretary Stanton told me I would be a big man in the new government.[39] The Secretary admitted to me on Monday in his office that it would be impossible for the Committee on the Conduct of the War to turn its three captives loose after they were kidnapped and the Rebels blamed."

"But John Wilkes Booth has thrown the whole thing into a cocked hat," sighed Andrew.

"Now I suppose Stanton and his crew are living in fear of their plot being exposed," Earl said.

"I admit my hatred and contempt for Edwin M. Stanton, but I also swear that what I'm saying is true. Stanton felt Lincoln, Johnson, and Seward would have to be executed. He told me it would be done quite legally, and in the proper manner for such officials," the Chief said.[40]

"Military trial," Earl guessed, "or maybe they would just disappear?"

"Seward may yet die, I understand," said Andrew.

"The last I heard, he was still alive," Earl told him. "But what about Johnson?"

"Somebody must have missed their assignment," Baker replied. "We'll have to look into that." Baker told the Potters to bring maps of Maryland and northern Virginia to the Tenth Street workshop that evening. "I'll discuss our next step after I meet with the Secretary," he said grimly.

Baker found Stanton a very different man. He seemed near panic. The dictator could be ruined by Booth's act.[41]

"Baker," the War Secretary said, almost in tears, "you've got to help me! You've got to find that man and his gang. You've got to do it promptly, or I'm ruined. My friends face ruin. Worse, we could be hanged as traitors."

Baker suppressed a smile. "Will there be rewards?"

"I'm having them drawn up now. It'll be a while before they are printed and on the streets. They'll be substantial. Very substantial. Naturally, you and your men stand to share in them."

Baker met Earl and Andrew Potter at the Tenth Street workshop.[42]

"How'd it go?"

"Booth's shooting the President was such a total surprise, Stanton and his friends are scared to death their plot will be uncovered, and they'll be hanged as traitors."

"Was Stanton rational?"

"For him, yes. But he was so disturbed and afraid that he wept in front of me."

The Potters grinned.

"You get those maps?" Baker asked.

"Right here," Earl said, unfolding them.

"Good. Now, let's work out our strategy. Since Booth is involved, and he knows smuggling, he'll attempt to get out of the country by ship."[43]

Baker ordered one team of detectives to head for Benedict's Landing. "It's a short run down the river to Chesapeake Bay and the ocean." Another team was ordered to Port Tobacco in Maryland. "Port Tobacco and Benedict's Landing are the two main smuggling ports. Watch for the assassins there. I'll also send the *Jenny B* down the river to St. Mary's, here in Maryland." He pointed to the site. "She'll also be available if needed in the lower Potomac."

Baker paused, "I want her to cruise up and down the river. She's the fastest boat on either the river or the bay. And she can be signaled in from shore."

Great rewards were at stake. Perhaps $200,000 would be split, man for man, among the secret service participants. "That way, all operatives will cooperate." Any NDP man turning up a fugitive would automatically earn a share for all his fellows.[44] The NDP would do its best to freeze out any military and civilian agencies simply by non-cooperation.

James Booth, the blacksmith, found his teenage son near Bryantown. Johnny Booth and David Herold were sleeping off a drunk on the front porch swing of a house owned by a Walter Edeline.[45]

The blacksmith gathered Johnny up in his powerful arms and loaded the youth into a buggy. Herold was left asleep. Father and son got home early Saturday morning, about six hours after Lincoln had been shot.

Two NDP detectives found Herold asleep Easter Sunday morning under a tree on a road near Hughesville in Maryland.

Detective William Bernard studied the bloodshot eyes of the young man, obviously suffering from a severe hangover. "He's one of Booth's smugglers."

Ernest Dooley said, "Let's arrest him and take him back."[46]

By 4 that afternoon, Herold was being photographed at the Tenth Street workshop.

"When you finish here," Earl Potter ordered, "take him over to the Pennsylvania Avenue headquarters for questioning."

There the experienced NDP operatives had no trouble

learning some vital information from the talkative Herold.

"He's not a party to the assassination," Andrew Potter told his brother, "but he had been planning to take part in the kidnapping. He seemed truly surprised the President had been shot."[47]

Once authorities had David Herold in custody, the roundup of other Booth acquaintances was rapid. On Monday, April 17, Sam Arnold was arrested in Fort Monroe, the result of a letter he'd written which was found in Booth's trunk.[48]

On Arnold's confession of kidnap knowledge, O'Laughlin was arrested the same Monday in Baltimore. Spangler was taken into custody at his boarding house.

About mid-day Monday, Provost Marshal O'Beirne's troops, led by Lt. Alexander Lovett, had arrested John Lloyd in Surrattsville. He had been visited Good Friday afternoon by Mrs. Surratt and Louis Weichmann.[49]

For two days, Lloyd had denied knowing anything until Detective George Cottingham used what he called "strategy." The alcoholic was denied all liquor for 48 hours. In addition, he was hanged from a tree by his thumbs for those 48 hours.[50] Lloyd was then ready to confess to anything.

Louis Weichmann was also given a choice of hanging as a conspirator or testifying against those accused.

About 10:30 that Monday night, Maj. H.W. Smith led an arresting party to the Surratt boarding house. As usual, no search warrants were used. When the widow opened the door for Smith, he asked, "Are you Mrs. Surratt?[51] I come to arrest you and all in the house, and take you for examination to Gen. Augur's headquarters."

Other officers took charge of Mrs. Surratt's daughter, Anna; her cousin, Olivia Jenkins, and teenage boarder, Honora Fitzpatrick.

As Mrs. Surratt was gathering a few necessities, the doorbell rang. Officers opened the door. Payne stood there.[52] He was dressed as a workman and had a pick over his shoulder.

Payne saw the frightened girls were under arrest and murmured, "I guess I'm mistaken." He turned to leave.

Capt. R.C. Morgan took Payne's pick and asked why he'd come that time of night.

Payne said Mrs. Surratt had sent for him to dig a gutter in the morning. The suspicious officers called the near-sighted Mrs. Surratt who swore, "Before God, I do not know this man and have never seen him before. I did not hire him to dig a gutter for me."

The officers seized Payne.

Mrs. Surratt asked and received permission to pray before being taken from the house.

Lafe Baker questioned Payne about the attack on Secretary of State Seward. Payne denied any knowledge of the bloody episode or any involvement with Booth's conspirators.[53]*

"You're a liar!" Baker cried.

The big man turned disdainfully away.

Baker ranted and accused, but Payne showed no concern.

The chief sent for William Bell, Seward's black servant. "Yessuh! That's him!" Bell declared.

"Take this prisoner to the ironclad, *Saugus*," Baker told two NDP operatives, "and secure him with irons and a ball about his ankle."

When the young giant left the room, Baker called another detective. "Take this description and get up a reward poster. Put THIRTY THOUSAND DOLLAR REWARD for a headline, followed by Booth's description. Keep that

---

Although the authors have supported the traditional view that Payne was the assailant at the Seward household, there is strong evidence indicating that Payne's cousin, Lewis Thorton Powell, carried out the bloody attack. The government contended at the 1865 Conspiracy Trial that Lewis Payne and Lewis Powell were the same individual and found Payne guilty. However, the authors have obtained Civil War service records on both individuals as well as confession statements by Michael O'Laughlin and George Atzerodt stating that Payne and Powell were separate individuals. The authors believe the new evidence indicates that Payne was arrested and framed for his cousin's evil deed. Since the Payne-Powell explanation would require a book in itself, the authors have shown how Payne was framed for the crime.

part brief. Then use the rest of the poster for this man's description."

The operative was puzzled. "But, Col. Baker, if you've already got him in custody, why. . . .?"

"Do as I say!"

"Yes, Col. Baker."

Six of the eight who would be formally accused in Lincoln's murder conspiracy were in custody within 72 hours after Booth fired his pistol at Ford's Theatre.[54]

Officer Charles H. Rosch had gone to Spangler's seldom used room and had found in the scene shifter's carpetbag, a coil of rope measuring a remarkable 81 feet long. The carpetbag disclosed a dirty shirt collar and some blank paper. Nothing very sinister in that.

But the investigation also turned up Spangler's two unfortunate remarks, the damning of Lincoln and Grant to fellow stagehands while preparing the presidential box, and the remark to Ritterspaugh after Booth had dashed out of the theatre.[55]

With the exception of John Surratt and Booth, all the accused conspirators were in the authorities' hands within a week of the shooting.

An aide tried to explain to Col. Baker that indiscriminate mass arrests for alleged involvement in the assassination was swelling the jails. "The prison superintendent says he's run out of room. . . ."

Baker interrupted, "Tell him to make room!"

The aide changed the subject. "Police Superintendent Richards has made an urgent request for fresh mounts for his special search unit. . . ."[56]

"Urgent? Why urgent?"

The aide said he understood some significant progress had been made in the search for Booth through lower Maryland.

"Impossible!" Baker said curtly. "We don't have any horses to spare."

"Sir, since you're head of the First District of Columbia Cavalry, it was thought . . ."

"No, I said! We've barely enough for all the NDP

search parties I have out. Where," Baker asked, "are Andrew and Luther Potter?"

The aide explained they were getting ready to ride south to join the search.

"Bring them in," Baker ordered. "And locate that Indian tracker—what's his name."[57]

"Nalgai. Whippet Nalgai."

"Best tracker in the world," Baker said. "I hear he can follow a bird through the air a week after it's flown by."

When the tracker entered NDP headquarters with Luther, another Potter cousin, and Andrew, Baker turned to maps spread before him. "I have more and more reason to believe this is the area we should concentrate on. Port Tobacco. Up and down the Potomac from there. It's been a smuggler's paradise all through the war. Many Reb sympathizers there. I know . . . I arrested a lot of them.[58]

Luther traced the road running from the Navy Yard Bridge south through Maryland toward Bryantown, Port Tobacco, and the Potomac. "It's reasonable to assume Booth would head south. He's undoubtedly got friends there. But that doesn't prove anything. He could also be heading for Canada."

Baker agreed. "That's why I've got agents watching in every direction. Bartenders, barbers, hotel clerks—everyone of our undercover operatives is on the watch. I still think that Southern Maryland's the most likely place. That's why I've sent some of my best teams there already. I'm sending more, including you three."

Luther straightened up. "Any special orders?"

"I want Booth found before the military and civilians mess up the trail. I want Booth dead or alive. As far as I'm concerned, I'd rather see him dead."

"But," Luther protested, "if he's killed, we won't be able to learn how he planned it. Who all's behind it."

Andrew shook his head. "Booth'll be dead soon enough, anyway, Right?"

Baker mused, "Not soon enough for me."

The aide entered. "Col. Conger's here."

The detectives and Nalgai left by the side door as Lt.

Col. Conger stepped past the aide. "Col. Baker, I thought you'd like to see this." Conger handed over a rough sketch of a reward poster without pictures. "The amount is $30,000, Lafe.[59] Be late Tuesday before we can get the poster out."

Baker shrugged. "As soon as you get that poster out, you'll have to start working on another version, adding pictures of suspects as we get them from their families. Of course, Booth's the valuable prize. Probably $200,000 or $300,000 for Booth and his immediate conspirators before it's over. And that doesn't count what rewards will be offered for Jeff Davis and his Reb friends."

Conger whistled softly. "Three hundred thousand dollars! Booth's going to be the most valuable carcass in the country. It'd be a shame for some ignorant farm boy to collect that much money."

The secret service chief nodded. "I've got our best people on it, Everton. I think we'll get our share of the reward money. But I want Booth dead. If he lives long enough to talk, it's not just his head in the noose."

The aide burst into the room. "Col. Baker, they've caught David Herold! They've just brought him in!"[60]

"Good! Where was he caught?"

"Drunk under a tree in Prince Georges County. Dooley and Bernard have him in the gallery, taking his picture!"

Conger was pleased. "One of Booth's well-known followers. At last we've got a prisoner that counts!"

Baker smiled, "He's more than a prisoner, Everton. He's a guide to take us where Booth is! Bring him in!"

When the young man was brought in, still nursing his headache, Baker got right to the point. "Herold, how much is your life worth to you?"

Herold had been in custody long enough to realize he was going to be charged with Booth's crime, even though he'd been surprised to learn Lincoln had been shot. "Well," Herold said, "everything, Col. Baker."

"Right now your life is forfeit. You don't own it; I do. And it doesn't make a penny's worth of difference to me whether I give it to the hangman or not."

Herold forgot his headache. "Please, Col. Baker, I didn't

know he was going to kill the President. I was just supposed to help capture . . ."

Baker interrupted. "I'm going to give you a chance to live, Herold. You were part of the plot. You knew the plans. You knew the escape routes. Right?"

"Well, yes . . ."

"Then you'll know where Booth is, or most likely to be. I'm going to send you to Maryland with some detectives. I want Booth. You lead us to him and you live. You're going to give me his life for yours. Is that clear?"

Numbly, Herold nodded.

In the swamp, Booth tried to ease his broken leg, now swollen and extremely painful. He back-dated entries in his diary about recent events.

"April 13, 14, Friday. Until today, nothing was ever thought of sacrificing to our country's wrongs. For six months we have worked to capture. But our cause being almost lost, something decisive and great must be done."[61]

Booth's pen continued on, making excuses. "But its failure was owing to others who did not strike for their country with a heart . . .

"I struck boldly, and not as the papers say. I walked with a firm step through 1,000 of his friends, was stopped, but pushed on. A colonel was at his side. I shouted, 'Sic semper' before I fired.

"In jumping, broke my leg. I passed all his pickets, rode 60 miles that night, with the bone of my leg tearing the flesh at every jump."

Booth frowned. "I can never repent it, although we hated to kill. Our country owed all her troubles to him, and God simply made me the instrument of His punishment."[62]

Detectives riding into Maryland on Monday, April 17, coached Herold in the part he was to play.[63] "You're to say, 'We're looking for our friend, John Wilkes Booth, so we can help him escape.' Do you understand?"

"I think so," Herold answered. "That way, somebody might tip us off to where Booth is hiding. Right?"

201

"That's the idea, Herold. It's worth your life to do it right."

David Herold swallowed hard and nodded.

Chapter 16

THE CHASE IS ON

The masquerade by Herold and the detectives almost ended in their death. The NDP team rode up to a Marylander's front porch. Herold knocked and spoke through the screen. "I'm a friend of John Wilkes Booth. Me and my friends are trying to help him escape."

A man's voice growled, "So why come to me?"

Herold lowered his voice. "We thought maybe you might have seen him."

The man exploded, "You thought I might be hiding him; that's what you mean!"

"No, we just thought . . ."

The door was thrown wide by a red faced farmer with a musket. Herold turned and jumped for his horse. The detectives turned with him. Crouching low in their saddles, they rode hard down the long, rutted lane, the musket blasting away behind them.

"One thing's for sure," an operative said when they reached the public road. "We'd better discontinue this masquerade."

His colleague suggested, "We may be overlooking one other man who could help us find Booth.[1] Boyd, the double agent. He's been working for the NDP. But he's a cold-blooded killer. None of us should trust him for a minute."

The two detectives and Herold headed for Col. Frank Beale's farm, where Boyd was reportedly hiding out.[2] Capt. Boyd did not want to cooperate in the detectives' plan involving Herold.

The first detective snapped, "We also know about the Watkins murder that was hushed up. Now do you want to cooperate with us or face murder charges, too?"[3]

Boyd, always cool under pressure, shrugged and nodded. He joined the detectives and Herold.

As they rode by a farmhouse, a detective jerked his thumb and asked, "Loyal or Secesh?"

Boyd replied, "Secesh."

"We'll wait." The detective motioned Boyd to inquire at the farmhouse.

Boyd turned his mount up the long muddy driveway, then called over his shoulder, "Coming, Mr. Herold?"

Herold urged his mount alongside Boyd as they moved up the lane. "So they made you a Judas goat for the Yankees," Boyd taunted.

Stung, David demanded, "And what are you?"

"The same."

"Then you should know that this family," he jerked his chin toward the house, "is Union."

Boyd nodded. "And if I'd said that, do you think they'd have sent us up here alone? Are you game to make a run for it, Herold?"

The younger man was startled. "I don't know what kind of a deal you've got with Baker, but if we find Booth he'll throw us both to the hangman."

"And if word gets out we're working for the North, we're just as likely to be killed by our friends as by our enemies. Play along for now, but let's watch for a chance to escape from these NDP boys."

The two men began watching for an opportunity to escape custody as they neared Port Tobacco.[4]

In Washington, the government's massive manhunt swung into high gear. On the first poster offering $30,000 reward for Booth and the man who attempted to assassinate Secretary Seward, Booth's description made no mention of the actor's famous mustache and covered only three lines totaling 42 words.[5]

The man who attacked Seward was described in great detail, requiring 12 lines of type and 160 words. He had attacked his victims violently and briefly in a darkened hallway lighted by gas jets, tried to kill others in a bedroom where the lights were even lower. Yet his description was detailed, including "hands soft and small, fingers tapering, shows no signs of hard labor . . ."[6] The answer of course, was that the NDP, with Payne already captured, still listed him as wanted.[7]

Rewards were also being prepared for Jefferson Davis and other Confederate leaders presumably involved in Lincoln's assassination.

In North Carolina, Union Gen. William Sherman met with Confederate Gen. Joseph Johnston to discuss surrending Johnston's army plus all remaining Confederate troops.[8] Jefferson Davis, still ahead of pursuing Federals, had reached Salisbury in his flight toward Charlotte, North Carolina.

That same day, Lincoln's body, autopsied and dressed in the same suit he'd worn to his second inauguration, was ready to lay in state until the funeral. Just as he had dreamed, the President lay dead by an assassin's bullet, and there was weeping in the East Room.[9]

By Tuesday afternoon, the detectives guarding Boyd and Herold had relaxed their vigil. Boyd had managed to whisper, "Tonight, when they're asleep, we'll make a run for it. Try to grab however many pistols they've got in their saddlebags. I'll go for one of those Spencer carbines and a couple of magazine pouches."[10]

That night, when the detectives were snoring, Boyd placed a gentle hand on the younger man's arm. They slid from their blankets. Herold found three pistols in the saddlebags. Boyd got one Spencer and three fully loaded magazine pouches. They slipped into the night.[11]

On Wednesday morning when the detectives awoke to find Boyd and Herold gone, they met with other nearby NDP men. "They've probably crossed the river," was the opinion.

A courier was sent to Washington with news of Boyd's and Herold's escape. The detectives split up. Two were to follow Boyd and Herold. Five others, including two of great experience, were to head north to Bryantown and look for Booth there.[12]

"Nobody's found a trace of Booth or his companion hereabouts," one of the operatives lamented.

"Ed Henson's the companion you can bet," a veteran officer said. "The two were friends and fellow smugglers during the war."[13]

Andrew and Earl Potter, with 10 detectives, headed down the Potomac on the *Jenny B.* The ship was signaled in from shore and a telegrapher handed over secret cipher messages from Baker.

Earl Potter read, "Booth's plans have undergone drastic changes. He's thought to be injured. He's traveling with a male companion. He'll have to hide and wait a chance to get away. If he can reach a ship, he'll probably take that. But the ships probably didn't wait. When they were alerted by the Navy's activity, the captains probably left without Booth."[14]

Andrew Potter studied the decoded cipher, "When the *Jenny B* cruised up and down the river right after the assassination, she didn't see a single patrol boat. Boyd and Herold have probably had a chance to cross the river, and it's possible Booth and his companion are across, too.

"But if Booth was on horseback and didn't catch the ship, he would try to get all the way down to St. Mary's and disappear in some Rebel's house there."

"There's also the possibility, as Lafe pointed out, that he could cross into Virginia," Earl said. "But Lafe doesn't think that's likely, since so many Federal troops are in the area."

The brothers figured Boyd and Herold had no trouble getting a boat to cross the Potomac. Therefore, they had to assume Booth and the other man would have no trouble either. There were boats all along that part of the river.

"If he came down into Port Tobacco," Earl theorized, "he could easily find someone to take him down the river and across to the Virginia side."[15]

The detectives could see by the map that the only logical place for Booth to cross would be from Chapel Point to Lower Cedar Point, Virginia, a distance of about 10 miles.

"He would then land between Mathias Point on the Virginia side and the mouth of Machodac Creek about four miles to the south."

"If Booth decided to cross the river, it would be much easier to cover four miles of Virginia shore than 10 miles of Maryland shore.[16] It'll also be easier to pick up two fugitives who've worn themselves out rowing across a river full of strong currents."

Earl said, "Andy, you drop Bernard and Dooley at Mathias Point. The only roads out of that area cross at Owen's Store. Send them there. If Booth and his companion crossed the Potomac, they would follow the road to Owen's store in order to get south. Bernard and Dooley could take them there."[17]

Dooley and Bernard were armed with Spencer carbines and pistols. Plenty of ammunition was provided. "Bring the fugitives back, dead or alive," Earl ordered.

"Does that mean no challenge required?"

"No challenge is required because Booth is believed to be heavily armed."

Andrew Potter took other detectives on to St. Mary's City. They landed Thursday with the evening tide, disembarked and hired horses.[18] Tack had been brought down on the *Jenny B*.

Like Bernard and Dooley, Andrew and his men each had breech-loading, repeating Spencer carbines.

The search widened.

The detectives had made only one mistake: none of the fugitives had crossed the Potomac. All four were still bottled up in Maryland. Unknown to each other, and unknown to the search parties fanning out over all of Maryland, Booth and Henson and Boyd and Herold were within a short distance of each other near Port Tobacco.

Each pair had the same primary goal—Gambo Creek across the Potomac and then Port Conway for a crossing of the Rappahannock to Port Royal in Virginia.

On Tuesday, April 25, Tom Jones went to Port Tobacco's old Brawner Hotel where a detective, introduced as Capt. Williams, invited him to have a drink.[19]

"I'll give $100,000," Williams said as they lifted their glasses, "to anyone who will give me the information that leads to Booth's capture."

Jones replied, "That's a large sum of money. It ought to get him if money can do it." He stayed away from the fugitives that night, the only time that week he had failed to deliver food and newspapers.

He saw that the neighborhood was filled with cavalrymen and detectives by Wednesday and Thursday. Each house in the area was visited by searchers, including Jones' house. Huckleberry was searched once and visited several times by officers.[20]

In the swamp, Booth grew more impatient to cross the river. His leg, terribly swollen and inflamed, was so painful he had a hard time keeping a grip on himself. His condition was made worse by cold, damp, and cloudy weather closing in, although no rain fell. Booth urged Jones to get him out of the swamp, but was refused.[21] "It's not the time. Too risky."

A week after the shot was fired in Ford's Theatre, Jones rode into Allen's Fresh. The small village was three miles east of Huckleberry at the point where Zekiah Swamp ends and the Wicomico River begins.

In the quiet evening, Jones saw a body of cavalry ride up and dismount. Some troopers entered Colton's store where Jones sat. The soldiers drank and talked until their guide, John R. Walton, burst into the store.[22] "Boys," he cried, "I have news that they've been seen in St. Mary's!"

The cavalrymen rushed to their mounts and thundered away. Jones watched them cross the bridge toward St. Mary's County and thought, "There won't be another soldier in the neighborhood. It's now or never."

Dusk was settling as Jones mounted his horse and rode casually out of the village.

At the swamp, Booth was trying to bear his pain by writing in his diary. A gray fog rose from the marsh and floated over the trees. He confided that he did not regret the blow he had struck, "I think I have done well . . .[23]

"And for this brave boy with me, who often prays (yes,

207

before and since) with a true and sincere heart, was it crime in him? If so, why can he pray the same?"[24]

Jones' low whistle sounded. Quickly he told what he'd heard at Allen's Fresh. "The coast seems to be clear. The darkness favors us. Let's make the attempt."

Jones led the way by 50 or so yards. Booth and Henson followed, Booth riding Jones' horse and Henson walking alongside.

The night was inky dark. Moisture clung to everything and splashed down in fat drops upon the men. They reached Huckleberry before 10 p.m.[25]

After eating the trio continued through the blackness until they reached the Potomac. A 12 foot long, flat bottomed boat was pulled from an almost impenetrable laurel thicket. Booth was eased into the stern and given an oar with which to steer. Herold took the bow seat to row. Jones shaded a candle under an oilcloth coat, since there was no lantern. Booth produced his compass. Jones pointed the direction.[26] "Keep to that," he whispered, "and it'll bring you into Machodac Creek. Mrs. Quesenberry lives near the mouth of this creek. If you tell her you come from me, I think she will take care of you."

Booth offered money to Jones, who took $18, the price he'd paid for the boat, which he never expected to see again.

Booth's voice broke with emotion. "God bless you, my dear friend, for all you have done for me. Good-bye, old fellow."

Jones heard them push off. They were swallowed by the night.

Boyd and Herold went to a Colonel Hughes' place between Burgess Creek and King's Creek arriving about daybreak on April 19. They were heading for a place west of Mathias Point to cross the river. Boyd's right leg was festering and so sore that he was reduced to using a crude crutch.[27]

Booth and Henson did not make it across the river the same night Jones saw them shove off. Jones had forgotten to caution them against the strong flood tide. Sometime that night the two men were swept to Naugemony shores. They were still in Maryland, on the same shore they'd left. They hid out again, intending to try for a crossing the next night.[28]

Another reward poster dated April 20 offered $50,000 for "the murderer of our late beloved President, Abraham Lincoln." Booth was not specified in the main body of the poster. His description was given in small type at the bottom. The poster had no pictures.[29]

The same poster offered $25,000 for John H. Surratt, "one of Booth's accomplices." He was also described at the bottom of the sheet.

An additional $25,000 was offered for David C. "Harold" as another accomplice. He was described in the bottom line of the poster as a "little chunky man, quite a youth, and wears a very thin mustache."[30] He had been in NDP custody from April 16 to 18.

On Friday, April 21, Booth wrote in his diary, "Tonight I will once more try the river with the intention to cross, although I have a greater desire and almost a mind to return to Washington, and in a measure clear my name, which I feel I can do."[31] That night Booth and Henson successfully managed the crossing.

Boyd and Herold had already crossed the Potomac the day before. They passed through or around Owen's Store before the detectives arrived Thursday morning and went on toward Dan Green's farm.[32]

On Saturday, April 22, a week after Lincoln's death, Booth and Henson reached the home of the Widow Quesenberry. They were met by Thomas H. Harbin, Jones' brother-in-law, and Joseph Badden of Prince Georges County. Harbin had been one of the original Maryland planter's group plotting Lincoln's kidnapping the previous autumn. Booth and Henson were sent on to a Dr. Stuart's summer home.[33]

Sometime Saturday night, they moved on to Gambo Creek, north of Dr. Stuart's place. They had doubled back past Mrs. Quesenberry's with the idea of hiding out in the area of Gambo Creek, which emptied into the Potomac, then apparently fled around dawn Sunday, leaving behind Booth's coat, his diary and other items. They were headed for a crossing at Port Conway. The two fugitives would reach there Monday morning, and so would Boyd and Herold.[34]

On Saturday morning, Andrew Potter left his brother in charge of the search and started out for Washington on the *Jenny B*. Rumors varied about where the fugitives had been seen. All had been checked out and proven false.

At Mathias Point, north of Gambo Creek, where all four fugitives were, the *Jenny B* was signaled in from shore. The captain pulled in and Andrew learned what "buck fever" had done to some of the over eager hunters.

"Mr. Potter, one of our detectives shot another detective."[35]

Ernest Dooley had been waiting with William Bernard at Owen's Store since Thursday. The two operatives had spelled each other, day and night. They had arrived at Owen's Store the same morning Boyd and Herold had passed through or near the site.

Bill O'Dwyer and another detective, also pursuing Boyd and Herold, had missed the fugitives at Col. Hughes. By Saturday morning, April 22, Bernard and Dooley were wearily watching at Owen's Store when O'Dwyer and his partner arrived. They ran headlong into Dooley and Bernard.[36]

There was a challenge either ignored or unheard. Dooley began firing. He hit O'Dwyer, 28, a former New York City policeman with seven years' service. O'Dwyer died on the boat back to Washington. His killing was hushed up by the NDP.[37]

Andrew Potter heard the report, then turned back to the pursuit. "If Boyd and Herold have gotten by us, it's entirely possible Booth and Henson have made it, too. I'm going south again. Bernard, I want you and Dooley to come with me. James and Thomas, you Potters, come along, too. And bring Whippet Nalgai."

The Indian scout had met Booth and would be able to recognize him. The men headed for Gambo Creek on their way to Port Conway.[38]

Booth and Henson were nearing Port Conway.

Chapter 17

PURSUERS CLOSE IN

The Potter brothers were gaining on the fugitives who had crossed the Potomac but still faced the Rappahannock into Virginia.

Meanwhile, back at NDP headquarters, detectives were in the wholesale arrest business. At 4 on the morning of Thursday, April 20, officers arrested George Atzerodt, following a tip from his brother, John, a detective.

The entire company and the owner of Ford's Theatre had been seized, as had Booth's close relatives, including his brother, Edwin. Edwin and John Wilkes had always been on the opposite sides of the political fence.

Altogether, about 2,000 people were arrested on suspicion of involvement in the Lincoln assassination conspiracy.

Three reward posters were issued with an April 20 date.[1] One raised the amount to $100,000. There were no pictures, only the physical descriptions of the wanted men.[2]

Fifty thousand dollars was offered for Booth, although his name was not mentioned except in small print at the bottom where his description was given. This time, his "heavy black mustache" was mentioned.

Twenty-five thousand dollars was offered for John H. Surratt and another $25,000 for the escaped Herold. Seward's attacker was not mentioned after Baker's first poster.

Another poster carried a picture labeled "Surratt," but it was a nearly full length photo of his older brother, Isaac, who had been with the army in Texas. The poster also carried Edwin Booth's photo instead of assassin John Wilkes, along with a picture of Herold.[3]

The third poster carried Surratt's picture, one of John Wilkes Booth, and Herold's Sunday NDP arrest photo. The Herold photo had his handcuffed hands cropped off so the public wouldn't know that he had been arrested earlier. The Herold frame-up was under way.

Secretary of War Stanton was listed on all the April 20 posters as the authority for the rewards. Additionally, a warning was included, issued by the War Secretary: "All persons harboring or secreting the said persons, or either of them, or aiding or assisting their concealment or escape, will be treated as accomplices in the murder of the President and the attempted assassination of the Secretary of State, and shall be subject to trial before a military commission and the punishment of death."[4]

Rewards were also being prepared for Jefferson Davis and other members of the Confederacy, but not a word about this was mentioned in any of the posters.

Ward Lamon's friend, Beverly Tucker, was arrested in Richmond on April 15. The Confederate agent, on Lamon's orders, was secretly transported to Lafe Baker's headquarters in Washington and given into the custody of the secret service chief while Lamon went to see Stanton.[5] On Stanton's order, Baker had Tucker taken to Rouse's Point by detective Allan Pinkerton. From there, Tucker was sent into Canada.[6]

Throughout the week of pursuit, arrests, escapes, and further deaths, the nation mourned Lincoln's passing.

The body was on view to the public Tuesday, April 18. The procession would wind from the White House to the Capitol. Eager spectators brought great umbrellas and chairs to perch on the portico of the Treasury building. Newspapers said early spectators held their positions "as though by squatter's rights."[7]

212

Mourners formed a mile long column six and seven abreast to file through the west driveway gate to the South Portico. The citizens, stifling sobs, passed on through the great hall to the darkened Green Room. There they turned left into the East Room.

Lincoln's $1,500 coffin, two inches longer than the body, rested on a catafalque in the center of the room. It had been hastily built of walnut.[8]

Officers divided the mourners into two single lines. The people mounted the steps and walked alongside the coffin, one a second, staring at the bearded, lined face. The head rested on a white silk pillow.

The public line was discontinued at 5:30 p.m., and special groups were admitted. Carpenters built bleachers, where the official funeral party would sit Wednesday morning, April 19.[9]

For two days, special trains had been bringing mourners into Washington. Officials estimated 6,000 people had to sleep on floors or wherever they could find space.

The booming of cannon and melancholy tolling of bells greeted the Wednesday dawn. The day was bright and beautiful. Not a business house opened.

By 11 a.m. Wednesday, the nation's great and near great were silently assembled in the East Room. Just before noon, President Johnson entered, trailed by former Vice President Hamlin and the Lincoln cabinet. Robert Lincoln, flanked by the late President's secretaries, John Hay and John Nicolay, stood at the foot of the casket.[10]

Mrs. Lincoln was confined to her room with grief. She had not seen her husband's body since she had been led from the Petersen house after his death."[11]

Gen. Grant sat alone at Lincoln's head. Johnson and the cabinet took positions by the side of the coffin.

Four ministers spoke,[12] the first one beginning with the Episcopal burial service: "I am the Resurrection and the Life, saith the Lord . . ."

A bishop from the Methodist Episcopal Church compared Lincoln to Moses. Dr. Gurley delivered the sermon. "It was a cruel, cruel hand . . . which smote our honored, wise, and noble President . . ."

The Senate chaplain, a Baptist, offered the benediction: "God of Justice and Avenger of the Nation's wrongs, let the work of treason cease, and let the guilty perpetrators of this horrible crime be arrested and brought to justice . . . Amen."

The 600 mourners filed out into the sunlight. The coffin, carried by 12 veteran reserve corps sergeants, was placed on a funeral cart, pulled by six white horses.[13]

A mile and a half down Pennsylvania Avenue, the funeral cart reached the east front of the Capitol. The coffin was carried inside to the rotunda and placed on a second catafalque. Here the body was to lie in state from Wednesday afternoon until Thursday morning.

Then through a light drizzle, the coffin was taken to a special railroad train made up of nine cars and the engine. Lincoln's body, attended by Robert, was in the second car from the rear. Three hundred people were to accompany the funeral train's sad burden 1,700 miles through almost every city where Lincoln had stopped in February, 1861 on his way from Illinois to be inaugurated.

At 8 a.m. after one final prayer by Dr. Gurley, the black-draped Baltimore & Ohio engine slowly moved toward Baltimore, the first stop on the long trip to Illinois.[14]

Abraham Lincoln was going home to Spingfield, not as he had talked of with Mary only a week ago, but on the iron wheels of his funeral train.

The nearly $300,000 finally offered in reward money had opened a cage of amateur bounty hunters. Booth, Surratt. and Herold were still at large. In the throngs of trigger-happy hunters, accidents were bound to happen. But it was the detectives and military men, immune from prosecution, who did the killing. In addition to Dooley shooting fellow NDP operative O'Dwyer, two civilians named Frank Boyle and William Watson were shot "because they resembled Booth."[15] The secret police even disposed of the two bodies. Watson was taken to St. Mary's City, put aboard the *Jenny B* and sent up river to the old Arsenal Penitentiary. Here an autopsy was done and the body sewn into a canvas sailcloth bag with a couple of cannon balls. Luther Baker, Lafayette Baker's cousin, and Thomas Potter took the body down the Anacostia River and sank it at the Potomac's junction.[16]

Boyle's remains were taken to the Armory Square Hospital for autopsy, then buried in an unmarked grave at the cemetery in Fort Lincoln.[17]

On Friday, April 21, Lt. Lovett and a squad of cavalry again called at the Mudd home.[18] Lovett asked, "May we have the razor the party shaved with when he was here Sunday?"

The physician was glad to cooperate with the authorities. Of course they could have the razor. "There's a boot here which I cut from the injured man, too. It was found in the room after he left. A servant had thrown it under the bed while cleaning the room."

Lovett examined the boot and said, "There's something written here: "J. Wilkes——.""[19]

One of the cavalrymen looked at the name and said, "A part of the name has been effaced."

The physician looked at the name and commented, "I've never looked inside the boot."

Lovett handed Dr. Mudd a photograph. "Does this bear any resemblance to the party?"

"I would not be able to recognize that as the injured man," Dr. Mudd replied after studying the photograph. "However, there is a resemblance about the eyes and hair."[20]

The picture was not of John Wilkes Booth, but of his brother, Edwin.

Lovett handed a second photograph to the physician and asked if he could identify it as the second man who had been with the injured person. The picture was of Herold.

"I cannot see any resemblance," Dr. Mudd answered. "But I can describe the horse. It was a spirited bay mare."

One of the detectives said, "That exactly answers the description of one taken from the stable in Washington."

"From the facts and circumstances given," Dr. Mudd said, "I have formed a judgment, which I express without

215

hesitation. I'm convinced that the injured man was Booth. He's the same man who visited my house last year in November and purchased a horse from my neighbor, George Gardiner. I'm saying this because I think my judgment in the matter is necessary to prompt pursuit of the assassins."

On Monday, April 24, an officer with three soldiers took Dr. Mudd to Washington. He would not return home for many years to come.[21]

Andrew Potter led operatives to Port Conway on Saturday, April 22. The fugitives had not been seen.

Indian scout Nalgai was told that all four fugitives were holed up some place with a sympathetic Rebel. "See what you can turn up and report back here."

Early Sunday, April 23, the Indian returned. Wordlessly, he displayed two quart brandy bottles, an ulsterette with bloodstains, a pistol, a compass, a wallet containing $2,100 in Union currency, several letters of credit on Canadian and British banks, and pictures of six pretty young women and a horse.[22]

The detectives' excitement had risen with each item. Nalgai had one last item. He held it out to Andrew.

"What's this?" Andrew took the small book. It was an 1864 pocket diary.

"Listen to this: 'I shouted, "sic semper" before I fired.' The written date: April 13, 14."[23]

"Booth's diary!" James Potter breathed.

"And he's got a broken leg," Andrew said. "Look: 'In jumping, broke my leg.' It's in the same paragraph!"

He flipped through the pages, stopping to read now and then. "Oh, oh!" James interrupted. "Stop! Go back a page. There!"

The brothers were reading the December 1864 entry of Booth's meeting with Jay Cooke, Henry Cooke, Thurlow Weed, Chandler, Conness and Lafayette Baker.[24]

Page after page contained names: Jefferson Davis, Judah Benjamin, Montgomery Blair, Conger, Baker, Eckert, "The Secretary," John Surratt, Herold, O'Laughlin, Arnold, Payne, Beverly Tucker, Senator Wade.[25]

Andrew flipped back to the damning mentions of Baker. Beverly Tucker and Baker. Baker and Conger. Booth's distrust of Baker. Booth's belief that Baker, Eckert and Stanton were in control.

Andrew turned to the Indian. "Whippet, where'd you find this?"

"By Gambo Creek. The coat was spread on the ground, like somebody had been sitting on it.[26]

Tom Potter frowned. "Why would Booth be such a fool as to run off and leave that diary and these other things?"

"He was in a mighty big hurry, I'd say," Andrew declared, "We're closing in on them. Jim, you and Tom go with Whippet and scout around the area where the diary was found."

Andrew called out, "Bernard and Dooley, I want you to come with me."

"Where we going?" Dooley asked.

"To Belle Plain. I hope we can catch a boat to take us to Washington." Andrew Potter wanted the diary there as soon as possible and thought it better to take it himself. The *Jenny B* was just docking as the three secret service men arrived. Andrew's older brother, Luther, was on board.

Andrew showed his brother the various items and the damning diary. The entry about breaking a leg reminded Luther Potter of the boot found at Dr. Mudd's home near Bryantown. Luther added, "While he was there, Booth shaved off his mustache."[27]

"Did Dr. Mudd see which way Booth and this companion went?"

"After the doctor splinted the leg, Booth and his friend headed for Zekiah Swamp."

"What'd his companion look like?"

"His description matches David Herold's. But that can't be, because we had Herold in custody Sunday morning through Tuesday night, before he escaped with Boyd."

"You remember Ed Henson, Luther? Used to be a member of Booth's smuggling ring? He resembles Herold a lot." Andrew found the place in the diary and read to Luther about the "young man praying." "Booth's travel-

217

ing with somebody who sounds like he's involved. I'll bet that's who it is, Henson with Booth."

Luther said, "It's been more than a week since Booth and Henson, if that's who it is, left Mudd's. The map shows it's possible. In fact, it seems fairly certain, that they reached Gambo Creek Friday night. There's a widow who lives near there, Mrs. Quesenberry. If she didn't take them in, they must have spent at least part of Saturday night in one of the thickets along Gambo Creek."

The two quart brandy bottles suggested someone was supplying the fugitives and that the two men may have been drunk when they had left personal items, including the diary.

The brothers decided to get some ham and eggs at the provost marshal's shack in Belle Plain. As they sipped coffee, they reached a conclusion. "Let's stay," Luther urged. "Let's not go back to Washington just yet. We've got a good chance to capture Booth, I think.

"Booth wouldn't head for Richmond," Luther contended. "He'd be more likely to head for the Shenandoah Valley and then north for Canada."[28]

Andrew blinked in surprise. "He's been heading south toward Virginia. We know that. Why should he suddenly turn north?"

"I've been thinking," Luther said. "He really wanted us to think that he ran off in a hurry. But in reality it was a ruse, a false trail. He's turned north, but wants us to continue searching south toward Richmond."

Luther explained, "If Booth had really wanted to go south, he could have made it easier by boat from St. Mary's County. Or he could have crossed to the eastern shore and found refuge there, taking his time to go south. Since he didn't do this, I contend he's headed west, and then he'll cut north."

Luther recalled that he'd heard Booth had a farm somewhere in the valley of northern Virginia, on the Appalachian Trail. The Trail ran along the top of the Massanuttea Mountains just west of Culpepper Court House, Orange Court House, and Charlottesville in Virginia.[29]

"Culpeper is heavily garrisoned," Luther said, "and

so's Charlottesville. But Orange Court House is relatively clear of all but a contingent of troops."

"And we know, Booth, when he was smuggling, made his way to Richmond by this route. Luther, the more you talk, the more I'm beginning to think you've got something."

"Shall we play my hunch, Andy?"

"Why not? What about the diary and other stuff?"

"Dooley and Bernard are good men. We can trust them."

It was agreed. The two detectives were given the evidence and told to deliver it personally to Lafe Baker.[30]

Chapter 18

THE DIARY TELLS A WICKED STORY

On Monday, April 24, political lightning struck Washington. Rep. George Julian of Indiana sped to the War Department. The abolitionist leader had stood with the Radical Republicans in opposing the late President's reconstruction plan. Julian entered Secretary Stanton's office and knocked on the closed inner office door.[1]

Maj Eckert opened the door slightly. The co-chairman of the congressional Joint Committee on the Conduct of the War saw immediately that something was up.

"Well, Major," Julian said, "your face looks as if the Capitol dome just collapsed on you."

"Come in," Eckert whispered.

"What in the world . . .?" Julian saw Sen. Zachariah Chandler mumbling over a small book. The Michigan political boss' face was gray.[2] "Zach, you look as though you're about to have apoplexy."

The War Secretary said, "Sit down, George." Stanton turned impatiently to Eckert. "What's keeping Conness? Where is he? He should be here by now!"

Julian sat uneasily. "Mr. Secretary, will you tell me what in the name of . . . ?"

"We've got Booth's diary," Stanton announced. "And he's recorded a lot in it."[3]

Chandler, still transfixed by his reading, exploded with an oath, "Oh, that scoundrel!"

Chandler read, " 'With Jay Cooke at the Astor Hotel, I met Thurlow Weed, Sen. Chandler, and a Mr. Bell who said he was a friend of John Conness. . . . The speculators in cotton and gold would do anything—including murder—to make the amount of money they have. . . .' "[4]

A knock at the door interrupted him. Eckert let Sen. Conness into the room.

Stanton spoke up. "Zach has Booth's diary. You and George had better read it."

Conness' face registered shock. "For God's sake, Chandler, let's have it!"

The first words Conness read were, ". . . 'Conness said he would supply the new passwords every six weeks . . . oh, my God!"[5]

Conness took a quick breath and read, his voice shaking, ". . . 'Thompson gave me $50,000 in bank notes with instructions to take $15,000 to Sen. Conness'. . . . "[6] The Californian raised his eyes in a frightened sweep of his audience then went back to his recital. ". . . And to leave in a sealed envelope $20,000 in notes at the home of Sen. Wade. . . .'"[7]

Julian looked around the room at the naked fear in the faces of Conness, Chandler, Stanton, and Eckert. The Indianian felt a flash of anger at the men.

" 'Baker comes'," the Californian continued, his voice a whisper. ". . . 'Baker comes and brings with him Col. Conger. I told Baker to have him leave because I did not know him, and talking to too many people can be dangerous. . . .'"[8]

"Louder," Chandler demanded.

". . . 'No matter who speaks for Baker, I do not like him and will not trust him . . . I believe that Baker and Eckert and the Secretary are in control of our activities. . . .'"[9]

"Read on," Chandler said harshly.

" '. . . Eckert and the Secretary are in control of our activities, . . . and this frightens me. . . .' "[10] Conness raised his head. "Oh, my God! If this gets out, I'm ruined."

"You're ruined!" Chandler roared. "What about me? Wade? The Secretary, the Major, Jay Cooke?"

Stanton grunted, "We'll all be in worse trouble than ruination."[11]

Conness handed the diary to Julian, but the congressman shook his head.

"I don't want to read it. I've never met Booth. And since there seems to be something going on with some of you about which I know nothing, I think I'm better off not reading it."[12]

"You're not mentioned, George, nevertheless, it does concern you. Quite simply, we either stick together in this thing or we all hang together," Stanton shouted.[13]

"Mr. Secretary," Julian said. "Perhaps you're right. But there is a difference among us. As you all know, no one has been more opposed to the late President and his policies than I. Like you, I felt it was most important that Lincoln be removed from office . . . but I favored means the Constitution provides us. Apparently you gentlemen didn't, and perhaps that's why you kept me in the dark. I fear that everyone here knows more about the President's removal than anyone has admitted to me."[14]

He paused, searching their faces, and seeing guilt in each. "Let each of you deal with his conscience as he will. But I don't wish to be a party to it."

Stanton reached out quickly and took the diary from Conness. All eyes watched as he dropped the diary inside an envelope and carefully sealed it. "Here, Tom," Stanton handed it to Eckert. "Put this in the safe at once. Under no circumstances is it to be released to anyone—to anyone—without my personal order."[15]

Julian watched with a certain detachment. "You may lock up Booth's diary, Mr. Secretary," he said quietly, "but how're you going to silence him when you bring him into open court for trial?"

"He will not be tried in open court."

"How're you going to stop him? Military tribunal?"

Chandler said emphatically, "We have Booth's diary, but we do not have Booth."[16]

Julian wondered how they had gotten Booth's diary but not Booth. He decided not to ask.

"We expect to capture him tomorrow."

Julian squinted one eye. "You still do not have him. You do expect to capture him tomorrow. But you've been hoping to do that since Good Friday night."

That night, the Indianian wrote in his diary: "It was disgusting to see those men grovel in fear because of their immoral activities."[17] The cover-up of the Lincoln conspiracy could be traced to the very top. Julian wondered if the lid could be kept on such a sordid mess.

Lafayette Baker took prompt action when he learned he also faced possible treason charges because of entries in Booth's diary. The diary was never supposed to be released, but Baker didn't trust Stanton. The colonel would have to make sure Booth's diary would never implicate him.

Baker had seen the Booth diary Sunday evening, April 23, and had immediately given it to Stanton. That same day, Baker summoned the First District of Columbia Cavalry, which he headed and used as a military police unit to make arrests.[18] On Monday morning, Baker had called for two of his most trusted men, his cousin, Luther, and Col. Everton Conger. "I've got a special assignment for you two," he began. "With a bit of luck, we shall all be a little richer very soon. We've got a good line on Booth. But a lot's going to depend on how well each of you does what you're supposed to. . . ."

An aide admitted a young cavalryman, Edward P. Doherty. The NDP chief hurried around the desk and shook hands.[19] "You're the man Gen. Hancock loaned me for a special mission?"

Doherty snapped a brisk salute. "At your service, Col. Baker."

Baker quickly introduced the others. "These men are

from my agency. They will accompany you. Col. Conger, although in mufti, will have courtesy rank. But you, Lt. Doherty, will have direct charge. Understood?"

"Yes, sir."

"Good. Now, let me make this clear, Doherty. Your mission may well be the most important you will ever have." The colonel held out a photograph and asked, "Do you recognize this man?"

"Booth, Sir?"

"Booth. I take it you've never seen him—on or off the stage?"

"Never, Sir."

"Take the picture with you. Make sure your men are familiar with this face. Mark every feature. It's your duty —and theirs—to find him, catch him, and bring him back."

"And if he resists, Sir?"

"I want him," Baker said, glancing at Conger and his cousin with meaning. "I want him alive, if possible. Alive, do you understand?"

"Yes, Sir."

"Good. Now, where are your men?"

"Mounted and waiting outside, Sir."

"How many?"

"Twenty-five, Sir."

"Excellent! Your ship is already waiting at the Sixth Street wharf. Now, if you gentlemen will follow me to this wall map, I'll explain the strategy."

Baker's fingers moved rapidly from Washington down the lower Potomac and the Rappahannock. Then swung southward from the Port Conway-Port Royal crossing.[20] He picked up a draftsman's compass, placed the point on Port Royal and described a small circle. "This is approximately 15 miles in diameter. On the basis of information in our hands, you will find the men we want inside that circle."

Baker was right. Inside the bull's-eye he had drawn, Booth and Henson had already approached Port Conway in a wagon driven by the free slave, Willie Lucas.[21]

In Washington, Sen. Conness stopped by the office of

Rep. George Julian. "It's now known Booth sent several letters to newspapers."[22]

"I wonder," Julian said, "what Booth wrote in those letters he sent to the various newspapers."[23]

Conness nodded, "Some of those," he said with meaning, "will never be published."

Julian wanted to ask how the Californian knew that but decided not to ask. He guessed they would be suppressed. "I understand," Julian continued, "that Booth gave one such letter to an associate of his to deliver to the British Embassy. However, knowing protocol, I'm sure that Lord Lyons will return it, unopened."[24]

Julian sat thinking after Conness had left. If John Wilkes Booth lived to tell his story, the nation's biggest scandal would wash over Washington like garbage scattered by a tornado.

Julian was afraid, for he was a member of the two elements which obviously had done something terribly wrong —the Radical Republicans and the Committee on the Conduct of the War. If the cover-up didn't work, would he be sucked in with the guilty ones?

He didn't feel like working anymore. He pushed the papers back on his desk and walked to the window. Julian stood staring into the spring sunlight.

Chapter 19

HOT TRAILS GROW HOTTER

On Thursday, April 20, Dandridge Mercer Green stopped sawing a piece of timber to stare at two men coming toward him. One was a stranger, the other Green recognized as James William Boyd, hobbling along on a crutch.[1] "Well, I'll be . . ." the 46-year-old farmer exclaimed, "Lookee who's here! Captain Boyd himself!"

Leaning on his crutch, Boyd shook hands with the former blockade runner. "Good to see you, Dan," Boyd said, not introducing his companion. Green noticed the young man seemed "skeered and skittish."

"Leg bothering you again?" Green asked, wiping sweat from his forehead with the back of a hand.

"Starts draining every time I walk too much."

Green knew better than to ask too many questions. He motioned his callers to the shade of the William Spellman barn, where he worked for $2 a day. Green knew Boyd had also worked for Spellman off and on since the captain had been released from a Union prison. Boyd had used the employment to front for his movements around Southern Maryland.

"Dan," Boyd began, "I'll give you $20 in gold if you'll take us to your farm and hide us.[2] We jumped a guard over in Maryland and the provost marshal's looking for us. We want to get down south to Tennessee, or maybe Mexico."

Green squinted. He didn't want to get into trouble again, but he had nine children to support. "I'll go tell Mr. Spellman I'm sick and will be back tomorrow."

At his home, Green put Boyd and Herold in the wash house, which contained two cots. Mrs. Green objected. "They look like desperate men to me, Dan."

When Boyd gave Green another $20 for a jug of whiskey and some food, Mrs. Green was even more apprehensive. "Why should they pay so much unless they're desperate?" she demanded of her husband.

On Friday, April 21, Green went back to Spellman's and worked through Saturday. When he returned Saturday evening, his wife was upset.[3] "Those two men are drunk! They're loud and they're cussing. They have to go, Dan."

Green went to the wash house and told Boyd and his companion they'd have to leave.

"Look," Boyd pled, "my leg is killing me! Just let us stay the night, and we'll give you $20 more."[4]

Green hesitated. That would mean he would have made $60 in a few days, more than in a month of carpentry. "Well, just so you don't upset my missus again."

The two fugitives were quiet enough on Saturday, but by Sunday morning they had again raised the ire of Mrs. Green. She personally went to the wash house and threw them out.[5]

Boyd went to Green. "Will you take us south to Port Royal?"

"I'd like to, Boyd, but I can't today. Tell you what," Green said. "There's a free darkie lives nearby, Willie Lucas, who might take you to the port."[6]

The fugitives went to find Lucas, but that night they returned to the Green's. "Lucas can't take us," Boyd explained. "But Lucas says his boy Charlie can go tomorrow morning on the condition you go along? How about it, Dan?"[7] Boyd held out another $20.

"All right," he said. "I'll do it." He gave Boyd and Herold some more whiskey, and they returned to Lucas' cabin.

Green reached the Lucas cabin about daybreak. Boyd and Herold were ready to leave in an old wagon, with young Lucas up front.

The wagon rolled off toward Port Conway. Charlie Lucas at the reins didn't tell his passengers that this was already the second trip the wagon had made to Port Conway that morning. His father, Willie Lucas, had driven the mule toward the Rappahannock and returned before dawn.[8]

Young Lucas was puzzled. His father's passengers had been a short, talkative man and a man with a bum leg who walked with a crutch. It was powerful strange. If Charlie hadn't known for a fact what his father had done, Charlie would have sworn he was hauling the same two men.

While Boyd and Herold were rolling toward Port Conway, Booth and Henson were there seeking a way to cross the Rappahannock. About 9:30 that morning, they had reached the north side of the river and approached William Rollins, who lived nearby.[9] "We'd like to cross the river."

"Take the ferry," Rollins said. "It's on the other side

right now. Can't cross 'til the tide comes in and the river rises."

"We can't wait."

Rollins shrugged. "No other way across I know about." Rollins went fishing, but returned in about an hour. The two men were still there. "I'll take you across now."

"No, thanks. We've decided to take the ferry. It's coming now."[10]

William Rollins shrugged. He owned the ferry. Peyton Washington, a black man, was now pushing the scow across the 300-yard wide Rappahannock. Booth and Henson crossed from Port Conway in King George County, Virginia, to Port Royal and moved on down the road.[11]

A short distance away, the road twisted into a stand of pines. Booth stopped, looked around, and gave a low whistle.

A slender black man emerged from the woods. He was a fancy dresser with the look of a dandy. He sported a vest with a watch fob, an immense knot in his bright tie, and a narrow-brimmed hat. He led two saddle horses. He grinned broadly at Booth.[12] "Yessuh, Massa Booth, it's me, Henry Johnson, sho' nuff! I got yo' message and come lak you all said."

"Henry! I never thought I'd be so glad to see your shining black face!"

"We'd best hurry, Massa Booth." Booth's former valet, whom the actor had set up in the barbering business in Washington, joined Henson in helping Booth into a saddle.[13] Henson swung easily onto his horse, then reached a hand down to Johnson.

"No, suh," he protested, "Ah'll walk."

Booth said softly, "Henry, you're no longer a slave and we're in a big hurry. Now ride behind my friend and get us out of here."

"Yes, suh," Johnson said, settling himself behind the white man. "Fredericksburg's that way, gennlemens." He pointed northwest along the Rappahannock.

Early that same Monday morning, Andrew and Luther Potter with their party of secret police were hot on Booth's

227

trail. They arose in Belle Plain from a good night's sleep, drew fresh mounts from the quartermaster, and headed toward Fredericksburg to play Luther's hunch that Booth had deliberately left his diary and other items behind to disguise a switch in direction.[14]

From Fredericksburg, it would be a fairly easy trip for the fugitives to the Shenandoah Valley and north to Canada.

The Potters reached Fredericksburg about 9 a.m. that Monday, April 24. When the detectives began making inquiries, Booth and Henson had not yet crossed the Rappahannock at Port Conway.[15]

"Well, now, yes," a stableman said. "Now that you gentlemen mention it, I did see a man answering that description."

"When?" Andrew Potter demanded.

"Well, now, let me see. A man on a crutch with a full beard—but without a mustache, like you just asked about—well, sir, he rented a wagon from me along about, oh, maybe 10 o'clock last night."

The Potter brothers exchanged triumphant glances. "Was he alone?" Luther asked.

"Yes and no," the stableman said. "He was alone when he come in, all tuckered out from hobbling on the crutch, but when I rented him the wagon, this here man waved and a darkie come up. He'd been hanging back some. I reckon the darkie was drunk; 'peared to me so, anyhow."

Andrew Potter was having a hard time controlling his impatience. "Which way did they go?"

The stableman pointed northwest. "Toward Culpeper Court House."[16]

The detectives knew the Shenandoah wasn't much farther beyond Culpeper.

Andrew asked the stableman, "Are you sure there wasn't anyone else with him?"

"No. No. Just him and that drunk darkie."

The Potters walked away from the stableman and held a quick conference. Luther said, "Maybe Henson left. But that sounds like Booth and his nigger valet. Let's follow them."

Shortly after the noon hour, Charlie Lucas reined in his two tired old horses before the ferry at Port Conway.[17] "We's heah, gennlemens," he said.

In the back of the wagon, Boyd sat up. His leg had bothered him too much for real rest. Herold jumped down, stretched, and handed Dan Green some money.

"Here's a little extra something for your trouble, and give that darkie this."

Herold approached Rollins, the ferryboat owner.[18] "How much to take us across the river?"

Rollins looked at the two strangers and judged their net worth to be very little. He named a price and was surprised when paid in gold.

The crippled man was helped into the flatbottomed, square ended scow. He seemed to be suffering a great deal of pain.

The crossing was made to Port Royal in Caroline County, Virginia. The crippled man was helped out of the scow and onto the shore where they met three young men in Confederate uniforms.

The youngest was Private Willie S. Jett, former member of the Ninth Virginia Cavalry, stationed in Caroline County as commissary agent for the late CSA. His companions were Lt. M. B. Ruggles and Maj. A. B. Bainbridge.[19]

Herold walked up to them. "Our name is Boyd. My brother was wounded below Petersburg."[20]

The three uniformed youths glanced at the older man's leg, but said nothing.

Herold asked, "Can you take us through the lines?"

Jett replied, "We haven't said where we're going."

"As long as it's south," Boyd said, "we'd be obliged to go along."

Jett said, "The only place I know where a wounded soldier might be welcome is at Garrett's farm."

"How far's that?" Boyd asked.

"Maybe three miles south." Jett pointed toward Bowling Green.

Ruggles offered his horse to the injured man. Herold rode double with Bainbridge. They reached the Garretts about four o'clock Monday afternoon, April 24.[21]

Garrett came out.

"Mr. Garrett, my name's Capt. Jett. This is Lt. Ruggles and the other is my friend, Capt. Boyd. He's a wounded Confederate soldier, hit at Petersburg just before the close of the war. Lt. Ruggles and I were going on a little scout toward Richmond, and wonder if you can take care of my friend until Wednesday morning? He's suffered too much to travel with us."[22]

Garrett's religion required entertainment of strangers, especially anyone who seemed to be suffering. The farmer had previously ministered to about a dozen wounded soldiers who had been captured and brought to the neighborhood.

"Of course," Garrett said heartily. "Capt. Boyd, you are welcome in my home." Garrett opened the small yard gate as Boyd dismounted.

"Thank you, Sir," Boyd said, hobbling through and shaking hands.

Jett explained, "Mr. Garrett, the rest of us want to ride on into Bowling Green."[23]

Herold held up a boot with the sole slapping loosely. "I need new shoes," he called.

"Of course, gentlemen," Garrett said. "I'll expect you on Wednesday.

Herold shouted, "Maybe I'll come back sooner, if that's all right with you, Mr. Garrett?"

"Whatever you wish," he replied.

Boyd was introduced to the Garrett family.

"My wife, Captain Boyd. My sons, John, called Jack— he's just out of the army; my second son, William, and my namesake, Richard."

Boyd judged the older sons were in their early 20s, while Richard, Jr., could not have been more than 12.

He acknowledged the introductions, then turned to the women who had been standing in the background.

"My sister-in-law, Miss Lucinda Holloway. And these are my daughters," his host continued. "Kate's in her early teens and doesn't like me to tell exactly how early or late," the father said with a teasing smile. "This is another daughter, Lilly, nine; and Cora, the youngest, is just four."

Mrs. Garrett asked, "Captain Boyd, do you have a family?"

"I have seven children," he said. "But I haven't seen much of them."

"You must be weary. Please come in and sit down. Rest your leg. Girls, get our guest some refreshments."

"Thank you, Mam." Boyd took off his coat, unslung his field glasses, and sank gratefully into a porch chair.

Luther and Andrew Potter's NDP search party reached Culpeper Court House late that afternoon. They asked about a man with a crutch who wore a full beard and soon picked up the trail.[24]

"Man answering that description came in this morning in a wagon with a darkie driving," a lounger told them.

"Know where he is now?"

"He went on toward Sperryville."

The Potter brothers touched heels to their horses and raced toward Sperryville near the Shenandoah.

But alas for the Potters, the look-alike "man with the beard and the drunk darkie" turned out to be complete strangers.

Booth and Henson, with Henry Johnson, moved toward Fredericksburg, well behind the detectives, who had over-run their quarry.[25]

At Garrett's farm, the two youngest daughters shyly peered at their guest from behind the shelter of a big chair. Boyd smiled warmly and held out his hands to the smaller one. "Come here, Little Miss Blue Eyes."

It had been a long time since Boyd had been anywhere near a real family. It made him feel good.

Chapter 20

MURDER AT GARRETT'S FARM

Capt. Boyd relaxed on the porch of the Garrett farm during the late afternoon of Monday, April 24.

In the hammock Cora pointed to Boyd's hand. "What's that?"

"That? Why, that's my tattooed initials. Can you read them?"

"I can," Lilly announced. "They're J.W.B. What's that mean?"

"They stand for my name, James William Boyd."[1]

Booth's initials were also on one of his hands.[2]

The little girls then studied Boyd's gold watch chain with a small gold ring on it.

"What's that?"

"Why, Little Miss Blue Eyes, that's my watch chain."

"What's that on it?"

"That? That's a gold ring."

Lilly asked, "Why do you wear it on the chain?"

"My wife gave it to me, but it's too little for my finger."

"Where's your wife, Capt. Boyd?" Cora asked.

He was silent a moment. "She died," he said finally. He pulled out his watch. "You ever see anything like this?"

Both girls gazed at the enameled face with the two holes for the winding key under the raised 18-karat cover.[3] "Remind me when it's time for the hour to strike and I'll let you hold it."

"Watches don't strike the hour. Only big clocks do."

"This one strikes so you can feel it through the case. I can feel it strike against me when it's in my vest." Boyd grinned. "You'll see."

The next morning Boyd's leg seemed a little less painful. He wound his watch, replaced it in the vest, and hung the garment in a downstairs hall closet filled with winter clothes.

After breakfast, Jack the oldest Garrett son, rode about a mile to a shoemaker's to have his boots repaired. When he returned, the Garretts had their first news of Lincoln's assassination and the huge rewards offered.[4]

At dinner Jack asked, "Captain Boyd, since you told me earlier you're a native of Maryland, I wonder if it's possible that you've seen Booth, the man the authorities are charging with the offense?"[5]

"Once," Boyd replied. "I saw him in Richmond about the time of the John Brown raid."

His host asked, "Is Booth a young man or old?"

"He's rather young."

The father mused, "I've never heard of but one Booth as an actor, and I thought his name was Edwin."

Lt. Doherty, Col. Conger and former Lt. Luther Baker left the Sixth Street dock in Washington about 3 o'clock the previous afternoon. Seven hours later the government tug, *John S. Ide*, docked at Belle Plain. The Sixteenth New York Cavalry disembarked, mounted horses and began scouting the countryside for clues to Booth's whereabouts.[6]

Although it was just past 10 at night, Conger and Baker, both in plainclothes, called on prominent Rebels. The two detectives assumed names of well-known Confederate blockade runners and mail carriers "with little regard for the truth," as Luther Baker admitted. The agents said they were being pursued by Yanks and had become separated from their companions while crossing the Potomac.[7]

"One of our companions is lame," the NDP men exclaimed to the Rebels. "Have you seen him?"

No one had.

At daylight, Baker and Conger ate breakfast and remounted. "We've decided," Luther Baker told Lt. Doherty, "to change our course and strike across the country in the direction of Port Conway."[8]

The 25 cavalrymen, who had been ordered to keep the two secret policemen in sight throughout the night, moaned in unison. Nobody had slept. Now they faced another day without rest.

Doherty turned to his sergeant, Thomas "Boston" P. Corbett. "Mount up, Sergeant," Doherty ordered.

"Yes, Sir!" Corbett replied.

At 43, Corbett was a religious eccentric. His wife and infant had died in childbirth. Corbett became an alcoholic. Picked out of the gutter by a New York religious mission group, he was baptized and took the name of Boston in imitation of biblical characters whose names were sometimes changed after momentous events. He had become a street preacher, wore his hair to his waist, and was known as the "glory to God man" on Fulton Street in New York City.

Though just five-feet-five, Corbett was a stirring speaker. In 1858 in order "to be holy," as Corbett said, he had castrated himself after being approached by two prostitutes who had offered him their favors.

This mentally unstable soldier fell in behind Lt. Doherty to lead part of Company L toward Bowling Green on Tuesday morning, April 25. Doherty was questioning local physicians now that Booth was known to be injured.

At the same time, Conger took four soldiers and a corporal and moved along the Rappahannock.

Luther Baker made inquiries at planters' homes throughout the morning and into the early afternoon when the search parties rendezvoused at Port Conway. Baker took a man with him to the hut of William Rollins beside the Rappahannock.

Baker asked, "Have you seen a lame man cross the river in the last few days?"

"Yes," Rollins answered. "He had another man with him."

The NDP man showed Rollins photographs of Booth.

"Yes," the ferry owner pointed at the pictures, "these are the men."[9]

Baker could barely control his excitement. "When did you see these men?"

"Yesterday."

"Where did they go?"

"I don't know for certain. They hired me to take them across the river, but some men seemed to know them, and they went off together."

"Who were the men they met?"

"One was called Capt. Jett, I think. The other was a Lt. Bainbridge. They've just been mustered out of Mosby's Cavalry."[10]

"And you don't know where they went?"

"Well," the fisherman drawled, "this Capt. Jett has a ladylove over at Bowling Green, and I reckon they might have gone there."[11]

Baker demanded Rollins show the way but the ferryman shook his head. "Few people around here favor the Union cause. It'd be mighty unpleasant for me if they thought I was willing to help Yankees."[12]

Baker blinked in surprise. While he was thinking, Rollins made a sly suggestion. "You might put me under arrest," he said. "Then I would have to go with you."

Baker made the arrest as Conger approached with the rest of the command. The leaky old ferry took the group over the Rappahannock in three trips.

Boyd's leg seemed better. Herold would soon be back from Bowling Green. Tomorrow they could ride on through Virginia toward Mexico, Boyd hoped.[13]

In the late afternoon horses approached from the direction of Bowling Green. One carried double. Herold slid off a horse at the main gate, waved to the two other riders, and walked up the dusty farm lane in his new shoes. Boyd introduced him to the Garretts as Dave Boyd, a cousin.

A short time later, the senior Garrett looked up. Horses were coming at a gallop from the north. They were the same two men who'd dropped Boyd's cousin off. They reined in at the front gate and Garrett recognized Lt.

235

Ruggles.[14] "The Yankees are crossing at Port Royal! You must take care of yourselves as best you can!" They galloped on down the road.

The Garretts were surprised to see Boyd and his cousin hurrying toward the tobacco barn.[15] Their guests vanished into the pine woods. A short time later, a troop of Union cavalry clattered by, riding hard to the south.

"They must be going to Bowling Green," Jack Garrett guessed.

The family was suddenly alarmed. When the two men returned from the woods, the farmer and his soldier son demanded some answers.[16] Jack asked, "Why'd you both run for the woods when those bluecoats rode by?"

Boyd tried to explain. "We had a little trouble with the Federals up in Maryland. Those cavalrymen made us nervous."

"If you're paroled Confederates, as you claim," Jack said, "there's no reason to be alarmed."

"We just thought it better to remain out of sight," Boyd replied.

Jack Garrett rode off to a neighbor where he heard disturbing news. When he returned he went directly to Boyd and Herold. "The cavalry is hunting a crippled man and a companion," he told them. "If you've gotten into any difficulty, you must leave at once. I don't want to bring any trouble upon my father. He's too old for it."[17]

Boyd tried to calm young Garrett. "The trouble's over. But maybe we had better leave."

"I would rather you would not stay here tonight at all. Anyhow, I don't want you to stay in the house tonight."[18]

Boyd nodded toward the tobacco barn. "How about there?"[19]

"There's hay and fodder in there. You can sleep there tonight, I suppose."

The fugitives were shown to the storeroom in the tobacco barn. Jack Garrett closed the door on Boyd and Herold and locked it. He took the key inside and handed it to his aunt. "I'll leave this in your care," he said to Miss Holloway. "Don't let anyone else have it. It's my opinion those men intend to try stealing our horses. I'm going to

236

sleep in the corncrib and watch them."[20]

The Sixteenth New York Cavalry, having ridden past Boyd and Herold on Tuesday afternoon, caught up with Willie Jett near midnight. It was dark and cloudy, but there was no rain as Doherty, Conger, and Luther Baker dismounted at the Goldman Hotel near Bowling Green.[21] The troopers were dispersed around the structure.

A dog began to bark. A black man opened the back door to investigate. Conger pushed his way in behind a revolver.

At the front, Baker pounded on the front door until a frightened woman came down and unlocked it. The detective shoved past her and met Conger in the hall.

Conger snapped at the terrified woman, "We're looking for two men who are your guests. Where are they?"

"There's just one man here," the woman managed to whisper.

"Where is he?" Baker demanded.

She pointed. "Upstairs with my son."

The detectives climbed the stairs and burst through the door the woman indicated. Two men sat up in bed under the detectives' guns.

"What do you want?" Jett demanded.

"We want you," Baker replied.

The revolvers held steady on the suspect as Baker continued. "We know you. You took Booth across the river. You must tell us everything you know."

Jett managed to say, "You're mistaken. . . ."

Conger interrupted. "You lie!" He shoved the revolver against Jett's head. "We know what we're talking about. We're going to have Booth. Now you can tell us where he is, or die."[22]

Union cavalrymen were crowding into the bedroom. Jett's eyes were wide with fear. "He's at the Garrett's farm. But you may have frightened him off. You must have passed that place."[23]

Conger waved his gun. "Get out of bed and get dressed. You're going with us. And if you mislead us, you're a dead man."

Around 4 a.m. Wednesday, April 26, the command halted within shouting distance of the Garrett farm. There were whispered commands. The ferryman Rollins rode ahead with Lt. Doherty, the prisoner Jett following. Behind them, Conger and Baker were trailed by Sgt. Boston Corbett and the weary calvalrymen.[24]

The house was surrounded. Dogs barked furiously. Baker pounded on the front door. "Open up! Federal officers!"

A window near the door opened. Farmer Garrett put his head out. Baker thrust a pistol against his head. "Open the door! Get a light! Be quick about it!"

Mr. Garrett pulled pantaloons over his night shirt and came outside with a tallow candle.

Conger grabbed him. "Where are the men who stopped at your house?"[25]

"They've. . . . they've gone."

"Gone where?"

"To the woods."

"Whereabouts in the woods?"

The household was stirring in alarm. The little girls were calmed by their mother. Miss Holloway, peering down at the Yankees, saw that her brother-in-law was trying to explain something to a fierce man. "I don't want any long stories from you! I just want to know where those men have gone!" Conger roared. "You lying Reb! Men, take this man to the nearest tree! Stretch his neck a little! Maybe he'll tell us the truth!"

The father was hustled to a chopping block in the yard and lifted upon it. A rope was thrown over a limb of the locust branch above and one end looped.[26]

Luther Baker held a gun to Garrett's head while the victim's wife and three daughters sobbed. Miss Holloway was arguing with a trooper when she spotted Willie Jett. "You brought these Federals here!" she cried.

She broke off her accusations with a shriek as she saw, by the tallow candle's fitful light, a rope placed about her brother-in-law's neck.[27]

Baker jabbed the gun against Garrett's throat. "Are you going to tell us where the men are?"

Garrett stammered, "They went to the woods, when the cavalry rode by yesterday afternoon. Afterward," Garrett went on, his voice choking, "they returned and got their supper, and I don't know where they went. I don't know where. . . ."

"Wait!" Jack Garrett rushed out of the corn crib. Guns were trained on him and he slowed to a walk, his hands in plain sight. "The men you want are in the tobacco barn.[28]

The other Garrett sons came running from the corn crib.

"Seize them!" Conger ordered.

The three boys were herded toward the tobacco barn, while their father was left standing atop the chopping block, shivering in his night shirt and pantaloons.

Conger grabbed Jack by the collar. Young Garrett protested, "We'll need the key. My aunt has it." He told Conger he'd been suspicious that the two men would steal the horses and had locked them in.

There was no sound from the barn.

Jack Garrett was handed the key. "Go up and open it," Baker commanded. "Then go in and bring those men out."[29]

"They're armed," Garrett protested.

"Move!" Baker shoved him toward the barn, then shouted, "You, in the barn! We're going send in this man to get your arms! Then you must come out and give yourselves up."

Jack Garrett unlocked the door and stepped cautiously inside.

Baker could hear movement inside the barn, the rustling of corn fodder, a low-voiced conversation, then an exclamation. "Damn you! You've betrayed me! Get out of here or I'll shoot!"[30]

Young Garrett backed hurriedly out the barn door.

Baker called out, "Surrender or we'll burn the barn and have a shooting match."[31]

Boyd's voice came from the dark barn, "Who are you? What do you want? Who do you want?"[32]

"We want you! We know who you are. Give up your arms and come out!"

Baker placed a candle in the lane, near the barn door, and retreated into the shadows. The flame danced in eddies of air, then burned steadily. The front of the barn door was visible.[33]

Boyd called again, "Who are you? What do you want?"

Conger raised his voice. "It don't make any difference who we are!"

There was a silence then Boyd's voice, "This is a hard case. It may be I am to be taken by my friends."[34]

Boyd challenged, "Captain, if you'll take your men 50 yards from the door, I'll come out and fight you. Give me a chance for my life."

"No! Throw out your weapons and surrender."

"Well then, my brave boys, prepare a stretcher for me."

The silence grew.

Conger turned to Jack Garrett. "Pile some brush against the corner of the barn."

Garrett moved through the shadows, but in a moment hurried back to Conger. "This man inside says if I put any more brush in there, he'll put a ball through me."[35]

Boyd called, "There's a man in here who wants to come out."

Herold's voice was heard. "Captain, let me out. I'll do anything I can for you. Let me out."

Baker called, "Let me have your arms."

"I have none."

Boyd called, "The arms are mine. I've got them. Upon the word and honor of a gentleman, he has no arms. They're mine."

Conger moved to Baker's side. "Never mind the arms. If we can get one of the men out, let's do it and not wait any longer."

"All right," Baker called. "Come on out."

Herold stuck his hands through the door to show they were empty. Baker jumped forward, grabbed the youth and jerked him toward the cavalrymen.

Baker called into the barn, "You'd better come out and surrender."

Boyd called again, "Captain, I'm lame. Give me a chance. Draw your men back 20 yards from the door and I'll fight your whole company."[36]

"We're not here to fight, but to take you. You're now free to come out and surrender."

"Give me a little time to consider."

"Very well," Baker shouted. "You have two minutes."

Boyd's voice finally broke the silence. "Captain, I've had a half a dozen chances to shoot you. I have a bead drawn on you now. But I don't wish to do it. Withdraw your men from the door, and I'll come out. Give me a chance for my life, for I won't be taken alive."

Baker answered, "Your time is up. We shall wait no longer. We will fire the barn."

The senior Garrett, trembling with cold and fear heard Boyd call out, "Don't destroy the gentleman's property. He's entirely innocent. He doesn't know who I am."[37]

Conger skirted the barn's shadows and came around to the far side. He pulled some hay from a crack in the barn, twisted it into a small rope and set fire to it. It blazed up. He thrust it through the crack into the loose, dry hay inside. It caught instantly. He saw the man inside swing up his rifle toward the flames.

Conger glanced around. Nobody could see him. He reached for his revolver and took careful aim.[38] Suddenly, the loud crack of a pistol from the other side of the barn was heard. The man inside the barn fell forward. Baker rushed in, followed by young Garrett, and grabbed the prostrate man.

Conger, revolver reholstered, raced through the door. "It's Booth, sure! He must have shot himself."

"No," Baker said. "No, he did not. I had my eyes on him every moment. But the man who did do the shooting goes back to Washington under arrest for disobedience of orders."[39]

Conger demanded, "Whereabouts is he shot?"

Men raised the limp form. Blood was coming from the right side of his neck.

"Yes, sir," Conger insisted, "he shot himself."

"He did not."

241

"Let's carry him out of here."

Conger, Garrett, and Baker dragged Boyd's body away from the burning barn, across the farm lane, and onto the grass under a stand of locust trees.[40]

Conger straightened up and looked at the cavalrymen crowding around. "All right," the detective shouted. "Who shot him?"

Chapter 21

ANY CORPSE WILL DO

Lt. Edward P. Doherty echoed Conger's demand. "Who shot Booth?"

Nobody answered.

Still standing on the chopping block, the senior Garrett reached shaky hands to the noose around his neck. "Booth?" he quavered. "Did he say it was Booth in the barn?"

A soldier turned to Garrett. "John Wilkes Booth—who assassinated President Lincoln. Who'd you think it was?"

"He said his name was Boyd. Capt. Boyd. . . ."

Dawn was breaking as Conger saw Boston Corbett crossing the lawn. "Sergeant, did you shoot Booth against orders? Tell me."[1]

The soldier drew himself up to his full five-foot-five-inches, saluted smartly and replied, "Sir, God Almighty directed me."

Conger stared at the religious fanatic, then said, "I guess He did, or you couldn't have hit him through that crack in the barn."[2]

Baker faced the long haired madman. "How'd it happen, Sergeant?"

Still stiffly at attention, Corbett replied, "Sir, as long as he made no demonstration, I did not shoot him. I kept my eye on him steadily. He turned towards the other side.

He brought his piece up to aim. I supposed he was going to fight his way out. I thought the time had come, and I took steady aim upon him and shot him."[3]

Everton Conger, fingering his own pistol, smiled with satisfaction. He had been issued secret orders from the Secretary and Lafayette Baker. It was all working out easier than he had ever imagined.

At the Fredericksburg Inn, the Potter brothers were sleeping soundly. Outside, in the early dawn, John Wilkes Booth, Ed Henson and Henry Johnson passed through the community and on toward Orange Court House.[4]

In the grass of the Garrett front yard, Boyd still breathed. The doomed man was totally paralyzed; the pistol ball had damaged his spinal cord so severely that he was incapable of swallowing or talking.[5]

One of the Garrett boys dragged an old mattress to the front porch and helped lift the dying man onto it. Boyd's eyes were open and followed the movements of the NDP men as they turned out his pockets.[6] There was a knife, belt, cartridge box, pistols, pocket compass, and a file. A Spencer repeating carbine was placed on top of the little pile.

Conger was anxious to break the news to Washington. He took some of Boyd's possessions and headed for his horse. "I'm going to ride to the capital and report to Lafe Baker," he announced. He would head first for one of the field telegraphers.

Twenty minutes after Conger left the scene, Boyd was dead. His body was wrapped in an old saddle blanket.[7]

"Garrett," Luther Baker called, "have you got a wagon we can use?"

"No, I don't own a wagon. But there's a darkie, name of Freeman, lives near here. He might have one."

Troopers were sent to bring the wagon. Mrs. Garrett began making breakfast to feed the men in shifts. While Baker was eating, the senior Garrett looked reproachfully at Willie Jett. "Why did you bring that man to my house and leave him as a wounded Confederate soldier? Look at the trouble you've brought upon me!"[8]

Jett lowered his eyes. "I wanted to get clear of him, so I left him at the first house we came to after leaving Port Royal."

"Why didn't you tell me who he was? He told us his name was Boyd, but these officers say he's John Wilkes Booth."

"I told these men when they came to Bowling Green that I'd left him with you as a Confederate soldier. I told them you didn't know who he was."

Garrett replied, "I want you to make that declaration to an officer in my presence."

Jett nodded. Lt. Doherty was called, and Jett repeated the statement to him. "This gentleman didn't know who that dead man was."

Sgt. Corbett added his testimony to the senior Garrett's, "I heard Booth call out in the barn, 'I declare before my Maker, this man is innocent of any crime whatever.' "[9]

The two older Garrett sons were arrested on charges of harboring the President's assassin. The distraught Garrett family saw the company mount up about 7 a.m.

The body of "Booth," was placed in an old army ambulance. Freeman, the black owner, rolled his eyes in fright when he was ordered to drive the body to Belle Plain.

Luther Baker came out of the Garrett home after breakfast. "Corporal, bring the prisoner, Jett, and ride with me to guard the body. I'm going on ahead of the main troops to Belle Plain landing."

Miss Holloway found herself staring at a strange pair of what she called "opera" glasses on a bookshelf. The family didn't own a pair. Maybe, she thought, they belonged to the dead man. She took them to Richard, but he ordered them out of his sight. "I don't want anything to remind me of this dreadful night!"

Baker with Jett and the body reached the ferry and crossed the Rappahannock before Lt. Doherty and his men arrived. "Drive on," Baker ordered the black man.

"Belle Plain is another 30 miles. The others will catch up."[10]

A short distance north of Port Conway, the wagon turned onto a side road. Baker glanced back from time to time but didn't see the rest of the soldiers. "Driver," Baker demanded, "are you sure this is the right road?"

"Mass, dis is all right. Ah hab been over dis road many and many a time befo' de wah, and Ah's sure it's de shortes' road to Belle Plain."[11]

"Corporal," Baker ordered, "Return to the ferry and inform Lt. Doherty what road I've taken."

The rickety old ambulance moved through country which became more and more forbidding. Straggling squads of men in Confederate uniform were met. "What you got there?" some ragged rebel troops asked. "A dead Yank?"

In Washington that morning, Lafe Baker received a coded cipher from Conger: "Booth has been shot to death near Bowling Green. Herold is a prisoner. I'll be in Washington tonight with details. Body follows. Conger."[12]

Lafayette Baker received the news with an unusual display of emotion. He leapt to his feet and across the room. "It's not often that I'm unbalanced by tidings of any sort," he told the telegrapher who brought the message. "But I feel like raising a shout of joy over the triumph of justice."[13]

There was reason for joy. With Booth dead, the secret service chief's part in the Lincoln conspiracy could never come out. Booth couldn't talk. Herold would keep his mouth shut on pain of death.

Baker shouted for his orderly to bring a carriage. A fast dash across Washington took him to Stanton's residence on K Street where he brushed by a servant and pushed into the bedroom where the War Secretary was napping.

"We've got Booth!" Baker exulted.

The secretary placed his hands over his eyes and lay still, saying nothing. Then, very slowly and deliberately, Stanton arose and pulled on his coat.[14] Unusual behavior for the man who often shouted and carried on in frenzied outbursts. His relief must have been beyond expression.

The news was leaked to the press. Soon the nation's newspapers screamed the news: "John Wilkes Booth, who shot President Lincoln the night of April 14 in Ford's Theatre, has been killed. His body is being returned by steamer to Washington. Government authorities this morning shot Booth while he was trying to escape from a farmer's barn near Bowling Green."

Washington was wild with anticipation.

The day grew hot and sultry. Luther Baker had been in the saddle two days and nights, exhausted but too anxious for sleep.

The road, badly gullied, wound up and down, in and out among hills. The battered ambulance with the $50,000 corpse groaned on over it. Sometime during the day, the Confederate Jett had slipped away. Baker half expected to meet an ambush at very ravine.

The Potter brothers arose from a good night's rest in Fredericksburg. When they emerged from their room at an inn, they were told the news: "They shot John Wilkes Booth near Bowling Green, and David Herold has been taken prisoner."

The brothers looked at each other. Luther Potter shrugged. "Well, I guess we were wrong."[15]

Finally, Luther Baker and the body of "Booth" arrived in Belle Plain. Boyd's corpse was swung over the side of the *John S. Ide* and placed under guard until the ship could build up a head of steam for the trip upriver. Andrew and Luther Potter arrived in time to board and find Luther Baker.[16]

"So you've got Booth!" Andrew exclaimed.

Baker puffed up with satisfaction. "Right over there," he pointed.

Luther Potter asked for details, and Baker sketched

246

them in, asking, "Would you like to see the $50,000 body?"

The Potters followed Baker along the deck to where two guards stood by the corpse. Baker pulled back the old blanket with a flourish. The Potter brothers leaned closer. The dead man wore a long shaggy mustache. It was so long that the reddish-sandy hairs curled upward into his nostrils. The brothers straightened up. "Sure grew a mustache in a hurry. Red, too."

Baker protested, "Everyone knows Booth had a mustache!"

Luther Potter gently replied, "His was black. And Booth shaved it off the night he stopped at Dr. Mudd's."

"My God!" Luther Baker exclaimed. "We got the wrong man!" He raced from the boat to order a fresh mount. "I'm going back to Garrett's farm!"[17]

"Wait for us!" Andrew called.

Within an hour, the three detectives were galloping through the night. As they neared the farm, Baker slowed his foam-flecked mount. "I'm after a pair of field glasses the dead man may have had with him." Luther knew, through the gossipy Weichmann, that Mrs. Surratt had taken a pair of glasses to John Lloyd's Tavern in a package that he assumed was for Booth. If Booth had picked up the glasses on his escape route, Luther thought, and if he could find them at the Garretts, he might still be able to claim it was indeed Booth the trooper had killed in the barn.

The Potters didn't question Baker's motive for seeking the field glasses as they roused the family out of bed.

"We're looking for the identity of the man who was shot here this morning," Andrew told the Garretts.

"He told us his name was Boyd. Captain J. W Boyd of the Confederate Army.[18]

The Potters walked out onto the porch. "It's easy enough to see what happened, Andy," Luther Potter said. "The troops have taken Boyd and Herold, thinking they had Booth and Herold."[19]

"Too bad neither you nor I had ever seen Boyd," Andrew said. "Obviously it's not Booth's body on board.

247

There's nothing more we can do here. Let's find Luther Baker and see if he's ready to go back to Washington with us."

Baker had finished searching the house without a warrant, but he found no field glasses.

The three men walked down the hallway. Baker stopped in front of the hall closet and tapped the door. "What's in here?"

"Winter coats," Mrs. Garrett replied.

Baker opened the door and caught the smell of stored garments. He closed the door and walked out of the house. As the Potter brothers followed, the rare LaRoix watch in the dead man's vest tapped out the hour. But no one was there to feel or hear it.

When the detectives reached the capital, they found the city in complete bedlam. Stories in the newspapers and by word of mouth were fantastic, including the report that Booth and Herold had been traveling together.[20]

As they rode toward their Pennsylvania Avenue headquarters, Andrew sighed. "I sure wish we didn't have to tell Lafe Baker that's not Booth's body."

"Impossible!" Lafayette Baker said. "That's impossible! Conger was there, and he personally reported to me. . . . Oh, Good Lord!"[21]

"What is it?" Andrew asked.

"Herold was with him! He knew Booth! They were smugglers together. And now he's a prisoner. . . ."

"Yes," Luther Potter said. "Herold can testify that it wasn't Booth with him in the barn! In fact, he told some of the officers at the farm that the man was Boyd."

"He must never testify to that fact."

"But there'll be an inquest, there'll be a trial. . . ."

"He will never testify." Baker turned toward the door. "Wait'll Stanton hears!"

Lafe Baker went alone to see the Secretary of War.

Stanton jumped up and thrust his face up to Baker. "What're you trying to do to me, Baker?" Stanton roared. "How could they have shot Boyd?"

"You know the answer to that," Baker said loudly. "You ordered Boyd released from prison yourself. You released him.

"You know Boyd and Herold escaped Tuesday night a week ago. Lt. Doherty, Luther Baker, and Lt. Col. Conger picked up Boyd's trail and followed him to Garrett's farm. No one there had ever seen Booth. Boyd was shot because they thought he was Booth."

Stanton collapsed heavily into his chair, his voice a whisper. "This is a disaster! A disaster. We've already announced the death of Booth to the press. We'll be a laughingstock—a laughingstock!"

Baker's anger met the Secretary's. "There's something else you should know."

"My God! What now?"

"David Herold was with Boyd, and he's going on about the corpse not being Booth. He said that at the farm, and he'll be telling that to anybody who'll listen."

Stanton sputtered. "Herold's talking? What're you standing there for? Stop him! Stop him right now!"

Baker yelled, "I could stop him for now! But how're you going to stop him forever?"

Stanton said softly, "I'll see that Herold does not talk. Get him in isolation at once. Isolate all the prisoners."

Baker was doubtful. "I still don't see . . ."

"I'll take care of those details! In the meantime, we've got Booth to think about." He began snapping his stubby fingers. "It's very plain. If we let the country believe Booth is dead, well . . . Booth will be dead."

Baker blinked.

"Booth will be forgotten if we continue to let the nation believe he's dead. If we admit we killed Boyd by mistake, and continue the hunt for Booth, he might be captured alive . . . and talk. . . ."[22]

Stanton's face brightened. He smiled and extended his right hand. "Col. Baker, congratulations on the killing of John Wilkes Booth!"

Chapter 22

IDENTITY CRISIS

The corpse of the man everyone called John Wilkes Booth was placed on the deck of the *Montauk,* anchored at the Navy Yard in Washington next to the *Saugus.*[1] Both ironclads were used as prisons.

A terse telegram was sent by Com. J. B. Montgomery, Commandant, to Secretary of War Stanton on Thursday, April 27: "David E. Herold, prisoner, and the remains of J. Wilkes Booth, delivered at 1:45 this morning. The body of Booth is changing rapidly. What disposition should be made of it?"[2]

A reply was sent that day. "You will allow no persons on board the *Montauk* unless under the joint pass of the Secretary of War and Secretary of the Navy."[3] An unprecedented stipulation.

An Identification Commission was ordered. It was headed by Stanton's aide, Thomas Eckert. Other commissioners included Surgeon General Barnes and his assistant; Judge Advocate Joseph Holt; the honorable John A. Bingham, special judge advocate; William G. Moore, Stanton's personal secretary; NDP chief Lafayette Baker and his cousin, Luther Baker; Lt. Col. Everton Conger; a man by the name of J. L. Smith; photographer Alexander Gardner; his assistant, Timothy H. O'Sullivan, and Charles Dawson, a clerk at the National Hotel.[4]

The mock inquest would formally identify Boyd's body as that of Booth.

Witnesses summoned aboard the *Montauk* had one lack

in common: none knew Booth well. None of Booth's relatives or accused conspirators were called, although most were in custody on the adjacent *Saugus*.

One by one, the government witnesses stepped forward across the deck to the shade of a huge canopy which had been rigged over the body lying on a long, narrow table. Brig. Gen. Holt, Judge Advocate General of the U.S. Army, was charged with recording the questions and answers.[5]

Vague witnesses included Seaton Munroe, a lawyer whose qualifications for identifying Booth were not recorded. Did he recognize the victim before him?

"Only by close inspection of the features," he replied. "I am confident that it is the dead body of J. Wilkes Booth."[6]

Charles Dawson said he had often seen Booth sign the register at the National Hotel. The clerk identified the body by the initials J.W.B.

None of the witnesses were surprised that the face had a mustache, since apparently none had been told that Booth had shaved off his mustache at Dr. Mudd's on Easter Sunday.

Two days before the inquest, when Doherty had shown William Rollins a photo of the actor, the ferryman had replied, "That's the man who crossed. I recognize him all right, except that he's shaved off his mustache."[7]

The government cover-up needed a witness of impeccable qualification to identify the body. A summons was sent to Dr. John Franklin May. Some time before, a man identifying himself as Booth had come to the physician's office for removal of a neck growth.[8]

Dr. May ignored the Identification Commission's first summons; it showed no authority. A short time later, a second and more explicit message came, directing the doctor to appear before the commission. As Dr. May left his home, a third message arrived in the person of Lafayette Baker himself.

Escorted on board the *Montauk*, Dr. May was asked preliminary questions before viewing the body. How long had he known Booth?

"I was acquainted with him. I cannot with exactness give the date, but I should say 18 months or two years ago."

Dr. May gave the details of his treatment. He had removed a neck tumor. Before the wound healed, it was torn open and Dr. May had again treated it.[9]

Barnes ordered the covering removed from the dead man's face.

At once, Dr. May exclaimed, "There's no resemblance in that corpse to Booth, nor can I believe it to be him."[10]

Wrong answer. The doctor now began to realize the significance of the three summonses and the personal appearance of the NDP chief.

The physician asked, "Is there a scar on the back of the neck?" Dr. May described the scar, location, and general appearance.

Surgeon General Barnes said smoothly, "You've described the scar as well as if you were looking at it."

In Dr. May's verbal and written statement, there is no mention that he actually examined the scar for positive identification, and the bullet, of course, had made a bloody mess of Boyd's neck.[11]

Dr. May asked to have the body turned. Looking down at the body, which had been raised to a sitting position, Dr. May admitted in a troubled voice, "I am enabled, imperfectly, to recognize the features of Booth."

Did he recognize the body as Booth's?

"I do recognize it, although it is very much altered since I saw Booth. It seems much older and in appearance, much more freckled than he was. I do not recollect that he was at all freckled."

Booth was 28, famous for his ivory, perfect skin, free of blemish. Boyd, on the other hand, was 43, with reddish-sandy hair and a tendency to freckle.

The doctor added, "I have no doubt it is his body."

The recorder included that remark in the same paragraph in which Dr. May stated that he did not recollect that Booth was at all freckled.[12]

"From the nature of this wound, even apart from the

general appearance, you could not be mistaken as to the identity of the body?"

The recorder noted the doctor's answer. However, it was carefully altered by some government official before it was released. "Wound" was struck out and the word "scar" written above.

The next half dozen words of Dr. May's reply were carefully inked out, new words added. "In connection with this" was written above the words, "I also recognize the features, which, though much changed and altered, still have the same appearance." A caret or insertion mark, between those words and the next in the line was inserted above the words, "I think I cannot be mistaken."[13]

The record of the doctor's reply in another phonographer's hand, states, "I recognize the features. I have no doubt that it is the person from whom I took the tumor, and that it is the body of J. Wilkes Booth."[14]

The coerced physician was finally dismissed. Dr. May went home and penned a letter and a statement. To a relative, Dr. May wrote, "The mustache was so long and untrimmed that the hairs curled into the nose."[15]

In his statement, Dr. May declared, "Never in a human being had a greater change taken place from the man whom I had seen in the vigor of life and health than that of the haggard corpse which was before me with its yellow and discolored skin, its unkempt and matted hair, and its facial expression, sunken and chapped by the exposure and starvation it had undergone.

"The *right* limb was greatly contused and perfectly black from a fracture of one of the long bones of the leg."[16]

Booth had snapped the *left* tibia, about two inches above the ankle. Dr. Mudd's formal statement on April 21, 1865 read, "On examination, I found there was a straight fracture of the tibia about two inches above the ankle."[17]

The government mockery ended.

There were similarities between Booth and Boyd, some quite startling. Both had identical initials on one of their hands or wrists. A resemblance in facial characteristics was evident in comparative photographs. Both men were approximately the same height and weight. Each had a leg injury.

Before the body was disposed of, the well-known photographer, Alexander Gardner, was motioned forward and told to make only one plate. He was escorted by James A. Wardell, a War Department detective.[18] Wardell stood where he could observe Gardner every moment aboard the *Montauk*.

Gardner carefully slipped the lens cover from his camera, exposing the wet glass plate inside. When he had covered the lens, Wardell quickly escorted Gardner off the ironclad and to the darkroom, explaining, "I'm required not to leave your side until the plate is developed. You're to turn the plate over to me." Wardell watched the glass plate developed and the picture printed, then took possession of what amounted to the negative and the positive. It would be impossible for anyone else to duplicate the picture.

After Wardell studied the photograph, he commented, "Looks just like the pictures of Booth on the posters, except the hair is longer on the sides. The mustache is shaggy. There's a growth on the chin."[19]

Lafe Baker immediately confiscated the picture and plate.

Later, when Wardell was asked about the picture, he said, "I think it was Booth."[20]

The government officially denied that any picture had been taken of the corpse. But the Gardner photograph later ended up in the personal possession of Secretary of War Stanton.[21]

Lafe Baker called in cousin Luther. "The Secretary of War wishes me to dispose of 'Booth's' body. He does not want the Rebs to get it and make an ado over it. He does not care where it is put, only let it be where it won't be found until Gabriel blows his last trumpet."[22] The NDP chief paused. "Luther, I want you to come with me."

The cousins continued to the *Montauk*. As thousands of spectators watched from the shore, the two men placed

Boyd's body in a rowboat with a heavy ball and chain for sinking it to the river's bottom. A sailor scrambled in to help row. The cousins followed. Oars rattled in the locks, and the boat pushed off from the ironclad. Half rowing, half drifting, it moved down the Potomac.

The crowd followed the rowboat's progress until it arrived at a fork of the East Branch where marshy ground prevented spectators going farther.

Darkness came on quickly. On this moonless night, the boat halted two miles downstream at Geeseborough Point where the stream widened. Rushes and river weeds grew profusely.

"Far enough," Lafe Baker whispered.

The boat was run into a cover near the bank. "Rest your oars. I don't think any boats trying to follow us will come to this slaughtering ground."

Luther Baker knew what his cousin meant. Condemned government horses were regularly brought to this point and killed. It was an eerie place of stinking horse carcasses and putrid backwater.

A terrible silence descended. The stench of rotting flesh assailed their nostrils. The splash of feeding carrion fish occasionally broke the silence.

In a little while, the boat moved slowly out into the stream again and toward the grim old Arsenal Penitentiary walls.

"A few more strokes," Lafe Baker puffed, "and ease off in front of the door."

"Door?" Luther whispered. "All I can see is solid wall."

"It's almost at the water's edge. The officer in charge is waiting for us."

The boat grated against the stone walls. A massive door creaked open, and a man reached out to grab the craft's rope.

"Lift the body out first," Lafe Baker commanded.

The three rowers scrambled out of the boat when the corpse rested inside the doorway. The door closed. A lantern was lit. Arms lifted the body and bore it through echoing halls. Rats scampered ahead of them. The officer led the way through a little door into a convict's cell, the lantern casting shadows on the grimy walls.

"Careful," the prison official said. "The stone slab in the floor has been lifted. There's a grave dug."

Watching their footing on the slippery stone floor, the four men centered the body over the hole and dumped it into the blackness below.

"Give me a hand with this stone."

Lafe Baker sighed with satisfaction. "Now let anybody try to find the corpse."

A few minutes later, the lantern was extinguished. The heavy door groaned open, and three men stepped into the boat. The prison door closed.

The men began to row, leaving the Arsenal Prison, the sepulchre for the mortal remains of the man who had become "John Wilkes Booth."[23]

With the body of James Boyd disposed of, Lafe Baker called in the 26 detectives who had worked on the case.

"Men, Booth's body has been identified. The case is closed. In order that all claims for the reward be orderly, the War Department has decided to pay all you detectives who worked on the case a little something extra, a special reward."

There were pleased exclamations.

"This will be paid," the chief continued, "in return for a quitclaim."[24]

"What's that?"

"It means," Lafe Baker said, "that the chase is over. Booth's dead. You can go onto other assignments as soon as each of you signs this sheet of paper saying you have no further interest in the Booth case."

The operatives lined up and filed past Earl Potter. As each man signed, he was handed an envelope.

Andrew Potter, the last detective in line, scrawled his signature. His half brother handed him an envelope.

Andrew felt the contents with satisfaction. "Is mine the biggest or the smallest, Earl?"

Earl grinned, "Neither."

When Andrew counted the cash in the envelope, it added up to $5,000.

The hunt for Booth had officially ended. But Andrew

Potter and Lafe Baker were not through searching for the living John Wilkes Booth.

Chapter 23

CONSPIRACY TO COVER UP CONSPIRACY

On May 1, 1865, President Andrew Johnson issued an order: "Whereas the Attorney General of the United States has given his opinion that the persons implicated in the murder of the late President, Abraham Lincoln, and the attempted assassination of the Hon. William H. Seward, Secretary of State, . . . are subject to the jurisdiction of and legally triable before a military commission. . . ."[1]

The Assistant Adjutant General was to detail nine competent military officers to serve as trial commissioners.

The legality of a military court martial for civilians was then before the U.S. Supreme Court in the case of Lambdin P. Milligan. It was apparent to Stanton and the other government officials in the cover-up that they must rush the military trial of the accused Booth conspirators before the high court ruled, for the judges seemed certain to support Milligan and to declare military tribunals illegal for civilians when civil courts were functioning.

Milligan, an Indiana civilian, had been arrested in 1864 by military officers, charged with pacifist, anti-war activities, conspiracy against the government, aiding and comforting the enemy, and inciting rebellion. Tried by military authorities, his lawyer had pled in a federal circuit court that his client had been deprived of his constitutional right to trial by jury.[2]

Although President Johnson had announced that Attorney General James Speed had given his opinion that military trial for civilians was legal, no written opinion was offered.[3]

Edward Bates, the nation's retired chief law officer,

scoffed at Speed's ruling: "I am pained to be led to believe that my successor, Attorney General Speed, has been wheedled out of an opinion to the effect that such a trial is lawful. If he be, in the lowest degree, qualified for his office, he must know better."[4]

The government announced the members of the "Court of Military Justice." Bias was evident. Whispers swept through Washington. "The Court of Military Injustice has been organized to convict" became a derisive joke.

Through the chain of command, each commissioner named was under orders to Secretary of War Stanton. Several judges had close and obvious ties to Stanton or Lincoln.[5]

Maj. Gen. David Hunter was to be the presiding officer. Stanton's close friend, he had once been sent by the War Secretary to spy on Gen. Grant's drinking habits. Hunter had also been Lincoln's good friend.[6]

Lew Wallace was the second major general named. On May 2, his bias was shown in an order at Baltimore that "the sale of portraits of any Rebel officer or soldier, or of J. Wilkes Booth . . . is forbidden. . . ."[7]

Other commissioners included Maj. Gen. August V. Kautz, Brig. Gen. Alvin P. Howe, Brig. Gen. Robert S. Foster, Brig. Gen. T. H. Harris, Brevet Brig. Gen. James A. Ekin, Brevet Col. C. H. Tompkins, and Lt. Col. David R. Clendenin.[8]

Brig. Gen. Harris' personal opinion of Dr. Mudd typified the attitude of the commissioners and their incompetence to hear the case. "He had the appearance of a natural born liar and deceiver."[9]

The nine judges were to be aided further in their assignment by the government's choice of those to lead the attack against the defendants.

Brig. Gen. Joseph Holt was to be judge advocate and recorder, to act as prosecutor and keep the official court records. He was to be assisted by John A. Bingham and Gen. Henry L. Burnett. Brevet Maj. Gen. John F. Hartranft was special provost marshal, or head of the military police handling the prisoners.

Holt was a native of Kentucky, a lawyer who had been

Postmaster General under Buchanan. He was a long time associate of Stanton. Lincoln had appointed Holt Judge Advocate General of the United States Army.[10]

Burnett, also of Ohio, had been judge advocate in "treason" trials in the west. He had gained notoriety for his conviction in the Milligan case, which had brought him to Stanton's attention. He was a man who knew how to get a military court to convict civilians. Burnett also would rule on which objections to sustain or to overrule.[11]

Although the government's case had been building, specifications and charges had not yet been given the prisoners. The charge then being secretly drawn by the government against Lewis Payne. George Atzerodt, David E. Herold, Dr. Samuel Mudd, Samuel Arnold, Michael O'Laughlin, Edward Spangler, and Mrs. Mary E. Surratt was "for maliciously, unlawfully and traitorously, and in the aid of the existing armed rebellion against the United States of America, on or before the 6th day of March, A.D., 1865, and on divers other days between that day and the 15th of April, A.D., 1865, combining, confederating, and conspiring together . . ."[12] with Booth, John Surratt and members of the Confederacy.

There was no mention of kidnapping. The charge was to be murder of Lincoln and "combining, confederating, and conspiring" to murder Andrew Johnson, William H. Seward, and Ulysses S. Grant. Additional charges of "lying in wait with intent" to kill Johnson and Grant were also to be levied.[13] The defendants were under the further handicap of not being able to obtain lawyers to represent them. And there was no higher court to which they could appeal.

Maj. Thomas Eckert had dealings with only one prisoner, the giant Payne. On April 22, Eckert wrote Lafe Baker: "I questioned the traitor who admits having gone to the Navy Yard on the 20th instant and that he was present when Booth purchased the carbine which was used by Booth to shoot at the President on the evening of 22nd of March.

"He states that after Booth fired, he fired twice and that

259

John Surratt ran away. He said that Booth purchased the carbine for $5 at the Navy Yard from a man named Wakefield or Wakeley.

"He refused to identify any of the members of the conspiracy to kidnap the President on March 16th, 18th, 19th or 20th. He admits he was present on three occasions.

"Given some time, I might yet obtain the confession you seek."[14]

There were suspicions that the powerful Maj. Eckert had tried to beat a confession out of Payne.

Part of Lafayette Baker's job was to get statements from the various participants in the chase that had ended in Boyd's death. Baker assigned Everton Conger, who ran into some problems, but solved them in a typical secret service way. On May 2, 1865, he wrote, "Colonel Baker, I have directed each detective, officer and private soldier who took part in the pursuit, capture and death of Wilkes Booth to prepare a written statement concerning those events and to submit the statements to myself.

"Some of these statements upon receipt I found wanting. I found it necessary to add to the narrative in some statements and to rewrite others.

"Lt. Doherty and [Lt. David] Dana presented some difficulty. However, I was able to convince them of the necessity involved.

"Each man seems concerned with the size of each reward and his portion of that and little else.

"Having now completed the task, I am forwarding them to you."[15]

The massive government cover-up continued.

Col. Baker called Luther and Andrew Potter into his office. Their older brother, Earl, was already there. The Colonel said, "There's been too many reports that Booth has actually escaped. We need to get on top of this situation."

Although Andrew had been paid $5,000 to give up the chase, he could see that new orders would override the quitclaim he'd signed.

"I want you to follow up reports of the two men and a darkie who went through Orange Court House by way of Fredericksburg."

"You mean, pick up where we left off the morning we heard about the shooting at Garrett's?" Andrew asked.

"Exactly. Go back there and see what you can find."

"The trail's cold."

"Not too cold, we trust," Baker said. "Draw what you need in the way of supplies and move out."

On the way toward Fredericksburg, Andrew asked, "Luther, what happens if we run into Booth?"

"We should've asked Lafe Baker that before we left Washington. Way I see it, we were assigned to pick up Booth's trail if we can. I figure if we get him, then it becomes Lafe's problem, and Stanton's."

At Orange Court House, Andrew and Luther Potter did pick up Booth's trail.[16]

"Yes, suh," a black man told them, "Ah remembers them. They spent de night at my house. This heah one," he said, tapping the Booth photograph, "paid me $5. Gold, too."

The Potter brothers pushed on toward Stanardsville.

A store owner confirmed that the three men had come through on Friday, April 28.[17] "They spent the night in that barn," the merchant said, pointing. "Before they left they bought some canned food, a ham, and a bushel of oats."

The detectives followed Booth's trail to Lydia where a widow told them the men had spent the night of Saturday, April 29, at her place.[18] "They gave me a ham."

The trail now vanished, although the Potters could not doubt that John Wilkes Booth was very much alive. So were Ed Henson and Booth's former valet, Henry Johnson.

While the Potter brothers tried to pick up further clues, and the government prepared for trial, the accused conspirators were undergoing cruel and unusual punishment.

On April 23, jailers had received strange instructions: "The Secretary of War requests that the prisoners on board the ironclads belonging to this department, for better security against conversation, shall have a canvas bag put over the head of each and tied about the neck, with a hole for proper breathing and eating, but not seeing, and that Payne be secured to prevent self-destruction."[19]

Stanton had imagination as a torturer.

The bags were padded with one inch thick cotton. A ball of extra cotton padding covered the prisoners' eyes to cause painful pressure on the closed eye lids.[20] Sight and sound were cut off, a mental torture that never ceased for the devices were to be worn 24 hours a day.

Mrs. Surratt alone escaped the hood and "leg irons" which tortured the seven male prisoners, who were also restrained by stiff-shackles, a form of handcuff with a solid iron bar between. It was impossible to move one hand independently from the other. The shackles were also designed to give pain. In addition, Payne was shackled with a heavy iron ball and chain about his ankles. He had gone for weeks without footwear.[21]

Dr. George Loring Porter, prison physician, was concerned for the prisoners' sanity and complained to Stanton.[22]

"The brutality with which the prisoners are being treated must be modified, Mr. Secretary," said Dr. Porter. "The constant pressure of those thickly padded hoods may induce insanity."

The Secretary of War looked coldly at the physician as Dr. Porter continued, "The hot summer weather is coming on. The lack of proper sanitary facilities, such as bathing, contributes to their suffering. They also need daily exercise."

Stanton indicated that the suffering would be alleviated. But he did not order any relief.

Except for Mrs. Surratt who was sent to Old Capitol Prison, the prisoners were later transferred from the iron-clads to the Arsenal Penitentiary on the old arsenal grounds and placed in different cells and on different levels. "Each prisoner virtually occupies three cells. That is, there is a vacant cell on each side of the one occupied by a prisoner."[23] Placed thusly between empty cells to prevent communication by knocking or rapping, the silence of the hoods was further aggravated by isolation.

William E. Doster, an attorney, said Mrs. Surratt had been suffering from a change of life sickness and at Old Capitol "her cell, by reason of her sickness, was scarcely habitable."[24]

All the prisoners had been denied the most basic sanitary needs.

Thomas B. Florence, editor of *The Daily Constitutional Union,* described Mrs. Surratt, who had been arrested in April when the weather was cool and she still wore winter clothing: "She was confined to an inner cell of the prison, the dimensions of which were about seven feet long and three feet wide. It had a stone floor, stone walls and an iron-grated door.

"Its only furnishings consisted of a very thin straw mattress, an army blanket and an old pail. She had neither washing utensils, nor a chair to sit in, nor a single comfort for her toilet or dress.

"A year or so previous to her incarceration she had been cured of a serious private malady. She had not been sitting on that cold stone floor but for three or four days when it was brought on again with redoubled violence."[25] Mrs. Surratt began to hemorrhage.

The plight of Mrs. Surratt finally moved Col. William P. Wood to compassion. As superintendent of Old Capitol Prison, he intervened with his friend, Stanton, on her behalf. With Stanton's authority, Wood made a deal to spare Mrs. Surratt if she cooperated in giving certain information. She furnished information about possible places Booth might have taken refuge in exchange for promises of leniency.[26]

Stanton had no intention of keeping this promise. As soon as he had what he wanted, he promptly had Mrs. Surratt transferred from Wood's charge at Old Capitol Prison and put into the unscrupulous hands of Lafe Baker, who sent her to the Arsenal Penitentiary where the rest of the conspirators were housed.

David Herold was also offered a deal, and cooperated with the Secretary of War. The naive Herold had no idea he was in mortal danger; he trusted Stanton's word.

Technically, the prisoners were allowed visitors. Actually, they were denied even religious counselors. Arnold was to say later, "Some kind Christian heart provided us with Bibles, from which some consolation could be obtained by the perusal of its pages, but these were soon removed and taken away."[27]

To see a prisoner, a pass had to be signed by Stanton and Secretary of the Navy Welles.[28] There were no visitors.

Except for Dr. Porter, no one except the guards were allowed to see the accused, and even they were strictly forbidden to converse with them. An infantry company, constantly on duty, was placed so that each guard could be seen in front of the cells.[29]

As the coolness of April gave way to a hot, humid May, the airless, prison cells became almost intolerable.

Other prisoners were treated far less harshly. Most of them had been confined because they were related to or acquainted with one or more of the defendants. A cousin, at whose home George Atzerodt had been arrested, was held. As were Asia Booth and her husband, John Sleeper Clarke; Isaac Surratt, just returned from the war in Texas; Anna Surratt, the teenage daughter of the widow, and the entire cast of "Our American Cousin." Hundreds of innocent citizens from lower Maryland were also in custody.[30] Most were released after several days of confinement.

Two prisoners turned state's evidence to save their lives. Louis Weichmann was held in solitary confinement at Carroll Prison after accompanying Superintendent of Police Richards on a fruitless search in Canada for John Surratt and Booth.[31]

James J. Gifford, confined with Weichmann, said: "I heard an officer of the government tell Weichmann that unless he testifies to more than he already had, they would hang him."[32] A detective placed in Weichmann's cell wrote out a statement that he claimed Weichmann had made in his sleep, and demanded the prisoner swear to it. "Sign it, or face prosecution as one of the conspirators."[33]

A Col. Foster demanded that John Lloyd—Mrs. Surratt's drunken tenant at Surrattsville—make a statement.

"Do you know what you're guilty of, Lloyd?" the colonel demanded.

"Under the circumstances, I don't think so."

"You're guilty as an accessory to the crime, the punishment of which is death."

The tenant protested he had already made a statement to a Col. Wells at Bryantown.

Col. Foster shoved the new statement before Lloyd with the explanation that the first "is not full enough."

Earlier Lloyd, an alcoholic, had been denied liquor for 48 hours and hung by his thumbs.[34] Ready to swear to anything, he had turned state's evidence.

Lloyd and Weichmann's testimony was primarily intended to ensure that Mrs. Surratt would die on the gallows—the first woman in the history of the United States to hang.

Further to assure the success of the cover-up, a school for perjury was set up in Washington's National Hotel where witnesses were coached on how to testify for the government against the defendants.

Several witnesses with unsavory backgrounds were to be paid for offering certain perjured testimony. The first witness was to be Richard Montgomery, a Union spy who had also taken money from the Confederacy. The double agent was to say on the witness stand that Jacob Thompson, Rebel Secret Service Chief in Canada, had told him that Lincoln was to be "put out of the way." In January 1865, Montgomery was to add, Thompson had also said "that a proposition had been made . . . to rid the world of the tyrant Lincoln, Stanton, Grant and some others." Those involved were, "bold, daring men, and able to execute anything they would undertake without regard to cost."[35]

There was a danger in this, for the Union government would be shown by the testimony to have known about the conspiracy in January 1865 and to have taken no safeguards.[36] But the court was so stacked against the defendants that this point could be easily overcome.

Dr. James B. Merritt of Canada was to be the second

Union witness. On April 21, Gen. James B. Fry, Provost Marshal General of the United States, had sent Dr. Merritt a message: "The Secretary of War authorizes me to pledge your protection and security, and to pay all expenses connected with your journey both ways, and in addition to promise a suitable reward if reliable and useful information is furnished."[37]

Within a few days after Merritt arrived in the United States, the Canadian government warned the War Department that Merritt had an unsavory medical practice and was known as a Secession sympathizer. Still, the U.S. government was to put Merritt on the stand to testify that he had heard various Rebel agents in Canada damn Lincoln as a tyrant and declare that he would never serve out a second term if re-elected. For his perjury, Merritt was to be paid $6,000.[38]

Sanford Conover, who used various aliases, was to claim he was a newspaper correspondent for the New York *Tribune* and had, through contacts with Confederate agents, learned of plots to burn certain Northern cities, to poison municipal water supplies, and to spread yellow fever in the North by use of "infected clothing." Furthermore, Conover was to say under oath that he had learned of assassination plans in February 1865, and had notified his newspaper.[39]

There would be other government witnesses, too, such as Henry Von Steineker, who had "heard Booth discussing assassination details with Stonewall Jackson's officers while he was a member of the rebel forces."[40]

The government's principal witnesses were to be Conover, Merritt and Montgomery. The prosecution was so sure that perjury of these principal witnesses was safe from discovery that Judge Advocate Holt met with Stanton just before the military tribunal convened.

"I've just spoken with each of the commission members," Holt began. "Each believes the conspirators are guilty beyond doubt."[41]

The War Secretary nodded.

"But," Holt continued, "they feel the trial is necessary

266

in following the military method of hearing the evidence and following the code."[42]

Stanton stroked his perfumed beard. "Anything else, Gen. Holt?"

"Yes, Mr. Secretary. You can be assured that the commission will not allow the conspirators' attorneys to impeach the testimony of Conover, Merritt, or Montgomery in any matter whatever."[43]

The Secretary of War favored the general with a pleased smile. "Gen. Holt," he said, "I believe the government is ready for the trial of the conspirators to begin."

Chapter 24

TRAVESTY OF JUSTICE

The preliminary proceedings of the trial began May 8, 1865, when official charges and specifications were delivered to eight defendants: Herold, Atzerodt, Payne, Spangler, O'Laughlin, Arnold, Mrs. Surratt, and Dr. Mudd.[1]

The prisoners' counsel was to furnish the government with an advance list of witnesses. The rules added, "Counsel may have access to them [the prisoners] in the presence . . . of a guard."[2]

Lawyers also faced a remarkable handicap imposed by Attorney General Speed's opinion favoring a military trial for civilians. The tribunal was based on "the Laws of War." Former Attorney General Edward Bates, whose opinion no longer counted, noted, "There is no such thing as the Laws of War."

A defense attorney said of the Laws, "They mean whatever the court wants them to mean."[3]

At 10 a.m. on the morning of Tuesday, May 9, the military commissioners filed into the second-story courtroom inside the old Arsenal Penitentiary. The nine judges in their blue uniforms took seats at a long table. The judge advocate sat to the left of the commissioner's table.[4]

The eight prisoners shuffled in and hobbled, in manacles and leg restraints, to chairs on a raised platform.

"Do the defendants wish to employ counsel?"

They did.

"They may have until 10 o'clock tomorrow morning to do so."

The prisoners were led out.

There had been enough time to see what their courtroom was like—a grim, austere place which the humidity and oppressive heat of the coming summer would make more and more unbearable as the trial wore on.

As the trial began, Jefferson Davis was seized at Irwinsville near Macon, Georgia, but the ex-President of the Confederate States of America was not rushed back to stand trial with the eight defendants, although his name was to be read that day as one of the co-conspirators.[5]

At 10 on Wednesday morning, May 10, the trial officially began. The defendants had had only two days' notice of the charges against them. The prosecution had been preparing its case for weeks. Not all the prisoners had been able to obtain counsel.

The court had relaxed its ruling, allowing the press to be present on opening day. Benn Pitman, the official court reporter, began to take notes in shorthand. So did newspaper reporter T. P. Peterson, whose work was not subject to scrutiny by the judges, as Pitman's was.[6]

The male prisoners, except for Dr. Mudd, were stiff-shackled. Mudd wore handcuffs joined by a chain so he could move one hand independently of the other. Mrs. Surratt's hands were free.

Atzerodt, as well as Payne, was restrained by heavy iron balls which required two guards to lift each ball from the floor.

Andrew J. Rogers, Representative from New Jersey, was to comment later, ". . . Since the trial of Cranbourne in 1696 . . . no prisoner has ever been tried in irons before a legitimate court anywhere that English is spoken."[7]

Newspaper reporter Peterson described the prisoners.[8] Dr. Mudd looked calm, collected, and attentive. He leaned on the railing as if to relieve his wrists from the weight of his handcuffs.

Arnold was restless, raising his hand to his hair with a nervous twitching. He constantly glanced from face to face, then bowed his head to his hands.

Payne, dressed in grey woollen shirt and dark pants, seemed intent on trying to obtain a full view of the sunny landscape through the barred windows. "As he looked, a strange, restless dreaminess pervaded his face. His long dark hair, irregularly parted, hung over his forehead and often clouded his dark blue eyes. His thick, somewhat protruding lips were as if glued together," Peterson reported.

"O'Laughlin was observant of every move in the court. He leaned back, with his head against the wall . . .

"Atzerodt, a man five-feet-six or seven inches in height, might have been taken, had it not been for his manacles, as a mere spectator.

"Mrs. Surratt . . . is a stout, buxom widow . . . fair, fat and forty, although it is ascertained she is far beyond that period of life."[9]

The proceedings began with a reading of the presidential order convening the commission. The prisoners were asked if they had any objections to any member of the commission. They replied that they did not. What good would it have done to antagonize the court?

The court reporters, judges, and the advocate general with his assistants were fully sworn. The prisoners were arraigned. For the first time, the charges were read to them. There was a frightening implication in that kidnapping of Lincoln was not mentioned; the charge was treason and murder.[10]

Each prisoner entered a plea of "not guilty."

The defendants were told they had the right to an attorney, but they must supply such counsel; the government would not. Many lawyers had flatly refused to represent the accused. Edward Spangler had no counsel for the first three days of trial.[11]

On the defense team, some of the lawyers had to represent more than one client, with whom they could only confer in open court. In each case, arguments for the defense had to be formulated on the spot. A civilian court would have provided the accused with a copy of the charges in advance.

Mrs. Surratt had the best lawyer, Reverdy Johnson, a U.S. senator in 1845, U.S. Attorney General in 1849, and now a Maryland senator. He was such a formidable opponent, it was immediately apparent to the prosecution that he must be removed.[12] Johnson was to be assisted by Frederick Aiken and John W. Clampitt, each in practice only one year and each trying his first big case. Clampitt was 24, Aiken even younger.[13]

Mrs. Mudd had managed to get Gen. Thomas Ewing, Jr., as her husband's principal attorney. Ewing's presence was an unwelcome surprise to the prosecution. He was a war veteran and brother-in-law to the Union's famous Gen. William T. Sherman. Frederick Stone was to be Dr. Mudd's junior counsel.[14]

Atzerodt was defended by William E. Doster and Walter S. Cox. Spangler finally got Gen. Ewing to represent him. Herold obtained Stone's services, Arnold had Gen. Ewing and Cox, as did O'Laughlin. Payne was represented by Doster.[15]

The seven attorneys were to make on the spot defenses for eight defendants, an incredible burden.

On Friday, May 12, the prosecution immediately moved against Reverdy Johnson. Gen. T.M. Harris objected to Sen. Johnson on the grounds the Marylander "did not recognize the moral obligation of an oath of loyalty" to the government.[16]

Having anticipated the challenge, Johnson promptly presented the certificate of allegiance required of U.S. senators. Gen. Lew Wallace observed that this should suffice as evidence. Reluctantly, Harris withdrew his objection, and Johnson was allowed to proceed. But the continued attacks on his integrity and the obvious fact that the tribunal was compromised, caused Johnson finally to step down. He turned Mrs. Surratt's defense over to his younger, inexperienced colleagues.

The overworked, overburdened, and under prepared defense attorneys found the court required defense witnesses to face the judges. Questions had to be asked from behind, without seeing the face of the witnesses, who were under the court's stern eye.

The government's case proceeded smoothly as the days grew hotter. The ventilation of the courtroom became worse. The humidity taxed manacled prisoners and other participants without distinction. Anguished friends and relatives watched the one-sided progression. Mrs. E. W. Nelson, one of Herold's sisters, told an interviewer that "Davey had been told that if he cooperated, he would go free."[17]

John Lloyd helped convict Herold and Mrs. Surratt. "Some five or six weeks before the assassination," Lloyd testified, "John H. Surratt, David E. Herold and G.A. Atzerodt came to my house." Lloyd said John Surratt left him a rope, a monkey wrench, and two carbines with ammunition. Lloyd was asked to conceal them.

On Tuesday before the assassination, Lloyd told the court, he had met Mrs. Surratt. She had asked him about the articles. "I did not know what she had reference to," Lloyd testified. "Then she came out plainer, and asked me about the 'shooting irons.'" Lloyd claimed he had forgotten about them, but that he had hidden them well "because I was afraid the house might be searched. She told me to get them ready, that they would be wanted soon."

On April 14, Lloyd said he again saw Mrs. Surratt. "She told me to have those shooting irons ready that night, there would be some parties that would call for them." Lloyd said Mrs. Surratt gave him a wrapped package. He later peeked and saw it contained field glasses.

About midnight, Lloyd continued, "Herold came into the house and said, 'Lloyd, for God's sake, make haste and get those things!'" Booth waited outside, Lloyd said, although "he was a stranger to me." He testified that, by moonlight, he had seen "the man whose leg was broken was on a light colored horse. I supposed it to be a gray horse . . . a large horse . . . 16 hands high . . ."

Lloyd continued. As they were preparing to ride off, "the man who was with Herold said, 'I will tell you some news . . . I am pretty certain that we have assassinated the President and Secretary Seward.' "[18] Lloyd's perjury had fastened the noose around the necks of Herold and Mrs. Surratt.

Louis Weichmann pulled the hangman's rope tighter. The War Department clerk testified he had seen Booth at the Surratt boarding house on various occasions, especially on Good Friday afternoon when Mrs. Surratt and the actor talked briefly alone. Weichmann had then driven the widow, carrying two packages, to Lloyd's tavern.[19] From Lloyd's testimony, one of these packages contained field glasses.

Weichmann's testimony tied Atzerodt, Payne, Herold, and Dr. Mudd in with Booth. Also, the testimony revealed that Booth had been seen with John Surratt in the widow's boarding house.

The noose was dangled over Payne's head by Weichmann's testimony about the strongman's appearances at the Surratt place. Atzerodt's presence in the boarding house was established by Weichmann.[20]

John Lee helped convict Atzerodt when the detective testified that he had found in the defendant's room in the Kirkwood Hotel on the night of April 15, "a black coat hanging on the wall; underneath the pillow, or bolster, I found a revolver, loaded and capped."

The detective said he had also found a bankbook belonging to J. Wilkes Booth showing credit at a Montreal bank, a map of Virginia, a large Bowie knife, and other items. "The room in which these things were found was No. 126, and is on the floor above the room then occupied by Vice President Johnson."[21]

The government did not have as strong a case against Spangler, accused of helping Booth. The scene shifter had briefly held the actor's horse the night of the assassination. The 81 foot length of rope found in Spangler's carpet bag by officer Rosch was supposedly to be used to trip pursuing cavalrymen.

O'Laughlin's childhood friendship with Booth and Arnold was shown. He was known to have talked with the actor the day of the assassination, but witnesses proved O'Laughlin was with them at the time the fatal shot was fired. A statment made by O'Laughlin shortly after his arrest was not introduced. It would have shown treason on the part of some high government officials, including involvement of people in Judge Holt's office.[22]

The so called "Sam" letter, written by Samuel Arnold, was introduced in evidence against him. It was written March 27, 1865, and had veiled references to the plot. "You know full well that the G—t [government] suspicions something is going on there; therefore, the undertaking is becoming more complicated." The letter showed Arnold had pulled out of whatever plot was afoot and was writing to say he would not come in response to Booth's summons.[23]

Dr. Mudd had been identified by Weichmann as being seen with Booth. It was the government's contention that the physician had recognized Booth when he treated his broken leg. This constituted aiding the fugitive. Melvina Washington, former slave of Mudd's, claimed she had heard Dr. Mudd say that President Lincoln would not occupy his seat long.[24] It wasn't very strong evidence, but it was entered.

The arch perjurers, Montgomery, Conover, and Merritt, gave their suborned testimony. Montgomery declared, "In January of this year, I saw Jacob Thompson in Montreal several times. In one of these conversations he said a proposition had been made to him to rid the world of the tyrant Lincoln, Seward, Grant and some others." He claimed that Thompson declared he had been offered the proposition by men he knew were bold and daring, and quoted the Confederate agent as saying he favored the proposition but had decided to hold off a decision until he consulted with his government in Richmond. Montgomery also claimed that he had seen Payne in Canada talking with Thompson and rebel agent Clement C. Clay.[25]

Conover tied in Booth and John Surratt with Confederate agents in Canada. He quoted Jacob Thompson as saying, "Some of our boys are going to play a grand joke on Abe and Andy." The explanation, Conover said, was that Thompson "informed me it was to kill them, or rather, 'to remove them from office.'" He testified that the Confederate agent had explained he meant only removing them from office, but that killing of a tyrant was not murder.[26]

Merritt testified that Rebel agents in Canada had told him "'Old Abe would never be inaugurated;' that, I believe, was his expression." The witness claimed Booth's name was mentioned in connection with a plan "to engage in the undertaking to remove the President, Vice President, the cabinet, and some of the leading generals, and that there was any amount of money to accomplish the purpose."[27]

The trial stretched on toward the end of a sweltering June. The manacled prisoners sat through a total of 422 witnesses who were called and recalled.

Defense attorney Walter Cox summed up his arguments with a scathing attack on the single charge with which all prisoners had been tried. "And when we inquire by what legal code the charges are to be judged and punished," Cox declared, "we are referred to the 'Common Law of War.'

"The Common Law of War! What a convenient instrument for trampling upon every constitutional guarantee, every sacred right of the citizen! There is no invention too monstrous, no punishment too cruel, to find authority and sanction in such a common law.

"Is it possible that American citizens can be judged and punished by an unwritten code, that has no definitions, no books, no judges nor lawyer; which, if it has any existence, like the laws of the Roman Emperor, is hung up too high to be read?

"I deny that the Common Law of War has anything to do with treason; or anything traitorous, as such . . ."[28]

It was a noble sentiment, but again it was pistols against seige guns.

The testimony concluded on June 28, and the military

commission met in secret session to deliberate on the testimony.

The prisoners awaited the verdict.

The reaction against military court martial for civilians was increasingly critical. Orville H. Browning, former Illinois senator and Lincoln's very close friend, declared: "This commission is without authority, and its proceedings void. The execution of these persons will be murder."[29]

There were strong indications that the sentences would include hanging, although the belief was still widespread that the court would recommend clemency for Mrs. Surratt.

There was some curiosity about the backgrounds of government witnesses Montgomery, Conover, and Merritt. It would be some time before the truth came out—that Richard Montgomery was in reality James Thompson, a New York burglar with a long police record; that Dr. James Merritt was a fraud and a medical quack, so named by the Canadian government, and that Conover, alias James Watson Wallace, was a Charles Dunham who had secretly coached government witnesses on fictitious testimony for which they were paid. Conover would later go to prison for perjury.[30]

Defense attorney Doster had his own ideas of sentences the eight defendants would have received had they been tried according to their constitutional rights in a civil court: "Payne would either have been acquitted, on the grounds of insanity, or, if convicted, would have been sentenced to a long term in the penitentiary.

"Atzerodt would probably have been convicted, but would have received a light sentence.

"Herold would have been convicted and sent to the penitentiary for a long time."*

"Arnold, Spangler and Mudd would have been acquitted. Mrs. Surratt would have been confronted again

*Doster based this belief on incorrect information, since Herold had not been with Booth at all during the time both were fugitives. Herold had been with Capt. Boyd and no doubt would have been acquitted.

with the testimony of her tenant, Lloyd, and her boarder, Weichmann, who turned state's evidence to save their necks. The court would have been obliged to charge that they could believe these witnesses only as accomplices if they were corroborated.

"With the previous good character of the defendant, the jury would probably have regarded Mrs. Surratt's declarations as those of an embittered Southern woman, and nothing more, and acquitted her."[31]

That was civilian lawyer Doster's opinion. What counted was the military commission's decision.

On June 30, the uniformed military officers reached a verdict. It was forwarded to the War Department for review. From there, the verdict was to be sent to the President. It was suspected that he was so concerned over the rumors of his possible involvement in the Booth conspiracy that to prove his innocence, he would be more harsh than lenient. On July 5, President Johnson approved the military commission's finding and sentences, as yet unknown to the defense lawyers and defendants. The official court record stated, "David E. Herold, Lewis Payne, Mrs. Surratt and George A. Atzerodt are to be hung tomorrow, by proper military authorities.

"Dr. Mudd, Arnold and O'Laughlin are to be imprisoned for life, and Spangler for six years, all at hard labor, in the Albany Penitentiary."[32]

The prisoners were not notified of their sentences until noon of July 6, sentences which were to be carried out 24 hours later. These final hours could not go fast enough for the government conspirators.

The government was wasting no time in stilling forever the voice of David Herold, who knew the truth about Booth not being killed at Garrett's farm. But Herold was not to die alone.

Outside the prison walls, angry citizens, at last aroused to the frightening danger under which they lived, were shouting about the "judicial murder" of Mrs. Surratt.

For the convicted "conspirators," hope was all but gone. Only Mrs. Surratt might yet escape execution. To that end, her attorneys worked desperately.

Chapter 25

ALL EFFORTS FAIL

The government's cover-up seemed to be proceeding smoothly. However, a secret clemency plea for Mrs. Surratt was filed. As one of their last acts before adjourning the military commission, five officers signed a petition for leniency on her behalf.

Gens. Hunter, Kautz, Foster and Ekin, plus Col. Tompkins, signed the plea addressed to President Johnson. Although they had found the widow guilty and had pronounced the death sentence upon her as prescribed by law, "in consideration of her age and sex, the undersigned pray your Excellency . . . to commute her sentence to imprisonment for life. . . ." Gens. Wallace, Howe and Harris refused to sign, as did Brevet Col. Clendenin.[1]

The document, written by Ekin, was attached to the last leaf of the court transcript and sent to Secretary of War Stanton. Judge Holt carried the commissioners' verdict of guilty to President Johnson—the majority petition for commutation of sentence was missing.[2] Only Stanton would have dared remove the clemency plea.

Johnson signed the death sentences for Payne, Atzerodt, Herold, Mrs. Surratt, and prison sentences for the other four accused.

Mrs. Surratt's junior counselors had one recourse—a writ of *habeas corpus*. Appeal was made to have her brought before another court.[3] For the widow, that offered last minute hope. For Atzerodt, Payne and Herold, there was none.

The day the sentences were announced Col. Christian Rath assembled some of Washington's Invalid Corps. "I want four able-bodied men to volunteer for special duty."

William Coxshall, 22, was among those who stood up. With three other volunteers, Coxshall followed the colonel into the prison yard. The soldiers saw a new gallows about 20 feet square, the scaffold 12 feet high and braced by timbers. The front part of the scaffold had been divided into two traps, hinged to drop away when posts underneath were knocked out.[4] They were assigned to knock the posts out from under the traps.

For two hours, the invalids practiced their grim job. Then they dug four graves between the door through which the condemned would enter the yard and the scaffold.[5] Four pine boxes, similar to those in which guns were packed, rested between the gaping holes and the rude gallows.[6] At last the chore was completed.

On the last night of their lives the four condemned prisoners were finally allowed the comfort of clergymen. On April 23, Mrs. Surratt had written to the Rev. Jacob Ambrose Walter, a Catholic priest who had never met the widow. Father Walter arrived two days later only to be denied admittance.[7]

On the afternoon of Thursday, July 6, the priest went to Mrs. Surratt and made arrangements to give her Communion the next morning. Father Walter also accompanied Anna Surratt to the White House. Johnson's secretary, Gen. R. D. Mussey, Sen. Preston King of New York, and Sen. James H. Lane of Kansas, among others, barred the door. Vainly, the priest and the teenage girl begged for five minutes of Johnson's time. This was denied.[8]

The priest tried again. "General Mussey," he said, "tell the President that I don't ask for pardon or commutation of sentence, but I do ask for ten days' reprieve to prepare Mrs. Surratt for eternity."

The priest and Miss Surratt were referred to Judge Holt. Father Walter and the girl went to Holt, but "it was perfectly useless," Father Walter said.

Anna Surratt, her eyes streaming with tears, "was left without any sympathy from this cold, heartless man," the priest declared.[9]

278

The final night of life for the prisoners dragged on. Payne, who had seemed resigned to his fate and disdainful of the biased court, suddenly showed concern. He asked that a Baptist clergyman attend him that evening.[10]

Atzerodt couldn't think of any clergyman's name. The Rev. J. George Butler, of St. Paul's Lutheran Church in Washington, was recommended. Atzerodt spent his last night praying and weeping. Atzerodt's mother dressed in deep black carried a prayer book into his cell and wept and prayed with the carriage maker.[11]

Herold's sisters came. Two were adults, the other five, younger. One of the older sisters, Mrs. E. W. Nelson, asserted to the NDP's Andrew and Luther Potter, "Davey had been told if he cooperated, he would go free. He had no idea of his danger until it was too late." Even on the day of the execution, Herold told his sisters, "It's the others—not me. They won't hang me."

Mrs. Nelson believed her only brother was being hanged for what he knew. "There was no way that anyone could ever make Davey keep a secret," she explained.[12]

Friday, July 7, dawned hot and humid. The more fortunate prisoners—Dr. Mudd, Spangler, O'Laughlin and Arnold—were to be confined to the civilian penitentiary at Albany, New York. The other four were scheduled to die shortly after 1 p.m.

By 7:30 that sultry morning, Frederick A. Aiken and John W. Clampitt had secured their writ of *habeas corpus* from Andrew Wylie, a justice of the Supreme Court of the District of Columbia. U.S. Marshal David Gooding served the writ on Gen. W. S. Hancock, commanding the Middle Military Division. With U.S. Attorney General James Speed, Hancock appeared before Judge Wylie to acknowledge the writ and to refuse to obey it.

"I . . . respectfully say that the body of Mary E. Surratt is in my possession," Hancock's reply to the court stated. ". . . I do not produce said body by reason of the order of the President of the United States. . . ."

The attached note from Johnson was blunt: "I . . . do

hereby declare that the writ of *habeas corpus* has been . . . suspended. . . ."[13]

The court had to yield to the presidential suspension of Mrs. Surratt's constitutional right. All legal proceedings had ended.

At an early hour, people began making their way to the prison where the quadruple hangings were to take place. A hundred passes had been issued, 25 of these to the press.

The sun was becoming unbearably hot as the morning passed.

Father Walter arrived at Mrs. Surratt's cell. Her daughter, Anna, was with her. The priest declared, "I can never forget the scene. . . ." The widow had long been in ill health. She lay on a mattress placed on the cell's bare floor. The priest gave her Holy Communion. Then she dressed in a black dress, a black alpaca bonnet, and a black veil.[14]

Outside the prison walls a wild rumor raced through Washington. "Did you hear? Mrs. Surratt will not be executed! The President will commute her sentence to life imprisonment!"[15]

It was untrue. Johnson had become almost paranoid in his determination to squelch rumors that he was connected with the ugly plot that had made him President. The card Booth had left at his hotel on the afternoon of the assassination continued to haunt him. It had been intended for Col. Browning, Johnson's secretary, but many believed it had been intended for the then Vice President: "Don't wish to disturb you. Are you at home? J. Wilkes Booth."[16]

Lafayette Baker had written an undated letter to Secretary of War Stanton: "It is absolutely essential that I see you at once in regard to the card of Booth's left for Andrew Johnson. I have most confidential information to relate concerning Booth's acquaintance with President Johnson and others which you will find alarming. Your obedient servant, Lafayette C. Baker."[17]

Two of Herold's sisters made a final, desperate effort to

save their only brother. They fell on their knees before Judge Holt, clutching him about the legs, pleading tearfully for mercy. Holt referred them to Johnson, who had already refused to see them. To escape any more such scenes, the Judge Advocate left his office.[18]

Defense Attorney William Doster, who had vainly subpoenaed President Johnson at the conspirators' trial, made a final call at the death cells. It did no good, but Doster reminded himself "the prisoner (Payne) was never connected directly with the conspiracy to kill Mr. Lincoln and legally could be found guilty only of assault and battery on Mr. Seward, with intent to kill—a penitentiary offense."[19]

"Thanks for all your help," Payne said to the attorney. "Here, I'd like you to have my jackknife. It's the only earthly thing I have to give."[20]

Doster declined with thanks. Strange that Payne, described as a potential suicide, and against whom harsh restraints had been practiced during imprisonment, had been allowed only one possession—a knife by which he could have taken his own life.[21]

Outside the sweltering cells, the cry of commercial vendors was heard. "Lemonade! Get your lemonade here! Slices of cake. Get your cake now!"[22]

Gen. Hancock stationed swift mounts with expert cavalrymen between the White House and the penitentiary. If President Johnson had a last minute change of heart, no effort would be spared to get a stay of execution to the scaffold in time.

One o'clock arrived. Beneath the scaffold, in the only shade available, young Coxshall was having a hard time keeping his churning stomach still.[23]

More than 1,000 soldiers ringed the prison wall from the outside. Atop the walls, men from the Sixth Regiment Veteran Volunteers stood three feet apart, the sun beating down on their heads.

Mrs. Surratt was helped to her feet. She had been allowed to sit in a chair outside her cell. Her voice came clearly through her heavy black veil. "Father?"

The Rev. Walter and several officers turned toward her.

281

"Yes, my daughter?"

"Father, I wish to say something."

"What is it, my child?"

"I am innocent."

They were, Father Walter knew, words uttered on the verge of eternity. "They were the last confession of an innocent woman," the priest declared.[24] It was the only legacy of value Mrs. Surratt would leave her daughter. Anna collapsed in grief.

The dismal procession was led toward the small door that opened onto the prison yard. Every eye turned toward the door as it swung open.

Mrs. Surratt was first into the merciless sun. At the scaffold, Gen. John F. Hartranft turned to Gen. Hancock and cried, "My God! Not the woman, too?"[25]

Payne was next. The strongman was composed. He was upright, aloof, and calm, wearing a sailor's suit. He was flanked by a sergeant of the reserve corps and one of Lafe Baker's secret service detectives. The Rev. Dr. A. D. Gillett of Washington's First Baptist Church followed.

Herold was the third condemned prisoner through the prison door. All seven of his sisters sobbed wildly behind him. He walked with obvious nervousness between another secret service operative and a reserve sergeant. Herold wore a black cloth coat and light pants, a collarless white shirt and a black slouch hat. The pastor of the Old Christ Episcopal Church accompanied him.

Atzerodt was last in line. Another sergeant and an NDP man flanked him. He wore a dark gray coat and pants, a black vest with a collarless linen shirt. Woolen socks and slippers were on his feet. The Rev. Butler of the local Lutheran Church walked behind.[26]

Mrs. Surratt, minus her veil but still wearing the bonnet, moved her lips in prayer. Her eyes swept the scene before her, then dropped.

The procession advanced across the area toward the open graves and the crude coffins—a final demonstration of calculated cruelty for the four who saw, in their last moments, the silent, waiting slits in the clay earth and their pine coffins.

The prisoners walked up the scaffold's traditional 13 steps. Mrs. Surratt was seated in one of four simple arm chairs placed on the scaffold. The crucifix was held before her face. She leaned forward and kissed it. A large black umbrella was held over the head of each prisoner.

The spectators pressed forward. Armed soldiers stood three deep, bristling with fixed bayonets. The crowd grew quiet. The cries of the lemonade and cake sellers abruptly ceased. The sun continued to beat down on the soldiers standing atop the prison wall as they gazed down on the scene.

Mrs. Surratt was bound about the ankles and knees with white strips of cloth, her elbows secured behind her back. Beneath the scaffold, young Coxshall heard the widow complain, "It hurts."

A man's voice laconically assured her, "Well, it won't hurt long."[27]

The condemned men were also bound.

In the crowd, rising tension was expressed in terse whispers and anxious glances toward the main gate. Nobody really expected Mrs. Surratt to be hanged. Surely there would be a cry of "Wait!" and a lathered mount would be spurred through the gate.

But there was no cry and no horseman.

On the scaffold, Mrs. Surratt's black bonnet was removed by a soldier. Another reached for the rope. To attorney William E. Doster, this was the most harrowing part of the ordeal. Until that moment, he had truly expected an eleventh hour miracle.[28]

Except for Payne, the condemned showed great distress. He reached out, took a straw sailor hat off an officer's head and put it on his own bare head.[29]

The hat was removed and a white hood covered the handsome face. Hoods were secured over the heads of the others.

Under the trap door drop, Coxshall yielded to the strain and the heat. He took hold of the supporting post he was to knock away in a moment, hung on, and vomited.

The clergymen were ordered back. The four ropes were adjusted about the four necks.

The chairs were removed, the four umbrellas taken away.

The last arrangements on the scaffold were now complete. The clergy, detectives, and soldiers retired to the rear of the scaffold. The four condemned stood alone, their heads swathed in the white hoods. Stout ropes hung slack from necks to a crossbeam overhead.

Col. Rath came down the steps and faced the four invalided soldiers under the scaffold. Coxshall and his companions tensed. The colonel held his hands in front of his chest. He clapped his hands together sharply. Once. Twice. Three times.

On the third clap, the invalid soldiers swung with all their might.[30]

The heavy timbers moved forward. A dull thump—wood sounded against wood. The two support posts fell away. The double traps overhead plunged downward.

It was 1:26 p.m., one of the darkest moments in American history.

Chapter 26

THE COVER-UP UNCOVERED

Before Mrs. Surratt's body was removed from the gallows, people outside the prison were chanting, "Judicial murder!" It was the first explosion of anger following the hanging.

Anna Surratt begged for her mother's body so she could bury it outside the prison. The request was denied, as was a family request for Atzerodt's body.[1]

In November of that year, the reward for John H. Surratt was withdrawn. In the same month, the official publication of the conspirators' trial was released. Benn Pitman's version made no mention of the majority court recommendation for mercy to the President on behalf of Mrs. Surratt. The public still didn't know such a recommendation had been made.

The official order of July had specified that the four state prisoners, Spangler, O'Laughlin, Arnold and Dr. Mudd, were to be confined at a civil penitentiary in Albany, New York. Since this posed an obvious threat to the government conspirators because the prisoners might yet be pardoned or allowed to talk in this prison, Lafayette Baker carried out a plan to place them out of reach.[2]

On July 15, President Johnson signed the order "so as to direct that the said Arnold, Mudd, Spangler and O'-Laughlin be confined at hard labor in the military prison at Dry Tortugas, Florida."[3]

Secretary of the Navy Welles said Stanton had persuaded Johnson to move the prisoners that far away, where mosquitos and fever were likely to silence the four.[4]

Arnold wrote, "We were denied all intercourse with everyone upon the desolate island, and our footsteps were always accompanied by an armed guard."[5]

Dr. Mudd wrote his wife, "We can't move five steps without permission of the sergeant. . . ."[6]

Smallpox spread through the prison, and the victims were placed close to the dungeon shared by Dr. Mudd, Spangler, Arnold, and O'Laughlin. Arnold wrote, ". . . It was done for the express purpose of inoculating us with this fearful and loathesome malady. . . ."[7]

The subject of John Wilkes Booth seemed to have dropped from public life. But Lafayette Baker and the Potter brothers knew the killer of Abraham Lincoln was very much alive.

After Andrew and Luther Potter had lost the trail of Booth, Henson, and the Negro valet in May, the NDP men went to Elkton and then Harrisonburg in Virginia to warn the garrisons to be on the lookout. "They're suspected thieves," the Potters said. They dared not mention it was Booth, for Booth was officially dead and buried.[8]

On May 2, in Lydia, they stopped to water their horses at a widow's home. A small black boy sidled up to them. "You'ns still lookin' for them three men?"

"Yes," Andrew answered. "Why?"

"Ah kin take you'ns where they's been."

"You can, boy?"

"Yessum—fo' 20 dollahs."

The detectives followed the boy toward a mountain and up a trail which led along a gully. At the head of the gully, not more than a quarter of a mile from a trail at the top of the ridge, the boy pointed. "That theh's a b'ar hole."

It was a cave. The detectives entered and checked around. "No doubt about it," Andrew told his brother. "Booth, Henson, and the nigger holed up here for more than a week probably. Look at the sign."⁹

The black boy nodded. "Yessuh. My pa, he done work for the widder woman, and he brung them food and coffee all the time."

"When they left, which way did they go?"

"I dunno, suh."

Luther laid his pencil down on a map. "If we start here at Stanardsville, then use Lydia for the second spot, where we are now, the pencil marks a straight line across the Shenandoah to Elkton and Harrisonburg. . . ." He stopped, looking at the map in perplexity.

"But we've already been to those places, Luther."

"Maybe we didn't go far enough. Look what's northwest of there."

"Linville. Let's try there."

When the brothers began asking questions at Linville, they were in luck. They found a farmer named Louis Pence with a blooded horse that he admitted belonged to a man who looked like the photo of Booth.

"That's him, all right," the farmer said. "Only without a mustache. He had this tall black man with him and a shorter white man. But the one on the crutch was this here man." He tapped Booth's photograph.

"How come he left his horse with you?" Luther asked.

"He gave me the horse and some money to let them stay one night."

"And then what happened?" Andrew persisted.

The farmer grew cautious. "Am I going to get in trouble of some kind? I mean, I don't know these men, and they just wanted a place to stay. . . ."

Luther vigorously shook his head. He held up Booth's photo again. "We just want to know where this man went."

"Well, sir, I'll tell you. I took him and his friends up near Harpers Ferry."

The two brothers exchanged glances. "Mount Olympus!" Andrew whispered.[10]

The two detectives swung back to the northeast. They guessed why Booth was doubling back. Booth's farm, "Mount Olympus," was in Harpers Ferry, West Virginia. Booth's ex-wife lived there.

But Booth wasn't at the farm and Potters returned to Washington.

On September 23, Andrew headed for Harrisburg, Pennsylvania, on a planned hunting trip with Det. William Bernard of Ebensburg. There he got an unexpected tip which again put the NDP on the actor's trail.[11]

As they got off the train, they were immediately approached by the town constable. "Aren't you government men?"

The detectives admitted they were.

"I saw two men with a darkie leave town two days ago," the constable said in a low tone. "I recognized the darkie. It was Henry Johnson; you know, the nigger who used to be Booth's valet?"[12]

"What'd the two white men look like?"

"Both had full beards."

"Did you recognize them?"

"Well, now, if I was to say who I thought one was, you'd not believe me. But I sure enough recognized Booth's nigger. He's a dandy, Henry is. Always dressed like the heighth of fashion even though he is black."

The detectives knew they had hit Booth's trail again.

"Where were they bound?" Andrew asked.

"New York City. They left September 21 on the early morning train from here."[13]

Two days ago! Bernard and Potter caught the same train the next morning and questioned the conductor. "Oh, yessuh," he said with a broad smile, "I remembers them because I knows Henry Johnson. He's a valet, you know. One of the gentlemens with him walked with a cane. Had a bad limp, he did, yessuh."

Potter asked about the second man and nodded when Ed Henson was described. "Where did they get off?" the detective asked.

"Philadelphy. Yessuh, that's what they done."

The two detectives checked around Philadelphia. They questioned the crew of the afternoon train. The valet, the man with the limp, and the small talkative man had left that afternoon for New York.

The detectives went to New York, but were once more forced to give up the chase.[14]

Just before Christmas, 1865, Henry Johnson was recognized in the New York train station. He was carrying three valises. He vanished before the detective who had spotted him could get close.[15]

That same day, Booth's former wife, Izola, with whom Booth had been living again, was seen in a Baltimore railroad station. She also disappeared before a detective could question her.[16]

Other reports filtered in. Booth, Henson, or Johnson had been seen at various places with Izola Booth. But the reports could not be pinned down. As the year ended, Lafe Baker called the Potter brothers into his office and announced a decision.

"We're going to have to go on to other things," he began.

"You mean give up chasing Booth?"

"I mean, let Booth lie. We don't know what we would have on our hands, or what we could do, if we did find him."

"But he's still out there."

"True," Baker replied, "but the rewards have been paid on Boyd, who's dead and buried as Booth. We're calling off this chase. Permanently."[17]

More than 20 people who had helped Booth in his escape were never formally tried. Among those were Col. Cox and his half-brother, Thomas Jones. Jones certainly had given far more help than had Dr. Mudd, and Jones admitted his complicity when it was safe to do so.

Jefferson Davis and those named in the original charges, which brought hanging to four and imprisonment to four others, also escaped formal trial.

Key witness Louis Weichmann unburdened himself to John P. Brophy, a professor at Gonzaga College where John Surratt had been a student. Brophy signed an affidavit, which he took to the White House to seek perjury charges against Weichmann. Gen. Mussey barred the way to President Johnson. Brophy went to the *National Intelligencer,* but the editor refused to print the professor's affidavit on the grounds it was "too strong."[18] The affidavit quoted Weichmann as saying he had been arrested as a Booth conspirator. Stanton and Burnett had threatened Weichmann with death unless he turned state's evidence.

Brophy's long affidavit concluded ". . . that since this trial closed, he has admitted to me that he was a liar . . . that he swore to a deliberate falsehood on the witness stand . . . that he told me that he thought Mrs. Surratt to be innocent. . . ."[19]

The Milligan case was settled by the U.S. Supreme Court, which held that military trials for civilians were illegal under the Constitution. Stanton's military court which had hanged Mrs. Surratt, Payne, Herold, and Atzerodt had no authority.

A break between President Johnson and Secretary of War Stanton now exploded. Johnson, in spite of his hard line remarks before he became Chief Executive, turned more and more to his predecessor's soft reconstruction policy. This brought the ire of the Radical Republicans down upon him. The government conspirators joined forces to remove *this* President by impeachment proceedings.

While this was boiling, the House Judiciary Committee was formed. Andrew J. Rogers, Congressman from New Jersey, filed a minority report of the Select Committee on the Assassination of Lincoln.[20]

As a member of the committee, Congressman Rogers'

report was a stinging one that showed even his own colleagues were hiding documents from him. ". . . The majority of the committee determined to throw in my way every possible impediment. . . . Papers were put away from me, locked in boxes, hidden; and when I asked to see them, I was told . . . I could not." Rogers brought the matter before the House, but the Speaker decided Rogers was not entitled to see the papers.

His report continued, "Secrecy has surrounded and shrouded, not to say protected, every step of these examinations, and even in the committee room I seemed to be acting with a sort of secret council of inquisition. . . ."

The minority report added that Rogers had been "forced to travel over the nebulous and extended region of the so-called 'assassin trial.'

"There are two reports on this trial. One approved by Mr. Holt, revised by Mr. Burnett, and the Associated Press report, published by Peterson & Co. . . . Whatever suspicion may naturally attach to the former, none can to the latter." It had taken awhile, but the truth finally had come out.

The official court record of the assassination trial by Benn Pitman had been substantially "doctored" by Holt and Burnett.

Congressman Rogers' minority report also detailed the perjury of government witnesses Montgomery, Merritt, Conover, and others, with their true names and shoddy backgrounds.

"And thus, one by one," the Congressman continued, "I find each and all of the witnesses brought forward at the so called trial to implicate Jefferson Davis . . . and others, to be either convicted perjurers or men of infamous life. . . ."

Rogers covered in detail the government's school of perjury, including confessions by some witnesses. In conclusion, Rogers declared, "There is no credible evidence whatever to incriminate Mr. Davis as an accomplice . . . in the murder of Mr. Lincoln. . . ."[21]

On February 13, 1867, the House passed the Reconstruction Bill. It incorporated Stanton's plan laid before the cabinet the day of Lincoln's assassination. The proposal called for dissolving the Southern states into military districts, under the War Department jurisdiction. The military governors would be appointed by Grant, who was under Stanton's command.[22]

The Senate modified the bill, making it the President's prerogative to appoint the military governors. President Johnson vetoed the hard line plan.

The Radicals countered by passing the Tenure of Office Act, which bypassed the Constitution and took away the Chief Executive's right to remove appointed officials without Senate approval. This bill, along with the Reconstruction Act, passed Congress together, overriding Johnson's veto.[23]

Secretary of the Navy Welles came to see Johnson. "Mr. President, it is with reluctance I am compelled to express an unfavorable opinion of a colleague."

The two men talked of Stanton's growing arrogance and efforts to embarrass Johnson.

"The Radical Congressmen are acting in concert with the Secretary of War. Gradually, the administration is coming under the War Department."

Johnson nodded sadly. It was true.

Lafayette Baker and Stanton had a falling out after Baker was caught spying on President Johnson at the White House. Baker was discharged from the U.S. Army on February 8, 1866, and was no longer head of the secret service.[24] But he found a way to embarrass the War Secretary.

In 1867, his book, *History of the U.S. Secret Service,* was published. In it, he told about delivering Booth's diary to Stanton.[25] The disclosure created a storm in the Congress. Why had it been kept secret? Why hadn't it been mentioned at the conspiracy trial of 1865?

There had been a public reference to the diary's existence when the New York *World* had casually mentioned it on April 28, 1865, before the trial, but nobody had picked up on it.

The diary was found in a "forgotten" War Department file. In it was the ominous line, "I have almost a mind to return to Washington and . . . clear my name."[26]

Gen. Ben Butler, now a congressman, asked, "Clear himself how?" Butler answered his own question with a question: "By disclosing his accomplices? Who they were?" The House of Representatives set up a special commission to look into the matter. This produced another sensation— 18 pages of the Booth diary were missing. Before the House Committee, Baker testified that the diary was complete when he handed it to either Stanton or to Maj. Thomas Eckert.

Baker thundered, "Who spoilated that book?" He later testified, ". . . In my opinion, there have been leaves torn out of that book since I saw it."

Judge Advocate Joseph Holt, appearing as a witness, said the diary was in the same condition in which he had received it.[27]

Stanton was summoned by the House Committee. When he had first seen the diary, he declared, "I examined it then with great care . . . and noticed that leaves had been torn or cut from it at the time."[28]

Lt. Col. Conger was called as a witness on May 13, but he couldn't remember. He thought some of the leaves were missing.

Baker was recalled and was asked, "Do you mean to say that at the time you gave the book to the Secretary of War, there were no leaves gone?"

"I do."

"That is still your opinion?"

"That is still my opinion."[29]

Had pages been cut or torn from Booth's diary? If so, why? What could they have contained that caused them to be removed? The answer was that one or more persons didn't want those missing papers made public. The missing pages were not destroyed, although it would take more than a century before they would be discovered.

The conflict between Stanton and Johnson became public when John Surratt was finally brought to trial. The junior counsel for his defense addressed the jury at his trial in Washington. The lawyer pointed out that Mrs. Surratt's clemency plea from the five military commissioners was still attached to the official court record.[30]

President Johnson read the lawyer's comments on August 5, 1867, and sent for the records. Judge Holt and President Johnson got into a public dispute about the death sentence papers that had been brought to the Chief Executive for his signature. Johnson claimed the clemency paper had not been attached to the papers, that he had never seen it. Holt said the paper was attached.[31]

That same day, Johnson sent a blunt memo to Stanton: "Sir: Public considerations of a high character constrain me to say that your resignation as Secretary of War will be accepted."[32] But Stanton, the American dictator, refused to be fired!

Over a period of months, the President tried to fire Stanton, but the War Secretary, protected by the powerful Republican Radicals in Congress, stayed at his desk. The Radicals moved against Johnson, trying for impeachment. Proceedings were instituted on February 2, 1868.

On February 21, Johnson wrote Stanton another dismissal note: "By virtue of the power and authority vested in me, as President, by the Constitution and laws of the United States, you are hereby removed from office as Secretary of the Department of War. . . ."[33] Maj. Gen. Lorenzo Thomas, army adjutant general, was to take possession of all War Department papers upon Stanton's receipt of the dismissal notice.

Stanton reported Johnson's appointment of Thomas to his allies in Congress. The War Secretary's communication was referred without debate to the Committee on Reconstruction. The next day, the committee announced a resolution calling for the impeachment of Johnson.

Stanton himself dictated the 10 articles of impeachment on a Sunday. On Monday, the House adopted a resolution, 126 to 47, informing the Senate of the charges so the Upper House could try Johnson.[34]

On March 5, the articles were presented by the House to the Senate with Chief Justice Salmon Chase presiding. Johnson was charged with violating the Tenure of Office

293

law of March 2, 1867, wherein Johnson had tried to fire Stanton without Senate approval. Other charges against the President were for treasonable utterances against the Congress and public language "indecent and unbecoming" the nation's top office.

The vote on May 26 was 35 to 19—one short of the necessary two-thirds need to impeach.

Sen. Benjamin F. Wade, President pro tempore, and next in line of succession to the Chief Executive's chair, had been so sure that Johnson would be found guilty that the old Lincoln conspirator had already informally named his cabinet. Instead he was to lose re-election in 1869 and go home to Ohio an embittered politician. In Wade's cabinet, Stanton was to have been Secretary of the Treasury.[35]

Stanton was crushed by the surprise vote. On the same afternoon that Johnson's right to fire the War Secretary was upheld, Stanton sent a note to the President: ". . . I have relinquished charge of the War Department. . . ."

Gen. John M. Schofield was confirmed as the new Secretary of War.

Booth committed a great and terrible crime that had a significant impact on American history, a great tragedy which Americans could face and then move on.

But what defense does a nation have against a crime that it does not know has been committed against it, the crime of concealment, which has endured for a century and more after Lincoln's murder?

The Radical Republicans of Congress succeeded in keeping the total truth from the people who had elected them. Their spokesman was Congressman George S. Boutwell of Massachusetts. He was chairman of the House committee that had given Rep. Rogers such a hard time when he tried to get at the truth. Boutwell officially closed the books on the cover-up.

"The whole matter is really very simple," he declared. "John Wilkes Booth shot the President, and some dirty Rebs, including Jeff Davis, helped him do it. Nobody else! So far as I'm concerned, this case is closed!"[36]

Boutwell's statement, made more than 112 years ago, was wrong.

The case is still open.

Epilogue

FINAL CURTAIN

Many of the people who played roles in the Lincoln assassination, the conspiracy, and cover-up suffered ironic twists of fate in their own lives.

Col. Lafayette Baker threatened to expose those involved in the plot against Lincoln and attempts were made on his life to silence him.[1] In addition to newspaper reports of such attacks, Mrs. Jenny Baker's diary treats them at length. On January 2, 1868, Mrs. Baker writes, "Lafe's shoulder is healing but he complains of soreness. He'd been shot at just before Christmas. . . . Splinters hit him in the shoulder."

On January 3, the diary records, "Lafe cancelled the hunting trip he, Tom and Wally had planned. Lafe does not sleep, but walks the floor all night."[2]

"Wally" is Walter Pollock, Baker's brother-in-law, who was still a detective for the War Department. Baker and Pollock had married sisters. Because of the family relationship, "Wally" was not suspected of having been sent to recover Baker's confidential War Department papers.[3]

The next entry in Mrs. Baker's diary is on January 12: "Wally brought oysters and imported beer to Lafe. Lafe enjoyed both immensely.

"Wally, Mary, Lafe and I went to the Rathskeller for dinner. We got home about 8 and Lafe was sick."[4]

By chemical analysis of a lock of Baker's hair, acquired with Mrs. Baker's diary, Dr. Ray A. Neff has determined that Baker had been slowly killed by arsenic poisoning resulting from his beer being laced with it.

Using an atomic absorption spectrophotometer analysis, Dr. Neff has been able to show that on each occasion Pollock brought beer to Col. Baker, the arsenic content in his hair shot up until finally, on July 3, 1868, he died from the poisoning.

The fact that Baker died of arsenic poisoning seems even more irrefutable when we read more in Mrs. Baker's diary: "Something is amiss. Today I was brushing Wally's coat, and his cigar case fell out of his pocket. It is leather bound, quite expensive, and it came open at the bottom. It had in it little bottles of powder and in them a little silver spoon. I wonder what it means? Wally is so mysterious, and he travels so much. What does he do?"[5] Mrs. Baker was describing white arsenic.

After Baker's death, Pollock ransacked the house, looking for Baker's papers and possibly money. However, before he died, Baker had a servant come from his cousin Mary Baker's house next door and remove all the papers and money to her attic. These papers remained undiscovered until the 1880s, at which time a court hearing of Mary Baker's will decreed that the War Department could not have any of the documents unless they were read into the court records.[6] A daughter of Detective Baker's cousin finally acquired this collection and allowed Andrew Potter to copy some items from it. Today the collection is in a Philadelphia vault, still secret until the present heir dies.

As for Booth, Henson, and Henry Johnson, several documents pick up the trail when Andrew and Luther Potter were ordered off it by Lafe Baker. The fugitives had spent several months at Harpers Ferry on Booth's farm with Izola.[7]

About November, 1865, the trio were off to Pennsylvania, where Booth reunited with former girlfriend Kate Scott, who was expecting Booth's child within a month. Miss Scott signed a sworn affidavit that Booth was alive after the Garrett's farm shooting and that he visited her in Pennsylvania. After leaving her home, Booth, Henson and Johnson went to New York City.[8]

The ultimate demise of John Wilkes Booth needs additional research, but it is known that Booth did go to Canada and later to England, where he married Elizabeth Marshall Burnley, another girlfriend he had had prior to the assassination. He had changed his name to John Byron Wilkes, a name he used before he became famous on the stage. Reports have him staying in England for some time, then going to India, where, some say, he died.[9]

Other reports say that he spent time in California where he met his first wife, who became pregnant again and delivered a son. Another report claims that a man who died in 1900 in Enid, Oklahoma, on his deathbed stated he was John Wilkes Booth. This man was never buried. His body was mummified and still exists today. There is strong evidence that the man in Enid, whose name was David E. George or John St. Helen, was in fact John Wilkes Booth.[10] This is possible since Booth could have faked his death in India, returned to the United States, and assumed a new name.

During the days following Lincoln's assassination, Mrs. Lincoln was in an extreme state of hysteria. She did not appear at her husband's funeral and never again looked on his face after the tragic scenes of the morning of April 15.[11]

Five weeks after Lincoln's death, on May 22, 1865, Mrs. Lincoln left the White House for Chicago. At the time, Mrs. Lincoln was deep in debt to many Washington and New York merchants. Much of her clothing and jewelry was sold to pay off creditors. Also Mrs. Elizabeth Keckley, the Lincoln's White House maid, authored a book exposing Mrs. Lincoln's debts which caused much embarrassment.

Mrs. Lincoln went into seclusion. Three and a half years after her husband's death, she took Tad to Europe —the trip promised by Lincoln during one of their last conversations on the day of the assassination.

But by the spring of 1871, homesick, Mrs. Lincoln and her son returned to Chicago, where they had a joyous reunion with Robert Todd, his new wife, and their little daughter Mary. The happiness was short lived. Tad became ill and died suddenly in July of 1871 from what started out as a severe cold and developed into "dropsy of the chest."[12]

On one occasion in Chicago, Mrs. Lincoln attempted to leave her room in the nude. When Robert Lincoln tried to restrain her, she screamed, "You are going to murder me." She had hallucinations of being followed and feared for her life.[13]

To keep her from possible self-injury and get his mother proper medical treatment, Robert finally had her committed to an insane asylum. After spending four months there, Mary Lincoln managed to win her release and again took up residence in Europe.

In 1879, she suffered an accidental fall and returned to the States an invalid. She moved to Springfield to live. There she shut herself away in a darkened room, preferring candlelight to sunlight. During the next four years, suffering from diabetes, she lost weight, had disturbed vision, and distressing boils. During her final years, she complained of living in poverty, but when Mrs. Lincoln died in July of 1882, she left an estate of $84,035.

In 1869, when Stanton was 55, President Ulysses S. Grant fulfilled the fired War Secretary's final wish and appointed him to the U.S. Supreme Court. Muffled in heavy wraps, looking more dead than alive, Stanton tottered over to the White House to thank President Grant for the appointment. The cold damp of that December 20 worsened his health, and he died before he could be seated on the Supreme Court.[14]

In New York on the morning of November 12, 1865, ex-senator Preston King tied a bag of bullets around his neck and jumped from the Christopher Street Ferry. King was the politician who had prevented Anna Surratt and Father Walter from presenting President Johnson with a mercy petition in Mrs. Surratt's behalf.

John M. Lloyd, star witness against Mrs. Surratt, died of alcoholism. Willie Jett, the lad who had led the soldiers to Garrett's farm, became a traveling salesman and eventually died of syphilis.[15]

Genuine mystery surrounds the fate of John F. Parker, the delinquent White House guard who had failed to guard Lincoln's presidential box on the fatal night. Never reprimanded nor punished, he returned to duty at the White House. He remained on the White House police force until 1868, when he was dismissed for sleeping in a street car while on duty, something which he had frequently done. Strangely his dismissal came after Stanton was fired as the Secretary of War. Parker then simply disappeared.[16]

Tragedy struck Maj. Henry Rathbone and Clara Harris, who were married, had a family, and took up residence in Germany. Two nights before Christmas in 1883, Rathbone attempted to kill his children. When a nurse tried to intervene, he instead shot his wife to death and stabbed himself. Doctors saved his life, but he spent the rest of his years in a German asylum.[17]

Sergeant Boston Corbett who had "admitted" to the slaying of the man in the barn, for years enjoyed the fruits of fame as "the man who shot Booth." He traveled the country as a celebrity. In 1887, he was awarded a job as doorman to the Kansas State Legislature where he had charge of the ladies' gallery. One morning after the roll call, he appeared with revolvers in each hand and opened fire on the legislators and the ladies. Overpowered, he was committed to an insane asylum in Topeka, Kansas, from which he escaped. He was known to have gone to Texas, where he became a traveling medicine man for a few months before disappearing.[18]

Secretary of State William H. Seward survived the attempted assassination of April 14 to be ridiculed for Seward's Folly, the purchase of Alaska for a little over $7,000,000. Mrs. Seward and daughter, Fannie, died a short time after the attack, presumably of shock.[19]

Life didn't go too well for the Booth family either. Junius Brutus Booth, father of John Wilkes, was said to have become intermittently insane. Sister Asia and her husband, John Sleeper Clarke, quarreled savagely after the assassination, and went to England to live in semi-exile.

Edwin Booth Clark, Asia's firstborn child, had gone to Annapolis. The naval officer is believed to have committed suicide by jumping overboard while at sea.

Booth's sister Rosalie, a melancholic, died in January of 1880. Rumor spoke of a mysterious assailant. She had been living with her brother, Dr. Joseph Booth, in New Jersey. One evening when the doctor was out, a knock came at the door. Rosalie answered. A heavy object thrown from the dark hit her in the temple.

Edwin Booth's funeral was held on the morning of July 9, 1893. On the exact hour when his casket was being carried from the Little Church Around the Corner in New York City, Ford's Theatre in Washington, D.C., collapsed with a seismic roar. Twenty-two clerks were killed in the disaster and 68 others were injured. By eerie coincidence, among the records stored in the theatre that the government had taken over, were those of the Army Medical Corps, including the Surgeon General's reports of the inquest held over the body on the *Montauk*. It is believed that some of the records were lost in the avalanch of fire and mortar.[20]

Louis Weichmann, after the 1865 Conspiracy Trial, through the direct efforts of Stanton and Judge Holt, was appointed to a clerkship in the Philadelphia Custom House. He soon lost the job and moved to Anderson, Indiana, where he opened Anderson's first business college, and ran it until his death in 1902.[21]

John Surratt, charged with being a Booth co-conspirator, was captured in Italy. After his trial in 1867 resulted in a hung jury, he became a school teacher in Rockville, Maryland, and later took to lecturing. Following his first lecture in Rockville, the police prohibited a repetition of it in Washington. Eventually Surratt became an auditor of freight receipts at the Baltimore Steam Packet Company, a position he held until his death in 1916. Close friends said he had written his autobiography, but when publishers expressed little interest in it, he burned it in a bonfire as his family looked on.[22]

William Petersen, the German tailor in whose house the

President died, committed suicide. His body, loaded with laudanum, was found on the grounds of the Smithsonian Institute.[23]

Maj. Thomas Eckert, head of Stanton's military telegraph office, became the founding president of Western Union. He never revealed what he knew about the Lincoln assassination.[24]

William H. Crook, Lincoln's favorite White House guard, stayed on at the White House through five administrations and later wrote his memoirs.[25]

John T. Ford, the owner of Ford's Theatre, was thrown into prison as a suspect in the assassination, but was later released. The government confiscated Ford's Theatre, but he forced it to pay $100,000 for the building.[26]

United States Marshal Ward Hill Lamon claimed that he regretted for the rest of his life that he was in Richmond the night the President was shot. He lived 28 years after the assination and wrote his memoirs.[27]

Michael O'Laughlin died during a yellow fever epidemic at Dry Tortugas where he was imprisoned. The heroic efforts of his fellow prisoner, Dr. Samuel Mudd, during this epidemic prompted prison officers to appeal for his pardon. It was granted in February of 1869.

Sam Arnold and Ned Spangler were also released from the Dry Tortugas prison. Spangler, who was dying of tuberculosis, went home with Dr. Mudd, who cared for him until he died. Dr. Mudd died of pneumonia 18 years after Lincoln's assassination, while Arnold lived to old age.[28]

Robert Lincoln, only surviving son of the Lincolns, later became Secretary of War. He was a witness to two other presidential assassinations—James Garfield and William McKinley.

Colonel William A. Browning, Vice President Andrew Johnson's personal secretary and the man to whom Booth wrote a letter indicating his assassination intent, is believed to have been murdered.[29]

Edwin Henson traveled with Booth to England and India. He later returned to Fort Wayne, Indiana, where he

301

changed his name to Edwin Henderson. He married and lived the rest of his life as a farmer.[30]

Booth's valet and barber, Henry Johnson, who spent nearly a year with Booth after the assassination, finally settled in Boston, where he and his mother lived out their remaining years.[31]

Rep. George Julian stood with the Radicals in the battles with President Johnson, and in 1867 was one of a committee of seven appointed by the House to prepare the articles of impeachment against the President. Failing re-election in 1870, he devoted his time to recuperating from broken health and writing political articles.[32]

Sen. Zachariah Chandler was one of the few Radical Republicans to be re-elected to the Senate in 1869. He was a Republican presidential candidate in 1879 and died on the campaign trail while making a political speech.[33]

California Senator John Conness did not seek re-election in 1869, but retired and settled in Boston. He was later committed to an insane asylum, where he died.[34]

So the curtain is rung down, the theatre darkened as the tragic drama of conspiracy and assassination moves off stage.

If you have any comments regarding this book or additional information to contribute toward the solution of the Lincoln assassination mystery, please write to the address given below, stating what your historical documents are. Do not send actual documents. Information of a historical nature will be forwarded to Sunn's select group of Lincoln historians for further evaluation, study, and response. Sunn will not be responsible for the loss of any unsolicited historical documents.

Dave Balsiger
Research Department
Sunn Classic Pictures
556 East 2nd South
Salt Lake City, UT 84102

FOOTNOTES

CHAPTER 1 — Source Footnotes

1. Andrew Potter Papers, Ray A. Neff Collection, Marshall, II
2. Johnson, Robert Underwood and Buel, Clarence Clough, *Battles and Leaders of the Civil War*, Vol. IV (The Century Co., New York, 1888)
3. Eisenschiml, Otto, *Why Was Lincoln Murdered?* (Little, Brown and Co., Boston, 1937)
4. Arter, Bill, "Did Stanton Plot Lincoln's Death?," *Columbus* (Ohio) *Dispatch*, Dec. 10, 1961
5. Lewis, Lloyd, *Myths After Lincoln* (Harcourt, Brace and Co., New York, 1929)
6-7. *Ibid.*
8. Potter Papers, *op. cit.*
9. *New York Times*, Mar. 6, 1864
10. Flower, Frank Abial, *Edwin McMasters Stanton* (Saalfield Publishing Co., New York, 1905)
11. Potter Papers, *op. cit.*
12. Millard, J.J., "The Devil's Errand Boy," *True*, July, 1925
13. *Ibid.*
14. Potter Papers, *op. cit.*
15. *Ibid.*
16. *New York Times, op. cit.*
17. Johnson and Buel, *op. cit.*
18. *Ibid.*
19. Potter Papers, *op. cit.*
20. *Ibid.*
21. Booth marriage certificate. Ray A. Neff Collection
22. John Wilkes Booth's letter to Col. William A. Browning, Vice President Andrew Johnson's private secretary, Apr. 14, 1865
23. Potter Papers, *op. cit.*
24-25. *Ibid.*
26. Booth's letter to Col. Browning, *op. cit.*
27. *Ibid.*

CHAPTER 2 — Source Footnotes

1. Chittenden, L. E., *Recollections of President Lincoln,* (Harper and Brothers, New York, 1891)
2-3. *Ibid.*
4. Long, E. B., *The Civil War Day by Day: An Almanac, 1861-1865* (Doubleday and Co., New York, 1971)
5-7. *Ibid.*
8. Flower, *op. cit.*
9. Carman, Harry J. and Luthin, Reinliaid H., *Lincoln and the Patronage* (Columbia University Press, New York, 1943)
10. *Ibid.*
11. Committee on the Conduct of the War research files. Dr. Richard D. Mudd Collection, Saginaw, MI
12. Carman and Luthin, *op. cit.*
13. Benedict, Michael Les, *A Compromise of Principle: The Politics of Radicalism* (W. W. Norton & Co., New York, 1974)
14. Van Deusen, Glyndon G., *Thurlow Weed: Wizard of the Lobby* (Little, Brown and Co., Boston, 1947)
15. *Ibid.*
16. Basler, Roy P., *The Collected Works of Abraham Lincoln*, Vol. VI (Rutgers University Press, New Brunswick, NY, 1953-55)
17. Long, *op. cit.*
18. Carman and Luthin, *op. cit.*
19. Long, *op. cit.*
20. Williams, T. Harry; Current, Richard N.; and Freidel, Frank; *A History of the United States to 1877* (Alfred A. Knopf, New York, 1959)
21-22. *Ibid.*

23. Current, Richard N.; Williams, T. Harry; and Freidel, Frank; *American History: A Survey* (Alfred A. Knopf, New York, 1975)

24. Williams, Current and Freidel, *op. cit.*

25. Current, Williams and Freidel, *op. cit.*

26. Long, *op. cit.*

27. Lamon, Ward Hill, *Recollections of Abraham Lincoln* (University Press, Cambridge, MA, 1895)

28. Gerry, Margarita Spalding, *Through Five Administrations: Reminiscences of Colonel William H. Crook* (Harper and Brothers, New York, 1907)

29. Johnson, William J., *Abraham Lincoln: The Christian* (Mott Media, Milford, MI, 1976)

30. Unpublished Voluntary Statement of Michael O'Laughlin, Apr. 27, 1865. originally in the Benn Pitman Collection, Cincinnati, OH Ray A. Neff Collection

31. Barbee, David Rankin, "The Murder of Mrs. Surratt" (Speech at the Emerson Institute, Washington, D.C., Feb. 25, 1950). Margaret K. Bearden Collection, Rochester, NY

32-33. *Ibid.*

34. Missing Booth Diary Pages. In the private collection of Stanton descendants. Released in 1976 through the efforts of Americana appraiser, Joseph Lynch of Worthington, MA

35. Long, *op. cit.*

36. Schlesinger Jr., Arthur M., *History of American Presidential Elections,* Vol. II, 1848-1896 (McGraw-Hill, New York, 1971)

CHAPTER 3 — Source Footnotes

1. Barbee, *op. cit.*; Brennan, John C., "General Bradley T. Johnson's Plan to Abduct President Lincoln," *Chronicles of St. Mary's County Historical Society,* (Leonardtown, MD) Vol. 22, Nov. 1974; Weichman, Louis J., *A True History of the Assassination of Abraham Lincoln and of the Conspiracy of 1865,* ed. Floyd E. Risvold, (Alfred A. Knopf, New York, 1975) and Roscoe, Theodore, *The Web of Conspiracy* (Prentice-Hall, Englewood Cliffs, NJ, 1959)

2. Missing Booth Diary Pages, *op. cit.*

3. Clarke, Asia Booth, *The Unlocked Book: A Memoir of John Wilkes Booth* (G. P. Putnam's Sons, New York, 1938)

4. Missing Booth Diary Pages, *op. cit.*

5. Chaffey Shipping Company Papers, 1864. Ray A. Neff Collection

6. O'Laughlin Statement, *op. cit.*

7. Potter Papers, *op. cit.*

8. *Ibid.*

9. Chaffey Company Papers, *op. cit.*

10-11. *Ibid.*

12. Missing Booth Diary Pages, *op. cit.*

13. *Ibid.*

14. Gray, Clayton, *Conspiracy in Canada* (L'Atelier Press, Montreal, 1957)

15-16. *Ibid.*

17. Missing Booth Diary Pages, *op. cit.*

18-19. *Ibid.*

20. Gray, *op. cit.*

21-22. *Ibid.*

23. *Maryland Historical Magazine,* Vol. 68, "Martin Family," Fall, 1973

24. Peterson, T. B., *The Trial of the Assassins and Conspirators* (T. B. Peterson and Brothers, Philadelphia, 1865); and Weichman, *op. cit.*

25. John Wilkes Booth's November 4, 1864 Account Statement with Chaffey Shipping Company from the William Bernard Papers. Ray A. Neff Collection

26. Turner-Baker Papers, (National Archives, File No. 3416)

27. Missing Booth Diary Pages, *op. cit.*

28. O'Laughlin Statement, *op. cit.*

29. Lafayette Baker's Unpublished Ciper-Coded Book Manuscript, 1868. Dr. Ray A. Neff Collection

30. *Ibid.*

31. McLaughlin, Andrew C., *Cyclopedia of American Government*, Vol. III (Peter Smith Co., Gloucester, MA, 1963) and *The Public Statutes at Large of the United States of America*, Vol. I (Charles C. Little and James Brown, Boston, 1850)

CHAPTER 4 — Source Footnotes

1. Long, *op. cit.*
2-3. *Ibid.*
4. *Americana Encyclopedia* (Americana Corp., New York, 1977)
5. Long, *op. cit.*
6. *Americana Encyclopedia, op. cit.*
7. Potter Papers, *op. cit.*
8. Missing Booth Diary Pages, *op. cit.*
9. Unpublished voluntary O'Laughlin statement, *op. cit.*
10. Missing Booth Diary Pages, *op. cit.*
11. Baker, Lafayette C., *History of the United States Secret Service* (L. C. Baker, Philadelphia, 1867)
12. Missing Booth Diary Pages, *op. cit.*
13-21. *Ibid.*
22. Mogelever, Jacob, *Death to Traitors* (Doubleday and Co., New York, 1960)
23. J. V. Barnes Letter, Mar. 2, 1865. Chaffey Shipping Company Papers. Ray A. Neff Collection
24. Missing Booth Diary Pages, *op. cit.*
25-29. *Ibid.*
30. Mogelever, *op. cit.* and Ray A. Neff Interview, Oct. 1976
31. J. V. Barnes Letter, *op. cit.*
32. Missing Booth Diary Pages, *op. cit.*
33. Lincoln, Abraham, "Proclamation Concerning Blockade," Apr. 11, 1865; "Proclamation Modifying Blockade," Apr. 11, 1865; and "Proclamation Concerning Foreign Port Privileges," Apr. 11, 1865
34. *Ibid.* and Potter Papers *op. cit.*
35. Burke, Merle, *United States History* (American Technical Society, Chicago, 1970)
36. Missing Booth Diary Pages, *op. cit.*

CHAPTER 5 — Source Footnotes

1. Missing Booth Diary Pages, *op. cit.*
2-6. *Ibid.*
7. Missing Booth Diary Pages, *op. cit.*
8. *Selma* (Alabama) *Dispatch*, Dec. 1, 1864
9. Lamon, *op. cit.*
10. *Ibid.*
11 Potter Papers, *op. cit.*
12. *Ibid.*
13. Bates, David Homer, *Lincoln in the Telegraph Office* (D. Appleton-Century Co., New York, 1907)
14. Gerry, *op. cit.*
15. *Ibid.*
16. Eisenschiml, *Why Was Lincoln Murdered?, op. cit.* and Bishop, Jim, *The Day Lincoln Was Shot* (Harper & Brothers, New York, 1955)
17. *Ibid.*
18. Missing Booth Diary Pages, *op. cit.*
19. Baker's Cipher-Coded Book Manuscript, *op. cit.*
20. Missing Booth Diary Pages, *op. cit.*
21. *Ibid.*
22. Baker's Cipher-Coded Manuscript; Potter Papers, *op. cit.*
23. Baker's Cipher-Coded Book Manuscript, *op. cit.*
24. *Ibid.*
25. Turner-Baker Papers, *op. cit.*
26. *Ibid.*
27. Potter Papers, *op. cit.*
28. *Maryland Historical Magazine, op. cit.*
29-30. *Ibid.*

CHAPTER 6 — Source Footnotes

1. Roscoe, *op. cit.*
2. *Ibid.*
3. O'Laughlin Statement, *op. cit.*
4. *Ibid.*
5. Clarke, *op. cit.* and O'Laughlin Statement, *op. cit.*
6. Clarke, *op. cit.*
7. Weichmann, *op. cit.*
8. Townsend, George, *Katy of Catoctin* (D. Appleton and Co., New York, 1886)
9. Missing Booth Diary Pages, *op. cit.*
10. *Ibid.*
11. O'Laughlin Statement, *op. cit.*
12. Weichmann, *op. cit.*
13. Townsend, *op. cit.*
14. *Ibid.*
15. Weichmann, *op. cit.*
16. Roscoe, *op. cit.*
17. Townsend, *op. cit.*
18. *Ibid.*
19. Lee, Thomas C., "The Role of Georgetown's Dr. Samuel A. Mudd in the Lincoln Conspiracy," *Georgetown Medical Bulletin*, May 1976
20. *Ibid.*
21. Townsend, *op. cit.*
22-24. *Ibid.*
25. Missing Booth Diary Pages, *op. cit.*
26. Roscoe, *op. cit.*
27. Bishop, *op. cit.*
28-30. *Ibid.*
31. Roscoe, *op. cit.*
32. Bishop; Weichmann, *op. cit.*
33. Weichmann, *op. cit.*
34-35. *Ibid.*
36. Pitman, Benn, *The Assassination of President Lincoln and the Trial of the Conspirators* (Funk & Wagnalls, New York, 1954) and Weichmann, *op. cit.*
37. Wilson, Francis, *John Wilkes Booth: Fact and Fiction of Lincoln's Assassination* (Houghton Mifflin Co., New York, 1929) and Roscoe, *op. cit.*
38. *Ibid.*
39. Roscoe, *op. cit.*
40. Weichmann, *op. cit.*
41. Roscoe, *op. cit.* and the Bearden Papers. Margaret K. Bearden Collection
42. Weichmann, *op. cit.*
43. Townsend, *op. cit.*
44. Roscoe, *op. cit.*

CHAPTER 7 — Source Footnotes

1. Capt. James William Boyd letter to Secretary of War, Edwin M. Stanton, Feb. 14, 1865, Turner-Baker Papers, Case No. 718B, National Archives
2. Capt. James William Boyd photos. Ray A. Neff Collection
3. Capt. Boyd Letter to Stanton, *op. cit.*
4-6. *Ibid.*
7. Potter Papers, *op. cit.*
8-14. *Ibid.*
15. Turner-Baker Papers, *op. cit.*
16. Captain Boyd's Letter to Stanton, *op. cit.*
17. *Ibid.*
18. Capt. James William Boyd Letter to Moe Stevens, Boyd Papers. Ray A. Neff Collection
19-20. *Ibid.*
21. J. V. Barnes Letter, *op. cit.*
22-28. *Ibid.*

29. Thomas Caldwell Letter to Capt. John Scott, Mar. 12, 1865, Chaffey Shipping Company Papers. Ray A. Neff Collection

30. *Ibid.*

31. John Wilkes Booth's Nov. 4, 1864 Account Statement, *op. cit.*

32. Missing Booth Diary Pages; Chaffey Shipping Company Papers, *op. cit.*

33. Missing Booth Diary Pages, *op. cit.*

CHAPTER 8 — Source Footnotes

1. Potter Papers, *op. cit.*

2. Long, *op. cit.*

3-5. *Ibid.*

6. Williams, Current, and Freidel, *op. cit.*

7. Randall, Ruth Painter, *Mary Lincoln: Biography of a Marriage* (Little, Brown, and Co., Boston, 1953)

8. Bishop, *op. cit.*

9-10. *Ibid.*

11. Lorant Stefan, *Lincoln: A Picture Story of His Life* (Bonanza Books, New York, 1975)

12. Bishop, *op. cit.*

13. Lorant, *op. cit.*

14. Roscoe, *op. cit.*

15. Gerry, *op. cit.*

16. Hamlin, Charles E., *Life and Times of Hannibal Hamlin* (Riverside Press, Cambridge, MA, 1899)

17. Lorant, *op. cit.*

18-22.. *Ibid.*

23. Pitman, *op. cit.*

24. Long, *op. cit.*

25. Mogelever, *op. cit.*

26-28. *Ibid.*

29. Capt. Boyd Letter to Moe Stevens, *op. cit.*

CHAPTER 9 — Source Footnotes

1. Roscoe, *op. cit.*

2. *Ibid.*

3. Long, *op. cit.*

4. Weichmann, *op. cit.*

5. Roscoe, *op. cit.* and Oldroyd, Osborn H., *The Assassination of Abraham Lincoln: Flight, Pursuit, Capture and Punishment of the Conspirators* (Privately Published, Washington, D. C., 1901)

6. Weichmann, *op. cit.* and Arnold, Samuel B., *Defence and Prison Experiences of a Lincoln Conspirator* (The Book Farm, Hattiesburg, MS, 1943)

7. Long, *op. cit.*

8. Roscoe; Weichmann; Arnold, *op. cit.*

9. Long, *op. cit.*

10. John Surratt Lecture at Rockville, Maryland, December 6, 1870. (*Evening Star*, Washington, D.C., Dec. 7, 1870)

11-13. *Ibid.*

14. Arnold, *op. cit.*

15. Surratt Lecture, *op. cit.*

16. Roscoe; Weichmann, *op. cit.*

17. Surratt Lecture, *op. cit.*

18. Roscoe, *op. cit.*

19. Oldroyd, *op. cit.*

20. Weichmann, *op. cit.*

21. Lewis, *op. cit.*

22. Eisenschiml, *Why Was Lincoln Murdered?*, *op. cit.*

23. *Ibid.*

24. Oldroyd, *op. cit.*

25. Missing Booth Diary Pages, *op. cit.*

26-36. *Ibid.*

37. Maj. Thomas T. Eckert Letter to Col. Lafayette C. Baker, April 22, 1865. In the private collection of Stanton descendants. Released in 1976

through the efforts of Americana appraiser, Joseph Lynch; and the Missing Booth Diary Pages, *op. cit.*

38. *Ibid.*
39. Missing Booth Diary Pages, *op. cit.*
40. *Ibid.* and Maj. Eckert Letter, *op. cit.*
41. Missing Booth Diary Pages, *op. cit.*
42-44. *Ibid.*

CHAPTER 10 — Source Footnotes

1. Shutes, Milton H., *Lincoln's Emotional Life* (Dorrance and Co., Philadelphia, 1957)
2. Long, *op. cit.*
3-5. *Ibid.*
6. Gerry, *op. cit.*
7-11. *Ibid.*
12. Missing Booth Diary Pages, *op. cit.*
13-14. *Ibid.*
15. Flower, *op. cit.*
16. *Ibid.*
17. Long, *op. cit.*
18. Missing Booth Diary Pages, *op. cit.*
19-20. *Ibid.*
21. Shelton, Vaughan, *Mask for Treason: The Lincoln Murder Trial* (Stackpole Books, Harrisburg, PA, 1965)
22-23. *Ibid.*
24. Baker's Cipher-coded Book Manuscript, *op. cit.*
25. *Ibid.*
26. Potter Papers, *op. cit.*
27. Baker's Cipher-coded Book Manuscript, *op. cit.*
28. Weichmann; Roscoe, *op. cit.*
29. Baker's Cipher-coded Book Manuscript, *op. cit.*
30-32. *Ibid.*
33. Long, *op. cit.*
34. Baker's Cipher-coded Book Manuscript, *op. cit.*
35-38. *Ibid.*
39. Missing Booth Diary Pages, *op. cit.*
40. Flower, *op. cit.*
41. Missing Booth Diary Pages, *op. cit.*
42. *Ibid.*
43. Lamon, *op. cit.*
44-45. *Ibid.*
46. Pendel, Tom, *Thirty-Six Years in the White House* (Neale, Washington, 1900)
47. Weichmann, *op. cit.*
48. Townsend, *op. cit.*
49. Lamon, *op. cit.*
50. Basler, *op. cit.*
51. Lamon, *op. cit.*
52-54. *Ibid.*
55. Col. Lafayette C. Baker's Letter to Secretary of War Edwin M. Stanton, May 5, 1865. In the private collection of Stanton Descendants. Released in 1976 through the efforts of Americana appraiser, Joseph Lynch
56. Ray A. Neff Interview, *op. cit.*
57. Potter Papers, *op. cit.*
58. E. L. Emerson, Letter to R. D. Bowen, Paris, Texas, Apr. 21, 1920. Lawrence Mooney Collection, Alexandria, VA
59-62. *Ibid.*

CHAPTER 11 — Source Footnotes

1. John Surratt Lecture, *op. cit.*
2. Roscoe, *op. cit.*
3. Weichmann, *op. cit.*
4. Ray A. Neff Interview, *op. cit.*
5. Roscoe, *op. cit.*

6. O'Laughlin Statement, *op. cit.*

7-10. *Ibid.*

11. Weichmann, *op. cit.*

12. *Ibid.*

13. Olszewski, George J., *Restoration of Ford's Theatre* (U. S. Government Printing Office, Washington, D.C., 1963)

14. *Ibid.*

15. Gerry, *op. cit.*

16. Weichmann, *op. cit.*

17. Olszewski; Pitman, *op. cit.*

18. Potter Papers, *op. cit.*

19. Lola Alexander's Letter to Col. William A. Browning. 1865. Ray A. Neff Collection

20. Lola Alexander's Letter to John Wilkes Booth, Feb. 20, 1865. Ray A. Neff Collection

21. Lola Alexander's Letter to John Wilkes Booth, Mar. 19, 1865. Ray A. Neff Collection

22. Lola Alexander's Letter to John Wilkes Booth, Apr. 12, 1865. Ray A. Neff Collection

23-27. *Ibid.*

28. Roscoe, *op. cit.*

29. E. L. Emerson Letter, *op. cit.*

30. Pitman, *op. cit.*

31. Bishop, *op. cit.*

32. E. L. Emerson Letter, *op. cit.*

33. Roscoe, *op. cit.*

34. Booth's Letter to Col. William A. Browning, *op. cit.*

35-36. *Ibid.*

37. Ray A. Neff Interview, *op. cit.*

38. Pitman, *op. cit.*

39. *Ibid.*

40. Olszewski, *op. cit.*

41. Weichmann, *op. cit.*

42-44. *Ibid.*

45. John Wilkes Booth's Letter to Editor James C. Welling of the *National Intelligencer*, *Apr. 14, 1865.* In the private collection of Stanton descendants. Released in 1976 through the efforts of Americana appraiser, Joseph Lynch

46-47. *Ibid.*

48. Booth's Letter to Col. Browning, *op. cit.*

49-52. *.Ibid.*

53. Pitman, *op. cit.*

54. *Ibid.*

55. Weichmann, *op. cit.*

56. *Ibid.*

57. Potter Papers, *op. cit.*

58. O'Laughlin Statement, *op. cit.*

59-61. *Ibid.*

62. Roscoe, *op. cit.*

63. O'Laughlin Statement, *op. cit.*

64. Roscoe, *op. cit.*

65. Buckingham, J. E., *Reminiscences and Souvenirs of the Assassination of Abraham Lincoln* (Rufus H. Darby, Washington, 1894)

CHAPTER 12 — Source Footnotes

1. Bishop, *op. cit.*

2. Roscoe, *op. cit.*

3-6. *Ibid.*

7. Randall, *op. cit.*

8. *Ibid.*

9. Bishop, *op. cit.*

10-12. *Ibid.*

13. Lamon, *op. cit.*

14-16. *Ibid.*
17. Randall, *op. cit.*
18. Lamon, *op. cit.*
19. *Ibid.*
20. Welles, Gideon, *Diary of Gideon Welles: Secretary of the Navy Under Lincoln and Johnson* (Houghton Mifflin, New York, 1911) and Laughlin, Clara E., *The Death of Lincoln: The Story of Booth's Plot, His Deed and the Penalty* (Doubleday, Page & Co., New York, 1909)
21. Roscoe, *op. cit.*
22. Lamon, *op. cit.*
23. Bishop, *op. cit.*
24-25. *Ibid.*
26. Welles, *op. cit.*
27. Bishop, *op. cit.*
28-29. *Ibid.*
30. Lamon, *op. cit.*
31. *Ibid.*
32. Ray A. Neff Interview, *op. cit.*
33. Long, *op. cit.*
34. Bishop, *op. cit.*
35. *Ibid.*
36. Roscoe, *op. cit.*
37. Bishop, *op. cit.*
38-43. *Ibid.*
44. Randall, *op. cit.*
45. Shutes, *Lincoln's Emotional Life*, *op. cit.*
46. Carpenter, Frank B., *Six Months at the White House* (Hurd & Houghton, New York, 1866)
47. Bishop, *op. cit.*
48. *Ibid.*
49. Gerry, *op. cit.*
50-53. *Ibid.*
54. Bates, *op. cit.*
55-60. *Ibid.*
61. Gerry, *op. cit.*
62. *Ibid.*
63. Eisenschiml, Otto, *In the Shadow of Lincoln's Death* (Wilfred Funk, Inc., New York, 1940)
64-67. *Ibid.*
68. Bishop, *op. cit.*
69. Long, *op. cit.*
70. Bishop, *op. cit.*
71-73. *Ibid.*
74. Gerry, *op. cit.*
75. *Ibid.* and Bishop, *op. cit.*

CHAPTER 13 — Source Footnotes

1. Lorant, *op. cit.*
2. *Meteorological Observations During the Year 1865*, U.S. Naval Observatory, Washington, D.C.
3. Lorant, *op. cit.*
4. E. L. Emerson Letter, *op. cit.*
5-6. *Ibid.*
7. Olszewski, *op. cit.*
8. Gerry, *op. cit.*
9. *Ibid.*
10. Pitman; Peterson, *op. cit.*
11. Bishop, *op. cit.*
12. Randall, *op. cit.*
13. *Ibid.*
14. Pitman; Peterson, *op. cit.*
15. *Ibid.*
16. Bishop, *op. cit.*
17. Randall, *op. cit.*

18. Pitman; Peterson, *op. cit.*
19. Roscoe, *op. cit.*
20-23. *Ibid.*
24. Weichmann, *op. cit.*
25. Pitman; Peterson, *op. cit.*
26. *Ibid.*
27. Ferguson, W. J., *I Saw Booth Shoot Lincoln* (Hougton Mifflin, Boston, 1930)
28. Randall, *op. cit.*
29. Lorant, *op. cit.*
30. Roscoe, *op. cit.*
31. *Ibid.*
32. Ferguson, *op. cit.*
33. Roscoe, *op. cit.* and Existing Pages of the John Wilkes Booth Diary on display at Ford's Theatre National Historic Site, Washington, D.C.
34. Roscoe, *op. cit.*
35. Pitman; Peterson, *op. cit.*
36-44. *Ibid.*
45. Randall, *op. cit.*
46. Shutes; Bishop, *op. cit.*
47. Randall; Bishop, *op. cit.*
48. Bishop, *op. cit.*
49. *Ibid.*
50. Shutes; Bishop, *op. cit.*
51-52. *Ibid.*
53. Bishop, *op. cit.*
54. *Ibid.*
55. Lorant, *op. cit.*
56. Roscoe; Bishop, *op. cit.*

CHAPTER 14 — Source Footnotes

1. Flower, *op. cit.*
2. Shelton, *op. cit.*
3. *Ibid.*
4. Roscoe; Bishop, *op. cit.*
5. Roscoe, *op. cit.*
6-7. *Ibid.*
8. Weichmann, *op. cit.*
9. Roscoe, *op. cit.*
10. *Ibid.*
11. Bishop, *op. cit.*
12-13. *Ibid.*
14. Shelton, *op. cit.*
15. *Ibid.*
16. Bishop, *op. cit.*
17. Peterson; Pitman, *op. cit.*
18. Eisenschiml, *Why Was Lincoln Murdered?*, *op. cit.*
19. Roscoe, *op. cit.*
20. Eisenschiml, *Why Was Lincoln Murdered?*, *op. cit.*
21. Dewitt, David M., *The Assassination of Lincoln and Its Expiation*, (MacMillan Co., New York, 1909)
22. Roscoe, *op. cit.*
23. Bishop, *op. cit.*
24. *Ibid.*
25. Laughlin, *op. cit.*
26. Bishop, *op. cit.*
27. Shutes, Milton, *Lincoln and the Doctors: A Medical Narrative of the Life of Abraham Lincoln* (Pioneer Press, New York, 1933)
28. *Ibid.*
29. Gerry, *op. cit.*
30. Peterson; Pitman, *op. cit.*
31-33. *Ibid.*
34. Ray A. Neff Interview, *op. cit.*
35. Flower, *op. cit.*

36. Eisenschiml, *Why Was Lincoln Murdered?*, *op. cit.*
37-42. *Ibid.*
43. Potter Papers, *op. cit.*
44. Weichmann, *op. cit.*
45. Roscoe, *op. cit.*
46. Bishop, *op. cit.*
47. Kunhardt, Dorothy Meserve and Kunhardt, Philip B., *Twenty Days* (Harper & Row, New York, 1965)
48. Bishop, *op. cit.*
49. Eisenschiml, *Why Was Lincoln Murdered?*, *op. cit.*
50. *Ibid.*
51. Oates, Stephen B., *With Malice Towards None* (Harper & Row, New York, 1977)
52. Bishop, *op. cit.*
53. *Ibid.*
54. Weichmann, *op. cit.*
55-56. *Ibid.*
57. Bishop, *op. cit.*
58. Abott, Abott A., *The Assassination and Death of Abraham Lincoln, President of the United States of America,* (American News Co., New York, 1865)
59. *Ibid.* and Eisenschiml, *Why Was Lincoln Murdered?*, *op. cit.*
60. *Ibid.*
61. Weichmann, *op. cit.*
62. Eisenschiml, *Why Was Lincoln Murdered?*; Bishop, *op. cit.*
63. Chaffey Shipping Company Papers, *op. cit.*
64. Mudd, Nettie, *The Life of Dr. Samuel A. Mudd* (Neale Publishing Co., New York, 1906)
65. Peterson; Pitman, *op. cit.*
66. Mudd, *op. cit.*
67. *Ibid.*
68. Roscoe; and Eisenschiml, *Why Was Lincoln Murdered?*, *op. cit.*
69. Kunhardt, *op. cit.*
70-72.. *Ibid.*

CHAPTER 15 — Source Footnotes

1. Weichmann, *op. cit.*
2. *Ibid.*
3. Kunhardt, *op. cit.*
4. Eisenschiml, *Why Was Lincoln Murdered?*, *op. cit.*
5. Mudd, *op. cit.*
6. Roscoe, *op. cit.*
7. Eisenschiml, *Why Was Lincoln Murdered?*, *op. cit.*
8. Baker's Cipher-Coded Book Manuscript, *op. cit.*
9. Mudd, *op. cit.*
10. *Ibid.*
11. Long, *op. cit.*
12. Bishop, *op. cit.*
13. Potter Papers, *op. cit.*
14. Kunhardt, *op. cit.*
15. *Ibid.*
16. *National Intelligencer* (Washington, D.C.) Apr. 20, 1865
17. *Ibid.*
18. Mudd, *op. cit.*
19-21. *Ibid.*
22. Roscoe, *op. cit.*
23. *Ibid.*
24. Mudd, *op. cit.*
25-27. *Ibid.*
28. Oldroyd, *op. cit.*
29. Jones, Thomas A., "J. Wilkes Booth: An Account of His Sojourn in Southern Maryland After the Assassination of Abraham Lincoln," *The Amateur Book Collector*, Sept. 1954
30-37. *Ibid.*

38. Eisenschiml, *Why Was Lincoln Murdered, op. cit.*
39. Baker's Cipher-Coded Book- Manuscript, *op. cit.*
40-42. *Ibid.*
43. Potter Papers, *op. cit.*
44-47. *Ibid.*
48. Weichmann, *op. cit.*
49. *Ibid.*
50. Bearden Papers, *op. cit.*
51. Weichmann, *Why Was Lincoln Murdered?, op. cit.*
52. *Ibid.*
53. Shelton, *op. cit.*
54. Roscoe, *op. cit.*
55. Pitmann; Peterson, *op. cit.*
56. Weichmann; Roscoe, *op. cit.*
57. Potter Papers, *op. cit.*
58. *Ibid.*
59. $30,000 Reward Poster Issued by Col. Lafayette C. Baker, National Archives/Library of Congress
60. Potter Papers, *op. cit.*
61. Existing Booth Diary Pages, *op. cit.*
62. *Ibid.*
63. Potter Papers, *op. cit.*

CHAPTER 16 — Source Footnotes

1. Potter Papers, *op. cit.*
2-4. *Ibid.*
5. $30,000 Reward Poster, *op. cit.*
6-7. *Ibid.*
8. Long, *op. cit.*
9. Lamon, *op. cit.*
10. Potter Papers, *op. cit.*
11. Capt. Boyd Letter to Moe Stevens, *op. cit.*
12. Potter Papers, *op. cit.*
13-18. *Ibid.*
19. Jones, *op. cit.*
20-22. *Ibid.*
23. Existing Booth Diary Pages, *op. cit.*
24. *Ibid.*
25. Jones, *op. cit.*
26. *Ibid.*
27. Potter Papers, *op. cit.*
28. Existing Booth Diary Pages, *op. cit.*
29. $100,000 Reward Poster Issued by Edwin M. Stanton, Number One, Apr. 20, 1865. National Archives/Library of Congress
30. *Ibid.*
31. Existing Booth Diary Pages, *op. cit.*
32. Unpublished Voluntary Statement of Dandridge Mercer Green, Apr. 30, 1865. National Archives. Ray A. Neff Collection
33. Roscoe, *op. cit.*
34. Dandridge Green Statement, *op. cit.*
35. Potter Papers, *op. cit.*
36-38. *Ibid.*

CHAPTER 17 — Source Footnotes

1. Photo Files, National Archives and Library of Congress
2. $100,000 Reward Poster Issued by Edwin M. Stanton, Nimber One, Apr. 20, 1865 National Archives/Library of Congress
3. $100,000 Reward Poster Issued by Edwin M. Stanton, Number Two, Apr. 20, 1865. National Archives/Library of Congress
4. $100,000 Reward Poster Issued by Edwin M. Stanton, Number Three, Apr. 20, 1865. National Archives/Library of Congress
5. Col. Lafayette C. Baker's Letter to Edwin M. Stanton, May 5, 1865. In the private collection of Stanton descendants. Released in 1976 through the efforts of Americana appraiser, Joseph Lynch.

313

6. *Ibid.*
7. Kunhardt, *op. cit.*
8-14. *Ibid.*
15. Potter Papers, *op. cit.*
16-17. *Ibid.*
18. Mudd, *op. cit.*
19-21. *Ibid.*
22. Potter Papers, *op. cit.*
23. Existing Booth Diary Pages, *op. cit.*
24. Missing Booth Diary Pages, *op. cit.*
25. *Ibid.*
26. Potter Papers, *op. cit.*
27-30. *Ibid.*

CHAPTER 18 — Source Footnotes
1. Rep. George Julian Diary, Apr. 1865. Ray A. Neff Collection
2-3. *Ibid.*
4. Missing Booth Diary Pages, *op. cit.*
5-10. *Ibid.*
11. Rep. Julian Diary, *op. cit.*
12-17. *Ibid.*
18. Roscoe, *op. cit.*
19. Roscoe, *op. cit.*
20. Potter Papers, *op. cit.*
21. Dandridge Green Statement, *op. cit.*
22. Rep. Julian Diary, *op. cit.*
23-24. *Ibid.*

CHAPTER 19 — Source Footnotes
1. Dandridge Green statement, *op. cit.*
2-7. *Ibid.*
8. Ray A. Neff Interview, *op. cit.*
9. *Ibid.* and Roscoe, *op. cit.*
10. *Ibid.*
11. Ray A. Neff Interview, *op. cit.*
12-13. *Ibid.*
14. Potter Papers, *op. cit.*
15-16. *Ibid.*
17. Dandridge Green Statement, *op. cit.*
18. Roscoe; Pitman, *op. cit.*
19. Peterson, *op. cit.*
20. *Ibid.*
21. Weichmann, *op. cit.*
22-23. *Ibid.*
24. Potter Papers, *op. cit.*
25. *Ibid.*

CHAPTER 20 — Source Footnotes
1. Capt. Boyd Papers. Ray A. Neff Collection
2. Clarke, *op. cit.*
3. The Wilhelmina Titus (granddaughter of Capt. James William Boyd) monograph. Ray A. Neff Collection
4. Weichmann; Roscoe, *op. cit.*
5. *Ibid.*
6. Luther Baker Speech delivered in 1932 at Lansing, Michigan. Richard D. Mudd Collection
7-12. *Ibid.*
13. Roscoe; Potter Papers, *op. cit.*
14. Weichmann, *op. cit.*
15. *Ibid.*
16. Roscoe, *op. cit.*
17-18. *Ibid.*
19. Weichmann, *op. cit.*
20. *Ibid.* and Roscoe, *op. cit.*
21. Luther Baker Speech, *op. cit.*

22-24. *Ibid.*
25. *Ibid.* and Peterson, *op. cit.*
26. Roscoe, *op. cit.*
27. *Ibid.*
28. Weichmann, *op. cit.*
29. Luther Baker Speech, *op. cit.*
30-31. *Ibid.*
32. Pitman, *op. cit.*
33. Luther Baker Speech, *op. cit.*
34. Pitman, *op. cit.*
35. *Ibid.*
36. Luther Baker Speech, *op. cit.*
37. Weichmann, *op. cit.*
38. Col. Lafayette C. Baker's memo-letter to Edwin Stanton, Apr., 1865. In the private collection of Stanton descendants. Released in 1976 through an interview with Americana appraiser, Joseph Lynch.
39. Luther Baker Speech, *op. cit.*
40. Pitman, *op. cit.*

CHAPTER 21 — Source Footnotes

1. Roscoe, *op. cit.*
2. *Ibid.*
3. Peterson, *op. cit.*
4. Potter Papers, *op. cit.*
5. Ray A. Neff Interview, *op. cit.*
6. *Ibid.*
7. Baker, *History of the United States Secret Service*, *op. cit.*
8. Weichmann, *op. cit.*
9. Peterson, *op. cit.*
10. Luther Baker speech; Roscoe, *op. cit.*
11. *Ibid.*
12. Potter Papers, *op. cit.*
13. Roscoe, *op. cit.*
14. *Ibid.*
15. Potter Papers, *op. cit.*
16-22. *Ibid.*

CHAPTER 22 — Source Footnotes

1. Roscoe, *op. cit.*
2. *Ibid.*
3. Ray A. Neff Interview, *op. cit.*
4. Roscoe, *op. cit.*
5-6. *Ibid.*
7. Oldroyd, *op. cit.*
8. Eisenschiml, *In the Shadow of Lincoln's Death*, *op. cit.*
9. Roscoe, *op. cit.*
10. Eisenschiml, *In the Shadow of Lincoln's Death*, *op. cit.*
11-12. *Ibid.*
13. *Ibid.* and Roscoe, *op. cit.*
14. Roscoe, *op. cit.*
15. Ray A. Neff Interview, *op. cit.*
16. Roscoe, *op. cit.*
17. *Ibid.*
18. Potter Papers, *op. cit.*
19-20. *Ibid.*
21. Joseph Lynch telephone interview conducted Oct. 1976.
22. Luther Baker Speech, *op. cit.*
23. Roscoe; Potter Papers, *op. cit.*
24. Potter Papers, *op. cit.*

CHAPTER 23 — Source Footnotes

1. Eisenschiml, *Why Was Lincoln Murdered?*, *op. cit.*
2. Americana Encyclopedia, *op. cit.*
3. Eisenschiml, *Why Was Lincoln Murdered?*, *op. cit.*
4. *Ibid.*

5. *Ibid.* and Weichmann, *op. cit.*
6. Weichmann, *op. cit.*
7. Eisenschiml, *Why Was Lincoln Murdered?*, *op. cit.*
8. Roscoe, *op. cit.*
9. *Ibid.* and Eisenschiml, *Why Was Lincoln Murdered?*, *op. cit.*
10. Weichmann, *op. cit.*
11. Eisenschiml, *Why Was Lincoln Murdered?*, *op. cit.*
12. Pitman, *op. cit.*
13. *Ibid.*
14. Maj. Eckert's Letter to Col. Lafayette C. Baker, Apr. 22, 1865, *op. cit.*
15. Col. Everton J. Conger's Letter to Col. Lafayette C. Baker, May 2, 1865. In the private collection of Stanton descendants. Released in 1976 through the efforts of Americana appraiser, Joseph Lynch.
16. Potter Papers, *op. cit.*
17-18. *Ibid.*
19. Shelton; DeWitt, *The Assassination of Lincoln and Its Expiation*, *op. cit.*
20. Kunhardt, *op. cit.*
21. DeWitt, *op. cit.*
22. Eisenschiml, *Why Was Lincoln Murdered?*, *op. cit.*
23. *Ibid.*
24. Doster, William E., *Lincoln and Episodes of the Civil War* (G. P. Putnam's Sons, New York, 1915)
25. Eisenschiml, *In the Shadow of Lnicoln's Death*, *op. cit.* and DeWitt, David M., *The Judicial Murder of Mary E. Surratt* (J. Murphy & Co., Baltimore, 1895)
26. Eisenschiml, *In the Shadow of Lincoln's Death*, *op. cit.*
27. Arnold, *op. cit.*
28. Eisenschiml, *Why Was Lincoln Murdered?*, *op. cit.*
29. *Ibid.*
30. Bearden Papers, *op. cit.*
31. DeWitt, *The Assassination of Lincoln and Its Expiation*, *op. cit.*
32-33. *Ibid.*
34. *Ibid.* and Bearden Papers, *op. cit.*
35. Roscoe; Pitman, *op. cit.*
36-40. *Ibid.*
41. Judge Advocate General Joseph Holt's Letter to Secretary of War Edwin M. Stanton, undated. In the private collection of Stanton descendants. Released in 1976 through the efforts of Americana appraiser Joseph Lynch.
42-43. *Ibid.*

CHAPTER 24 — Source Footnotes

1. Peterson; Pitman, *op. cit.*
2. Roscoe, *op. cit.*
3. *Ibid.*
4. Peterson; Pitman, *op. cit.*
5. Roscoe, *op. cit.*
6. Shelton, *op. cit.*
7. Roscoe, *op. cit.*
8. Peterson, *op. cit.*
9. *Ibid.*
10. Roscoe, *op. cit.*
11. Eisenschiml, *Why Was Lincoln's Murdered?*, *op. cit.*
12. Weichmann, *op. cit.*
13-15. *Ibid.*
16. Pitman, *op. cit.*
17. Unpublished Interview with Mrs. E. W. Nelson (David Herold's sister) of Denver, Colorado, Aug. 22, 1873. Ray A. Neff Corporation
18. Poore, Ben Perley, *The Conspiracy Trial for the Murder of the President* (J. E. Tilton Co., Boston, 1865); Peterson; Pitman, *op. cit.*
19-21. *Ibid.*
22. O'Laughlin Statement, *op. cit.*
23. Weichmann, *op. cit.*
24. Pitman; Peterson, *op. cit.*

25. Poore; Peterson; Pitman, *op. cit.*
26-28. *Ibid.*
29. Kauffman, Michael W., *Report to the President on the Case of Dr. Samuel A. Mudd., M.D.* Richard A. Mudd Collection
30. Roscoe, *op. cit.*
31. Doster, *op. cit.*
32. Peterson; Pitman, *op. cit.*

CHAPTER 25 — Source Footnotes

1. Weichmann, *op. cit.*
2. *Ibid.*
3. Roscoe, *op. cit.*
4. Holt, Harlowe R., *Town Hall Tonight* (Prentice-Hall, Englewood Cliffs, NJ, 1955)
5-6. *Ibid.*
7. Weichmann, *op. cit.*
8-9. *Ibid.*
10. Peterson, *op. cit.*
11. *Ibid.*
12. Mrs. E. W. Nelson Interview, *op. cit.*
13. Weichmann; Roscoe, *op. cit.*
14. *Ibid.* and Peterson, *op. cit.*
15. *Ibid.*
16. Weichmann, *op. cit.*
17. Col. Lafayette Baker's Letter to Edwin Stanton, undated. In the private collection of Stanton descendants. Released in 1976 through the efforts of Americana appraiser, Joseph Lynch.
18. Weichmann, *op. cit.*
19. Doster, *op. cit.*
20. *Ibid.*
21. Shelton, *op. cit.*
22. *Constitutional Union*, July 7, 1865
23. Holt, *op. cit.*
24. Weichmann, *op. cit.*
25. Holt, *op. cit.*
26. *Ibid.*
27. Holt, *op. cit.*
28. Doster, *op. cit.*
29. Holt, *op. cit.*
30. *Ibid.*

CHAPTER 26 — Source Footnotes

1. Eisenschiml, *Why Was Lincoln Murdered?*, *op. cit.*
2-3. *Ibid.*
4. *Ibid.* and Roscoe, *op. cit.*
5. Arnold, *op. cit.*
6. Eisenschiml, *Why Was Lincoln Murdered?*, *op. cit.*
7. *Ibid.*
8. Potter Papers, *op. cit.*
9-17. *Ibid.*
18. Weichmann; Bearden Papers, *op. cit.*
19. *Ibid.*
20. *Report Relating to the Assassination of President Lincoln*, House Reports, No. 104, 39th Congress, 1st Session, Vol. 1, July 1866
21. *Ibid.*
22. Eisenschiml, *Why Was Lincoln Murdered?*, *op. cit.*
23. *Ibid.*
24. *Ibid.*
25. Roscoe, *op. cit.*
26. Eisenschiml, *Why Was Lincoln Murdered?*, *op. cit.*
27-31. *Ibid.*
32. Weichmann, *op. cit.*
33. *Letter on Removal of E. M. Stanton*, House Ex. Docs., No. 183, 40th Congress, 2nd Session, Vol. XV, Feb. 2, 1868
34. Flower, *op. cit.*
35. *Ibid.*
36. Roscoe, *op. cit.*